DOCTRINES FOR EXALTATION

THE 1989 SPERRY SYMPOSIUM ON THE DOCTRINE AND COVENANTS

Susan Easton Black
Richard O. Cowan
Richard D. Draper
S. Brent Farley
LaMar E. Garrard
Leland Gentry
Richard Neitzel Holzapfel
Clark V. Johnson
Daniel K. Judd
E. Dale LeBaron
Robert England Lee
Robert J. Matthews
Robert L. Millet
Monte S. Nyman
Alan K. Parrish
Chauncey C. Riddle
S. Michael Wilcox
Robert J. Woodford

Deseret Book Company
Salt Lake City, Utah

©1989 Deseret Book Company
All rights reserved
Printed in the United States of America

10 9 8 7 6 5 4 3 2 1

No part of this book may be reproduced in any
form or by any means without permission in writing
from the publisher, Deseret Book Company,
P.O. Box 30178, Salt Lake City, Utah 84130.
Deseret Book is a registered trademark of
Deseret Book Company.

Library of Congress Catalog Card No. 89-40394

ISBN 0-87579-245-6

Contents

Preface

The Doctrine and Covenants instructs us to "teach one another the doctrine of the kingdom. Teach ye diligently and my grace shall attend you, that you may be instructed more perfectly in theory, in principle, in doctrine, in the law of the gospel, in all things that pertain unto the kingdom of God, that are expedient for you to understand." (D&C 88:77–78.) This was the goal of the seventeenth annual Sidney B. Sperry Symposium, held Saturday, 4 February 1989, on the campus of Brigham Young University in Provo, Utah. The symposium, sponsored jointly by Brigham Young University's Religious Education and the Church Educational System, honors Dr. Sidney Sperry for his faithfulness and scholarship. Brother Sperry, a professor of religion at BYU for forty years, was a great student of the scriptures. As a teacher and writer, he set a high standard for scholarship and was a faithful defender of the faith.

The papers delivered at this symposium reflect similar scholarship and faith and were responsive to the Lord's challenge to "teach one another the doctrine of the kingdom." The theme of the symposium was "The Doctrine and Covenants: Doctrines of Exaltation." The Doctrine and Covenants contains the doctrines and covenants that will assist us in our quest for exaltation. Dr. Chauncey C. Riddle, the keynote speaker, discussed the role of the new and everlasting covenant in becoming Christlike. This theme was carried through the symposium, which concluded with a discussion by Dean Robert J. Matthews on the role of the dispensation of the fulness of times in the exaltation of man.

Although all of the contributors sought to be in harmony with the teachings of the Church, the views expressed in the papers are those of the individual writers and do not necessarily represent the position of Brigham Young University, the Church Educational System of The Church of Jesus Christ of Latter-day Saints, nor should they be viewed as a replacement for the standard works and the words of the latter-day prophets.

The Seventeenth Sperry Symposium Committee

H. Dean Garrett, Editor
Rex C. Reeve, Jr., Editor
Spencer C. Condie
Eldon L. Haag
Richard D. Draper

CHAPTER ONE

The Sacred Role of Women

Susan Easton Black

Associate Professor of Church History and Doctrine
Brigham Young University

Attempts to develop a universally accepted definition of a woman's ideal role have left scholars frustrated. Whatever model they propose, increasing numbers of women proclaim themselves to be the exception to the proposed norm. Few women today hold fast to long-held traditional standards, as they witness other women tossing off "apron strings" as vestiges of servitude.

Concurrently, the growing challenge of identifying a doctrinally unassailable definition of the role of women has also confronted gospel scholars. Some gospel scholars have concluded that a redefinition of traditional roles is necessary because of changing times. Others insist that the prophetic roles of antiquity are unalterably appropriate for all dispensations, including our own. Such polarization has prompted me to question why gospel scholars have not searched the modern scriptures found in the Doctrine and Covenants to discover divine direction for defining the role of women in these latter days.

The Doctrine and Covenants is a standard work, which by definition means a collection of prophetic writings against which our thoughts, actions, and even our chosen roles can be measured. It reveals the doctrines of salvation and the basic truths of the gospel of Jesus Christ that are necessary for women to understand and apply. It assures women of the validity, power, and efficacy of the continuing covenants between God and each of his sons and daughters. Careful perusal of this scripture clearly reveals a definition of the currently prescribed role of women in mortality and the promised blessings for faithful obedience to the laws of God.

My purpose is to assure today's women that the Doctrine and Covenants reveals the Lord's continuous approbation of the sacred phases of womanhood: it contains the Lord's continuous respect for the process of womanhood. This modern scripture delineates the prescribed path that illuminates the woman's course toward eternal life. (D&C 132:20; 138:39.) Also, an alternative perilous path is presented, which, if followed, will destroy each woman's potential fulfillment and lead to her destruction. (D&C 132:42.)

THE SACRED PHASES OF WOMANHOOD

The sacred phases of womanhood, reaffirmed and expanded for our day, are those taught to Eve and her daughters through the ages. In broadest terms they are the eternal roles of righteous daughter, wife, and mother. In each of these roles, there is a challenge to serve God and his children in such a way that, line upon line and precept upon precept, women become glorified in "a fulness and a continuation of the seeds forever and ever." (D&C 132:19.) These roles are as old as Adam and as new as today. The Doctrine and Covenants helps women see clearly each eternal role and how they can make the greatest growth and avoid the failures in each.

The role of daughter. The unfolding of the earthly plan of salvation, as reported in the Doctrine and Covenants, began for women when "the worlds are and were created, and the inhabitants thereof are begotten sons and daughters unto God." (D&C 76:24.) As daughters of God, women learn the ennobling truth that the Lord "created man, male and female, after his own image and in his own likeness, created he them." (D&C 20:18.)

Adam was the first man and Eve the first woman. Since that early creative period, "our glorious Mother Eve, with many of her faithful daughters who had lived through the ages and worshiped the true and living God," have experienced the opportunities for growth in mortal life. (D&C 138:39.)

As these daughters grow to the age of responsibility, they become subject to the laws and ordinances of the gospel. As such, they "must repent and be baptized." (D&C 18:42.) As daughters keep the Lord's commandments, they desire to progress by making further covenants with God. These covenants include commitment to personal worthiness.

The Doctrine and Covenants speaks of an exemplary daughter, Vienna Jaques.[1] In many ways Vienna becomes a representative model of the many women who respect their womanhood and by their words and actions become Saints.

Vienna was approximately the age of Joseph Smith's parents when she first became acquainted with the Church. She had been a devout Christian who had associated with the Methodists on Bromfield Street in Boston, Massachusetts. While in Boston, she became dissatisfied with her religion and began seeking for a church that evidenced the spiritual gifts described in the New Testament. Hearing of Joseph Smith and his newly published Book of Mormon, she requested a copy. At first reading she was not particularly inspired by the words of the Book of Mormon. One night, however, while she was praying, she saw a vision of the Book of Mormon and resolved to know of its truthfulness.

Her conversion was not instantaneous but came gradually through continual prayer and study of the scriptures. She read the Book of Mormon until she became convinced of its divinity. In 1831 she traveled alone toward Kirtland, Ohio, to meet Joseph Smith. She met the Prophet in Kirtland and accepted baptism. On 8 March 1833 she was instructed by revelation to give the money she had brought from the east to the Church and settle in Missouri: "It is my will that my handmaid Vienna Jaques should receive money to bear her expenses, and go up unto the land of Zion;

"And the residue of the money may be consecrated unto me, and she be rewarded in mine own due time.

"Verily I say unto you, that it is meet in mine eyes that she should go up unto the land of Zion, and receive an inheritance from the hand of the bishop;

"That she may settle down in peace inasmuch as she is faithful, and not be idle in her days from thenceforth." (D&C 90:28–31.)

Forty-six-year-old Vienna Jaques gave all of her money to the Lord's church. In return, she received a portion of her funds from the bishop to maintain herself. This contribution from a single daughter stands as a memorial to her sacrifice and love of God.

Joseph Smith wrote a letter to Vienna on 4 September 1833, in which he wrote: "I have often felt a whispering since I received your letter, like this: 'Joseph, thou are indebted to thy God for the offering of thy Sister Vienna, which proved a savior of life as pertaining to thy pecuniary concerns. Therefore she should not be forgotten of thee, for the Lord hath done this, and thou shouldst remember her in all thy prayers and also by letter. . . . Therefore let your heart be comforted; live in strict obedience to the commandments of God, and walk humbly before Him, and He will exalt thee in His own due time. I will assure you that the Lord has respect unto the offering you made.' "[2]

In Missouri, Vienna lost her deeded portion because of mobbing against all Latter-day Saints in that region. Nevertheless, she continued to give service. Heber C. Kimball noted her service in his journal entry concerning illness in Zion's Camp. He wrote, "We had to exert ourselves considerable to attend to the sick, for they fell on every hand." Then he added that there was one woman whom, "I received great kindness from . . . sister Vienna Jaques, who administered to my wants and also to my brethren—may the Lord reward . . . [her] kindness."[3] Vienna Jaques was an exemplar of a righteous daughter in her readiness to accept the laws of God, her devotion to the Lord, and her ability to serve others.

The role of wife. The pivotal covenant that enables a woman to reach her fullest potential is eternal marriage. (D&C 132:18–19.) She desires to be married to a companion who listens to the Lord's command that "thou shalt love thy wife with all thy heart, and shalt cleave unto her and none else." (D&C 42:22.) Such a man desires to begin his marriage union by "enter[ing] into this order of the priesthood [meaning the new and everlasting covenant of marriage]." (D&C 131:2.) In this bond of marriage, the couple becomes "one flesh, and all this that the earth might answer the end of its creation." (D&C 49:16.)

In this eternal bond, "women have claim on their husbands for their maintenance." (D&C 83:2.) The word *claim* means rights, privileges, and entitlements. Maintenance, according to President Spencer W. Kimball, includes the husband's "obligation to maintain loving affection and to provide consideration and thoughtfulness as well as food."[4]

In turn, the righteous wife is told to comfort her husband. (D&C 25:5.) Joseph Smith clarified this counsel to women as wives:

"Submit yourselves unto your own husbands, as unto the Lord, for the husband is the head of the wife, even as Christ is the head of the Church; and He is the Savior of the body. Therefore, as the Church is subject unto Christ, so let the wives be to their own husbands, in everything."[5]

Emma Smith is remembered as the woman who faithfully stood by her husband during his life.[6] Emma was a woman of great faith and courage whom the Lord addressed in Doctrine and Covenants, section 25, and again in section 132. Section 25 begins, "Hearken unto the voice of the Lord your God, while I speak unto you, Emma Smith, my daughter." This section is personal for Emma, yet latter-day prophets have used it as counsel for daughters of God and wives in Israel. (D&C 25:16.)

Emma is told by the Lord, "Thy sins are forgiven thee, and thou art an elect lady, whom I have called." (D&C 25:3.) The terminology of *elect* was defined by Joseph Smith on 17 March 1842 in Nauvoo, Illinois, when he told the sisters that "elect meant to be elected to a certain work . . . and that the revelation was then fulfilled by Sister Emma's election to the Presidency of the [Relief] Society."[7]

Her calling was to be the wife of a prophet. In this role she was told that "the office of thy calling shall be for a comfort unto my servant, Joseph Smith, Jun., thy husband." (D&C 25:5.) She was to use "consoling words, in the spirit of meekness" with him. (D&C 25:5.) Emma was to cleave to Joseph and to "go with him at the time of his going, and be unto him for a scribe." (D&C 25:6.) She was promised that for faithfully fulfilling her calling as a wife, her "husband shall support thee in the church." (D&C 25:9.)

In addition to these responsibilities as an elect lady and a called wife, Emma was to develop her talents. Emma's talents included expounding the scriptures, exhorting the Church, writing, learning, and selecting sacred hymns. (D&C 25:7–8, 11.) She was told that while fulfilling these responsibilities, she was not to murmur but was to "lay aside the things of this world, and seek for the things of a better." (D&C 25:4, 10.) She was also admonished to beware of pride. (D&C 25:14.) If Emma proved faithful, she was to receive "a crown of righteousness." (D&C 25:15.)

Joseph Smith loved Emma, for she did comfort him, she increased her talents, and she heeded the Lord's admonitions. In his love for her, Joseph pleaded with the Lord on her behalf, "Have mercy, O Lord, upon [my] wife . . . , that [she] may be exalted in thy presence, and preserved by thy fostering hand." (D&C 109:69.)

Following Joseph's pleading, Emma again became the subject of the Lord's revelation in Doctrine and Covenants 132. Emma is told "to abide and cleave unto my servant Joseph, and to none else." (D&C 132:54.) She is also told to "forgive my servant Joseph his trespasses; and then shall she be forgiven her trespasses . . . ; and I, the Lord thy God, will bless her, and multiply her, and make her heart to rejoice." (D&C 132:56.)

Emma is warned that despite her position as an "elect lady" and a called wife, she must endure faithfully to the end or risk losing all, for unless she does endure, "where I am you cannot come." (D&C 25:15.) "She shall be destroyed, saith the Lord; for I am the Lord thy God, and will destroy her if she abide not in my law." (D&C 132:54.)

Throughout her life as a wife to the Prophet Joseph Smith, she experienced persecution and Abrahamic tests. Despite the persecution and the severe tests, Emma was admonished to beware of pride and told to let her soul delight in her husband. Emma's responsibilities were many, and by comparison her weaknesses were perhaps few. Elder Bruce R. McConkie wrote, "Just as it is possible for the very elect to be deceived, and to fall from grace through disobedience, so an elect lady, by failing to endure to the end, can lose her chosen status."[8] The lessons from the Lord's revelation to Emma are clear: a wife is to cleave to her husband and comfort him, serve in the Lord's kingdom, and endure faithfully to the end.

The role of mother. As the wife enjoys the marriage relationship, she will anticipate with joy the opportunity of motherhood. As a mother, she will want her children sealed to her and her husband for all eternity by the ordinances and bonds of love. (D&C 138:48.) As parents, the husband and wife will teach the children "to understand the doctrine of repentance, faith in Christ the Son of the living God, and of baptism and the gift of the Holy Ghost by the laying on of the hands, when eight years old." (D&C 68:25.) These children will have "claim upon their parents for their maintenance until they are of age." (D&C 83:4.)

Although Lucy Mack Smith is not mentioned by name in the Doctrine and Covenants, she is mentioned by her designated role of mother in the life of Joseph Smith.[9] Joseph, in his vision of eternal realms, wrote, "I saw Father Adam and Abraham; and my father and my mother; my brother Alvin, that has long since slept." (D&C 137:5.)

This indisputable role of Lucy Mack Smith, mother of the Prophet, was also noted in the minutes of a Church conference held on 8 October 1845 in Nauvoo, Illinois. On that day, according to the minutes, Lucy Smith made the following remarks: "I raised up 11 children, 7 boys. I raised them in the fear of God. When they were two or three years old I told them I wanted them to love God with all their hearts. I told them to do good. I want all you to do the same. God gives us our children and we are accountable. . . . I presume there never was a family more obedient than mine. I did not have to speak to them only once. . . . I want you to teach your little children about Joseph in Egypt and such things, and when they are four years old they will love to read their Bible. . . . Set your children to work; . . . don't let them play out of doors. . . . I call you brothers and sisters and children. If you consider me a Mother in Israel, I want you to say so."[10]

According to the minutes, Brigham Young then arose and said, "All who consider Mother Smith as a Mother in Israel, signify it by saying yes." There were loud shouts of yes, according to the clerk.[11]

Eternal roles. The roles of womanhood found in modern scripture are the same roles found throughout ancient scripture. Furthermore, the roles for righteous women are parallel to those prescribed for righteous men. As the woman became a daughter of God, the man became a son. As the woman became a wife, the man became a husband. As the woman became a mother, the man became a father. These complementary roles and their divine order are basic to the framework of the gospel and the plan of salvation. They have been so since the beginning of time. These are the same roles as those of our ancient forebears, and they are the same as those expected and respected roles in the society of Saints today. Through these roles both men and women can learn the doctrines of salvation and how they are to participate in the laws and covenants of the kingdom of God.

THE LORD'S RESPECT FOR THE PROCESS OF WOMANHOOD

Complementary expectations and blessings dominate. The role of woman is much more extensively taught through the Doctrine and Covenants when it is realized that masculine references are almost always equally relevant to man and to woman. Thus the description of womanhood can be confusing to the hurried reader because it is interwoven into both masculine and feminine terminology. Throughout the Doctrine and Covenants the terms *man, he, him,* and *his,* when not referring to a specific man, also mean woman. For example, Doctrine and Covenants 1:32 states, "Nevertheless, he that repents and does the commandments of the Lord shall be forgiven." This passage is confidently interpreted to mean, "Nevertheless, he or she that repents and does the commandments of the Lord shall be forgiven." Another example of the generic use of the masculine terms is seen in Doctrine and Covenants 38:24, "And let every man esteem his brother as himself, and practice virtue and holiness before me." This passage is interpreted to mean, "And let every man and woman esteem his or her brother or sister as himself or herself, and practice virtue and holiness before me."

Such implied understanding or liberality with the word of God is accepted by latter-day prophets and Saints and considered appropriate understanding of the word of God. The substance and the essence, with respect both to prescription and to standards, is exactly parallel and complementary for man and woman. Such universality, or generic reference, is not apparent when the Lord uses the feminine terms *woman, she,* and *her.* Feminine references are generic for all women but are not applicable to any man. A search of the feminine terms in the Doctrine and Covenants reveals 239 references meant just for women.

Respect for womanhood is emphasized. One consistent theme noted in the 239 references is the divine injunction of continual respect for womanhood.[12] This respect is shown to woman by various titles that depict her role. These titles include "daughter," six times; "hand-maid," five times; "woman," fourteen times; "wife," twenty-six times; "mother," six times; and "widow," three times. These positive titles designate the expected and the respected roles in a woman's mortal life.

The Lord further indicated his respect for the roles of womanhood by teaching parables that feature women. These parables emphasize the importance of continually seeking the Lord (D&C 101:84), of being prepared when he comes again (D&C 63:54), and of his desire to gather the house of Israel (D&C 10:65; 43:24; 29:2).[13] He expects that his example of respect for womanhood will be followed by both men and women.

The Lord in the Doctrine and Covenants evidenced his high regard and respect for womanhood by noting significant concepts introduced by feminine pronouns. These concepts include *Zion* (D&C 68:26), *mercy* (D&C 88:40), *stakes* (D&C 68:25), *earth* (D&C 88:45, 89), and *moon* (D&C 88:45). Numerically the strongest of these feminine referents is *Zion.*[14]

The reason why a feminine pronoun was used for these concepts may be found in the virtuous nature of the concepts themselves. For example, mercy is the pure love of God. "Mercy hath compassion on mercy and claimeth *her* own." (D&C 88:40; italics added.) Another example is "Zion," which is a dedicated place or people with one heart and one mind. "For, behold, I say unto you that Zion shall flourish, and the glory of the Lord shall be upon *her.*" (D&C 64:41; italics added.) The sanctity of *mercy* and *Zion,* associated with a feminine pronoun, conveys the Lord's vision of the cherished and even sacred position of righteous womanhood. Using these concepts as a prototype shows that in the Lord's plan, women are to be respected and considered sacred and pure.

THE DOCTRINE AND COVENANTS ILLUMINATES THE WOMAN'S COURSE TOWARD ETERNAL LIFE

In addition to general and generic reference to women, there are specific scriptures in the Doctrine and Covenants for women that have universal application. These scriptures center on the laws of God. A woman must know that God lives and earn her testimony of the mission of Jesus, the same as does her father, brother, or husband. She must know that Jesus is the Christ, "that by him, and through him, and of him, the worlds are and were created, and the inhabitants thereof are begotten sons and daughters unto God." (D&C 76:24.)

This principle is highlighted throughout the Doctrine and Covenants in specific commandments, laws, and ordinances for women. The first of these is found in Doctrine and Covenants 20:73. "The person who is called of God and has authority from Jesus Christ to baptize, shall go down into the water with the person who has presented himself or herself for baptism."

Notice the parallel of men and women in this scripture centered on the first principles and ordinances of the gospel. Throughout the Doctrine and Covenants this parallelism is seen in all the laws and ordinances. (D&C 42:80–81, 85–92.) For example, "if a man or woman shall rob, he or she shall be delivered up unto the law of the land." (D&C 42:84.)

Also, Elder John A. Widtsoe noted the parallel of the ordinances and laws of the Church with respect to men and to women. He wrote: "This doctrine of equal rights is confirmed in the ordinances of the Church, which are alike for man and woman. Faith, repentance, and baptism are the same for all. The rewards, such as the gift of the Holy Ghost and the temple ordinances, are alike for men and women. The gifts and obligations of the gospel are alike for all. The man who holds the priesthood officiates in it, but the blessings of it descend upon the woman, also."[15]

President Joseph F. Smith wrote: "There are people fond of saying that women are the weaker vessels. I don't believe it. Physically, they may be; but spiritually, morally, religiously and in faith, what man can match a woman who is really convinced? Daniel had faith to sustain him in the lion's den, but women have seen their sons torn limb from limb, and endured every torture satanic cruelty could invent, because they believed. They are always more willing to make sacrifices, and are the peers of men in stability, godliness, morality and faith."[16]

WHEN RESPECT FOR WOMANHOOD IS DISREGARDED: THE PERILOUS PATH TO DESTRUCTION

Ancient roles of women are not accepted by all women in our dispensation. The clearly defined roles of women throughout the ages have never been the most popular or the most convenient roles. It takes effort to successfully function in each role because each role forms a relationship. For example, a daughter bonds with a parent, a wife unites with a husband, and a mother rears a child. No sacred role for a woman can be performed in isolation. A current trend of "do my own thing," without regard to an eternal relationship, is inconsistent with the plan of God.

Many women choose to reject a relationship in one or all phases of God's eternal plan and also the ordering of these phases. They advocate alternative life-styles inconsistent with the eternal plan of God for women. Yet, there are numerous faithful women who desire to be wives and mothers but for reasons often unknown, do not have these sacred privileges in mortality. Gratefully, these noble women will not be denied the responsibilities and blessings in the eternities.[17]

It is often inconceivable to those who desire these opportunities and to those who participate fully in these roles in mortality that increasing numbers of women do not seek to participate in one or more desired phases of womanhood. It is disconcerting also that some women accept the desired role on the surface but grudgingly perform it without "lift[ing] up thy heart and rejoic[ing], and cleav[ing] unto the covenants which [she] hast made." (D&C 25:13.)

Still other women claim that the righteous daughter-wife-mother plan is not easily discernible in the Doctrine and Covenants. Their difficulty in discerning this clearly revealed message is because the message is indeed hidden to the casual reader. Of the 184 individuals mentioned by name in the Doctrine and Covenants, only five are women.[18] Of the five women, three (Eve, Sariah, and Hagar) are seen first in the Old Testament, and only two (Vienna Jaques and Emma Smith) are contemporary with Joseph Smith. Of all persons named in the Doctrine and Covenants, only 3 percent are women, whereas 97 percent are men. Seventy percent of the men mentioned were living at the time of Joseph Smith, 20 percent were Old Testament men, 5 percent New Testament men, and 2 percent Book of Mormon men.

The critics' impression that the role of women is not clearly taught in modern scripture may also arise from their discovery that the Doctrine and Covenants does not contain any detailed, exemplary stories of women like those in the Bible of Ruth and Esther. They miss the women-oriented teachings in the Doctrine and Covenants, noting instead that women are not mentioned as listening to Joseph's sermons. This omission is contrasted by such critics who recall that women are often cited as listening to Jesus and his apostles in Jerusalem and America.

Yet, when the modern scripture is seen in objective clarity, we see that the quality and quantity of references regarding women is more pervasive throughout the Doctrine and Covenants than in any other scripture.[19] It is in the Doctrine and Covenants that the Savior calls specifically to women and extends to them the blessings offered in the plan of salvation. (D&C 10:65.) The blessing of being gathered in, plus other blessings, including the wife's ability to sanctify her unbelieving husband and the promises of eternal life, are contained in this holy writ. (D&C 74:1; 132:20.)

Even though the scripturally defined path is ancient and clearly restated in the Doctrine and Covenants, many women still reject one phase or all phases of the plan. Each time a woman rejects a portion of the plan, she not only loses a blessing but experiences a judgment. For example, for marrying outside of the temple, "if a man marry him a wife in the world, and he marry her not by me nor by my word, and he covenant with her so long as he is in the world and she with him, their covenant and marriage are not of force when they are dead, and when they are out of the world; therefore, they are not bound by any law when they are out of the world." (D&C 132:15.)

The woman's willful rejection will obviously affect not only her own life but also perhaps generations to come. The family unit is basic to mortality and will exist among the righteous in eternal realms. When a woman ignores her familial responsibility, frustration will become apparent in her divine nature — for a woman is to be a daughter, a wife, and a mother. A woman cannot reject any of these divine roles without rejecting the essential process of womanhood.

When respect for womanhood is disregarded. Both men and women are warned against even the mildest disrespect toward womanhood. Such disrespect can thwart the Spirit from abiding with the individual. David Whitmer told of an incident in the lives of Joseph and Emma Smith where the devastating effects of mild disrespect were present:

"One morning when he was getting ready to continue the translation, something went wrong about the house and he was put out about it. Something that Emma, his wife, had done. Oliver and I went upstairs and Joseph came up soon after to continue the translation but he could not do anything. He could not translate a single syllable. He went downstairs, out into the orchard, and made supplication to the Lord; was gone about an hour—came back to the house, and asked Emma's forgiveness and then came upstairs where we were and then the translation went on all right."[20]

In each of the Lord's warnings against disrespect for womanhood, the greatest condemnation is found in the mental or physical violation of the sacred tabernacle of the woman's body. Men are warned, "He that looketh upon a woman to lust after her shall deny the faith, and shall not have the Spirit; and if he repents not he shall be cast out." (D&C 42:23; 63:16.) Women are similarly warned, "If she be not in the new and everlasting covenant, and she be with another man, she has committed adultery." (D&C 132:42.)

The Lord emphasized his great anger for those who disrespect womanhood by referring to Babylon as a whore. A whore rejects her sacred opportunity to co-create life and even eternal lives through righteous union with another of God's servants. Instead, she uses her most sacred and eternal gifts to get worldly gain, to destroy others, and to create cults for personal, selfish power.

Babylon is the epitome of evil whoring for gain after other gods. The Lord refers to false churches resulting from such whoring as stemming from the "mother of abominations." (D&C 88:94.) To help us understand the concept of Babylon and the mother of abominations, let us look at the example of the woman in the Doctrine and Covenants who illustrates some of these characteristics: Ann Lee.[21] This example teaches us that whoring of the mind and heart, as in Ann Lee's case, are as abominable as whoring of the physical body with its overt destruction, as was characteristic of ancient Babylon.

Mother Ann claimed, "The duality of Deity, God both Father and Mother; one in essence — one God, not two; but God who possesses two natures, the masculine and the feminine, each distinct in function yet one in being, co-equal in Deity."[22] This proclamation led to her belief that she was Jesus Christ. This doctrine was believed by her followers in "The United Society of Believers in Christ's Second Appearing."[23]

This abomination of redefining the nature of Deity also included a redefinition of the divine role of motherhood. Ironically, Mother Ann taught, "You must forsake the marriage of the flesh or you cannot be married to the lamb, or have any share in the resurrection of Christ." She abominably concluded, "Those who are counted worthy to have any part in the resurrection of Christ neither marry nor are given in marriage, but are like unto the angels."[24] Ann did not triumph in her false doctrine but became as the mother of abominations, of whom it was written, "She is fallen, is fallen!" (D&C 88:105.)

As is true of all who subvert the sacred role of daughter, wife, and mother, Ann received the harshest condemnation of God. We hear in our day cries by those who insist, like Ann Lee, that women should be freed from the role of righteous comforter and given the role of priest. We hear that women should be released from the earthly role of mother, yet viewed in eternity as a goddess. We see on all sides women who desire worldly power and influence claiming, "Come worship me." Yet, we see the faithful women humbly praying, "I shall worship thee." The whore of Babylon comes in many guises. Each guise would destroy for personal, temporal gain the sacred roles of righteous daughter, wife, and mother.

CONCLUSION

The world gives women little convincing direction for the process of womanhood. There are conflicting advisers on every side, seeming to agree only that old ways are to be rejected and replaced by roles that emphasize today by discounting eternity. The role of obedient daughter, comforting wife, and inspiring mother are viewed as foolish residue of past ages.

The righteous woman recognizes the increasing peril of the world's destructive advice. She searches diligently in the Doctrine and Covenants to discover the revealed word regarding her appropriate role. She finds modern prophetic advice consistent with ancient scriptural text. As a result, she commits herself to being a faithful daughter, wife, and mother.

The unrighteous woman will not search the Doctrine and Covenants to discover the Lord's plan for women. She does not desire to know or to heed the Lord's warnings. This lack will result in her life on earth and in the eternal realms being tossed to and fro by worldly doctrines, which are in opposition to the Lord's plan.

Obviously, each woman needs to choose whether to accept the Lord's divine plan for womanhood or to embrace its counterfeit. The revealed roles in mortality and in eternity for the woman are the correct roles. If they are obedient and faithful, "a crown of righteousness" awaits all women who reach and then live for this conclusion. (D&C 25:15.)

NOTES

1. Vienna Jaques, daughter of Henry and Lucinda Jaques, was born 10 June 1787 at Beverly, Essex, Massachusetts. She died 7 February 1884 in Salt Lake City, Utah.

2. Joseph Smith, *Teachings of the Prophet Joseph Smith,* sel. Joseph Fielding Smith (Salt Lake City: Deseret Book Co., 1961), pp. 26–27.

3. "Extracts from H. C. Kimball's Journal," as cited in Jerrie W. Hurd, *Our Sisters in the Latter-day Scriptures* (Salt Lake City: Deseret Book Co., 1987), p. 65.

4. Spencer W. Kimball, in Conference Report, Oct. 1978, p. 63.

5. *Messenger and Advocate*, Nov. 1835; Smith, *Teachings of the Prophet Joseph Smith*, p. 89.

6. Emma Hale Smith, daughter of Isaac Hale and Elizabeth Lewis, was born on 10 July 1804 at Harmony, Susquehannah, Pennsylvania. She married Joseph Smith, Jr., on 18 January 1827 at South Bainbridge, Chenango, New York. She died 30 April 1879 at Nauvoo, Hancock, Illinois.

7. Joseph Smith, *History of the Church,* ed. B. H. Roberts, 2d ed. rev. (Salt Lake City: The Church of Jesus Christ of Latter-day Saints, 1932–51), 4:552–53.

8. Bruce R. McConkie, *Mormon Doctrine,* 2d ed. (Salt Lake City: Bookcraft, 1966), p. 217.

9. Lucy Mack Smith, daughter of Solomon Mack and Lydia Gates, was born 8 July 1776 at Gilsum, Cheshire, New Hampshire. She married Joseph Smith, Sr., on 24 January 1796 at Tunbridge, Orange, Vermont. She died 5 May 1855 at Nauvoo, Hancock, Illinois.

10. Conference in Nauvoo, 8 Oct. 1845, General Minutes Collection, Historical Department, The Church of Jesus Christ of Latter-day Saints, Salt Lake City, Utah.

11. Ibid.

12. This consistent norm is also evident in the Gospels, in which women are identified by various titles. "Mother" is mentioned eighty-five times; "woman/women," eighty-eight; "wife/wives," fifty-five; "daughter," thirty-nine; and "maid/maiden," fourteen. Each time Jesus designated a woman by a title denoting her role in life it was with respect. He refrained from referring to any woman as an adulteress, a harlot, a hypocrite, or any other degrading title. (Luke 7:45; Matthew 9:22; Luke 13:12.)

13. Often the Lord's respect for womanhood, as documented in the New Testament, was illustrated in his stories and parables. He chose as an exemplar of generosity and sacrifice a certain poor widow who threw two mites into the treasury. (Mark 12:43–44.) The Savior used one woman's joy at the recovery of a lost piece of silver to illustrate angelic joy over one soul that repents. (Luke 15:8–10.)

14. Zion is referred to 262 times in the Doctrine and Covenants.

15. John A. Widtsoe, *Joseph Smith, Seeker After Truth, Prophet of God* (Salt Lake City: Deseret News Press, 1951), p. 185.

16. Joseph F. Smith, *Gospel Doctrine*, 5th ed. (Salt Lake City: Deseret Book Co., 1939), p. 352; Conference Report, Oct. 1947, p. 152.

17. Harold B. Lee, *Ye Are the Light of the World* (Salt Lake City: Deseret Book Co., 1974), p. 292; Joseph Fielding Smith, *Answers to Gospel Questions* (Salt Lake City: Deseret Book Co., 1979), 2:36.

18. A sixth woman, Ann Lee, is mentioned by name in the headnote to Doctrine and Covenants 49: "Some of the beliefs of the Shakers were that Christ's second coming had already occurred and he had appeared in the form of a woman, Ann Lee."

19. The Doctrine and Covenants closely parallels the Book of Mormon, which mentions only three contemporary women, Sariah (1 Nephi 2:5), Abish (Alma 19:16), and Isabel (Alma 39:3).

20. B. H. Roberts, *A Comprehensive History of The Church of Jesus Christ of Latter-day Saints* (Salt Lake City: The Church of Jesus Christ of Latter-day Saints, 1930), 1:131.

21. Ann Lee, born 29 February 1736, was the daughter of a blacksmith. She married a blacksmith by whom she bore four children, who died in infancy. At age twenty-two, Ann was converted by Jane Wardley and began to preach. Ann came to America in 1774, and from then until her death in 1784, she was able to found three Shaker communities.

22. Anne White and Leila S. Taylor, *Shakerism, Its Meaning and Message* (1904); *Encyclopedia Americana* (1949), 24:642; in Roy W. Doxey, *The Doctrine and Covenants Speaks* (Salt Lake City: Deseret Book Co., 1964–70), 1:336–41.

23. Joseph Smith wrote, "A woman has no right to found or organize a church — God never sent them to do it." (*Teachings of the Prophet Joseph Smith*, p. 212.) "And again, verily I say unto you, that the Son of Man cometh not in the form of a woman, on the earth." (D&C 49:22.)

24. White and Taylor, *Shakerism, Its Meaning and Message*, pp. 41–42; in Roy W. Doxey, *The Doctrine and Covenants Speaks*, 1:341.

CHAPTER TWO

The Doctrine and Covenants on Temples and Their Functions

Richard O. Cowan

Professor of Church History and Doctrine
Brigham Young University

An understanding of temples in former dispensations enhances our appreciation of these sacred structures in our own day.[1] In Old Testament times, for example, temples served two distinct functions: God promised to manifest himself to his people in the Tabernacle made by Moses in the wilderness (Exodus 25:8, 22), and God revealed sacred ordinances, both in the Tabernacle and in Solomon's Temple (D&C 124:38). Summarizing these two functions, Elder James E. Talmage declared that a temple is "characterized not alone as [1] the place where God reveals Himself to man, but also as [2] the House wherein prescribed ordinances of the Priesthood are solemnized."[2] A perceptive article written by Dr. Sidney B. Sperry considered the extent to which these ordinances may have been performed in ancient temples.[3] Both temples and temple functions would need to be part of the latter-day restoration of all things.

God's people at different times have had a varying comprehension of temple functions. As Elder Talmage explained, there is "no close similarity" in temple designs from one era to another, because "there is a definite sequence of development in the dealings of God with man throughout the centuries."[4] Even in the present dispensation this understanding has been unfolded piecemeal, by means of revelations now contained in the Doctrine and Covenants.

THE SCHOOL OF THE PROPHETS

A forerunner to temple procedures and worship can be seen in the School of the Prophets that opened three years before the dedication of the Kirtland Temple. An 1832 revelation instructed Church leaders to convene this school, which was described as a "solemn assembly" to prepare and sanctify those who would go forth to preach. (D&C 88:70, 74.) Only the worthy were to attend: "He that is found unworthy . . . shall not have place among you; for ye shall not suffer that mine house shall be polluted by him." Subsequent revelations use almost identical language concerning those who should or should not be permitted to enter the temples. (D&C 88:134; compare with D&C 97:15–17, for example.) Participants in the school were to have their hands and feet washed as a symbol of this spiritual preparation and of their being "clean from the blood of this wicked generation." (D&C 88:75.)

Meetings of the School of the Prophets frequently included advanced discussion of gospel doctrines. Those participating accepted a commitment "not to willfully divulge that which is discussed in the school."[5] The school met initially in a room, measuring about twenty feet square, above Newel K. Whitney's store. During the school's first season, however, the Saints were already looking forward to building the temple in order to provide a permanent home for the school.

DESIGN AND CONSTRUCTION OF THE KIRTLAND TEMPLE

The building of the Kirtland Temple had its genesis in the December 1832 revelation that had directed the brethren to form the School of the Prophets. The Lord commanded them to "establish a house, even a house of prayer, a house of fasting, a house of faith, a house of learning, a house of glory, a house of order, a house of God." (D&C 88:119.)

In May of the following year, the Lord directed that the temple and two other sacred buildings should be planned for the heart of Kirtland. (D&C 94:1–12, especially 8–9.) Just a few weeks later the Prophet drew up a plat for the city of Zion. The plan he envisioned expanded the number of holy buildings at the center of the city from three to twenty-four. These "temples" were to be assigned to the various priesthood quorums and were to serve a variety of functions — "houses of worship, schools, etc."[6] Because all inhabitants of the city would be expected to be living on a celestial level (D&C 105:5), all these buildings could be regarded as "temples" — places of communication between heaven and earth — even though their functions were not restricted to ordinance work.

On 1 June 1833, the Lord admonished the Saints to move forward with the building of the Kirtland Temple in which "I design to endow those whom I have chosen with power from on high." (D&C 95:8.) He specified that the temple was not to be built "after the manner of the world," but according to a plan that he promised to reveal. (D&C 95:13–14.) The chapel on the main floor was to be used "for your sacrament offering, and for your preaching, and your fasting, and your praying." A similar hall on the second floor was to house "the school of mine apostles." (D&C 95:16–17.) Five small rooms in the attic were used as offices or classrooms.

Thus, "the design and construction of the Kirtland Temple," Elder Boyd K. Packer explained, "was different from that of all other latter-day temples because its purpose was different. While already in 1836 certain ordinances had been introduced in a limited way which later would form part of the regular temple ordinances, the sacred ordinances and ceremonies performed in today's temples were not done in this first temple."[7] Specifically, President Brigham Young pointed out, the Kirtland Temple "had no basement in it, nor a font, nor preparations to give endowments for the living or the dead."[8] The temple was more of a multipurpose building intended for general functions rather than only for sacred ordinances.

A RICH OUTPOURING OF SPIRITUAL BLESSINGS

Great spiritual blessings and remarkable manifestations followed the period of sacrifice during the temple's construction. These "pentecostal" experiences began just three days after the School of the Elders had moved into the attic of the nearly completed temple. On Thursday evening, 21 January 1836, "at early candle-light"[9] the First Presidency met with the Patriarch, Joseph Smith, Sr., in the west room of the temple attic, where they anointed one another with consecrated oil and pronounced blessings and prophecies. Then, "the heavens were opened," the Prophet recorded, and he "beheld the celestial kingdom of God, and the glory thereof." When he saw his brother Alvin in that kingdom, he "marveled" because Alvin had died before the gospel was restored, so had not been baptized. But the Lord declared: "All who have died without a knowledge of this gospel, who would have received it if they had been permitted to tarry, shall be heirs of the celestial kingdom of God." (D&C 137:1, 6–7.) This assurance became the foundation of the Church's doctrine of salvation for the dead and of its great vicarious service in the temples.

During early 1836, the Saints reported seeing heavenly messengers in at least ten different meetings. At five of these meetings individuals testified that they had beheld the Savior himself. Many received visions, prophesied, or spoke in tongues.[10]

Some of the most memorable spiritual experiences occurred on Sunday, 27 March, the day the temple was dedicated. Hundreds of Latter-day Saints crowded into the temple, anticipating the great blessings the Lord promised to bestow upon them, including a special gift or endowment of power from on high. The seven-hour dedicatory service began at 9:00 A.M. Joseph Smith's first counselor, Sidney Rigdon, spoke eloquently for two and a half hours, declaring that among all the buildings erected for the worship of God, the temple was unique, having been "built by divine revelation."[11]

The climax of the day was the dedicatory prayer, which had been given to the Prophet by revelation. This revelation was a fulfillment of the Lord's promises (D&C 46:30; 50:30) to guide us in knowing what to pray for, and it also showed the Prophet what was appropriate to include in a temple dedicatory prayer. After expressing gratitude for God's blessing, the Prophet, with hands raised to heaven and tears flowing freely, prayed that the Lord would accept the temple, which had been built "through great tribulation . . . , that the Son of Man might have a place to manifest himself to his people." (D&C 109:5.) Thus the Kirtland Temple, like holy sanctuaries in former dispensations, was to be a place of revelation between God and man. Joseph petitioned that the blessings promised in the Lord's 1832 revelation (D&C 88:117–20) might now be realized. The prayer also asked that Church leaders and members and the leaders of nations might be blessed and that the promised gathering of "the scattered remnants of Israel" might be accomplished. (D&C 109:67.) This prayer would become a pattern for other temple dedicatory prayers. Joseph Smith and others testified that they had beheld divine messengers and heard heavenly choirs during the services.

A transcendently important spiritual manifestation occurred on Easter Sunday, 3 April, just one week following the temple's dedication. After the close of the afternoon worship service, Joseph Smith and Oliver Cowdery retired to the Melchizedek Priesthood pulpits in the west end of the lower room of the temple. The "veil," a canvas partition, was lowered so that they might pray in private. Joseph Smith testified that "the veil was taken from our minds" (D&C 110:1) and that he and Oliver beheld a series of remarkable visions. The Lord Jesus Christ appeared, accepted the temple, and promised to manifest himself therein "if my people will keep my commandments, and do not pollute this holy house." (D&C 110:8.) Moses then appeared and bestowed "the keys of the gathering of Israel from the four parts of the earth, and the leading of the ten tribes from the land of the north." (D&C 110:11.) Elias next conferred "the dispensation of the gospel of Abraham." (D&C 110:12.) Finally, in fulfillment of Malachi's prophecy (Malachi 4:5–6) and Moroni's promise (D&C 2), Elijah committed "the keys of this dispensation" in preparation for the "great and dreadful day of the Lord" (D&C 110:16). Through the sealing keys restored by Elijah, priesthood ordinances performed on earth can be "bound," or "sealed," in heaven. Latter-day Saints can also perform saving priesthood ordinances in behalf of loved ones who died without the opportunity of accepting the gospel in person. In this way the hearts of the children are turning to their fathers.

"The prime purpose in having such a temple," Elder Harold B. Lee believed, "seems to have been that there could be restored the keys, the effective keys necessary for the carrying on of the Lord's work." He therefore concluded that the events of 3 April 1836 (as recorded in D&C 110), were "sufficient justification for the building of [this] temple."[12]

Not long after these glorious occurrences had lifted the Saints, the forces of persecution increased. In less than two years the faithful were compelled to flee from their homes in Kirtland, and shortly afterwards, the Saints in Missouri were ordered to leave that state or be exterminated. By 1839, they found a new haven in Illinois, where they built the city of Nauvoo. Here the Lord unfolded to their understanding the doctrine of salvation for the dead and restored vital temple ordinances — the second of the two main functions of temples.

BAPTISM FOR THE DEAD

The New Testament indicates that the early Christians performed vicarious baptisms for the dead. (See 1 Corinthians 15:29.) This practice was taught for the first time in the present dispensation on 15 August 1840 at the funeral of Seymour Brunson, a faithful member of the Nauvoo high council.[13] The Prophet indicated that the Saints could "now act for their friends who had departed this life, and that the plan of salvation was calculated to save all who were willing to obey the requirements of the law of God."[14] Almost immediately Church members began receiving the ordinance of baptism in the Mississippi River in behalf of deceased loved ones.

In October, the Prophet explained this ordinance to the Twelve who were then in England: "The Saints have the privilege of being baptized for those of their relatives who are dead, whom they believe would have embraced the Gospel, if they had been privileged with hearing it, and who have received the Gospel in the spirit, through the instrumentality of those who have been commissioned to preach to them while in prison."[15]

The Prophet, on another occasion, referred to "the wisdom and mercy of God in preparing an ordinance for the salvation of the dead." Then, in the spirit of warning, he concluded: "Those Saints who neglect it in behalf of their deceased relatives, do it at the peril of their own salvation."[16]

With such encouragement, the Saints eagerly took advantage of the opportunity to make gospel ordinances and blessings available to their departed loved ones. By 1844, the year of the Prophet's martyrdom, some 15,722 baptisms had been performed in behalf of the dead.

NAUVOO TEMPLE CONSTRUCTION COMMANDED BY REVELATION

As early as August 1840 the First Presidency declared that the time had come "to erect a house of prayer, a house of order, a house for the worship of our God, where the ordinances can be attended to agreeably to His divine will."[17]

A revelation received 19 January 1841 specifically pointed out the need for the temple. Echoing instructions given to Moses concerning the ancient Tabernacle, the Lord now commanded his latter-day Saints to gather precious materials from afar and build a house "for the Most High to dwell therein. For there is not a place found on earth that he may come to and restore again that which was lost unto you, or which he hath taken away, even the fulness of the priesthood." (D&C 124:27–28; compare Exodus 25:8, 22.) Specifically, the Lord declared that the ordinance of baptism for the dead "belongeth to my house," and that he had temporarily allowed the Saints to perform this ordinance outside of the temple only "in the days of your poverty." He therefore commanded them to provide an appropriate font in the temple. (D&C 124:30–33.) Hence the Nauvoo Temple, like holy sanctuaries in former dispensations, was to serve the dual purpose of being a place of contact between God and man where sacred priesthood ordinances are also performed. The Lord promised to show the Prophet "all things pertaining to this house," including "the place whereon it shall be built." (D&C 124:42.)

THE ENDOWMENT AND OTHER BLESSINGS

Speaking in 1853 at the cornerstone-laying ceremonies for the Salt Lake Temple, President Brigham Young declared that in Kirtland the "first Elders" received only a "portion of their first endowments, or we might say more clearly, some of the first, or introductory, or initiatory ordinances, preparatory to an endowment."[18] "It should be remembered," Elder Bruce R. McConkie concurred, "that the endowment given in the Kirtland Temple was only a partial endowment, and that the full endowment was not performed until the saints had established themselves in Nauvoo."[19]

Elder James E. Talmage described the temple endowment as a "course of instruction," reviewing key events in the history of mankind—the Creation, the fall of Adam, the Great Apostasy, the Restoration, and our eventual reunion with God—giving emphasis to the plan of redemption and to our living according to the high standards of the gospel.[20] These instructions would need to be given in a place of privacy because they were sacred and would make known "things which have been kept hid from before the foundation of the world." (D&C 124:41.) Such a facility became available when Joseph Smith opened his store early in 1842. The second storey of this twenty-five-foot by forty-four-foot red brick structure included the Prophet's small personal office and a large area that came to be known as the assembly room. Here the Relief Society was organized on 17 March 1842, and the first endowments were given seven weeks later.[21]

With the assistance of five or six workmen, the Prophet divided the main room to represent the various stages in man's eternal progress. "We therefore went to work making the necessary preparations," one of the workmen later recalled, "and everything was arranged representing the interior of a temple as much as the circumstances would permit, [the Prophet] being with us dictating everything." These preparations were completed before noon on 4 May 1842, and later that same day the first endowments were given.[22] As the instructions of the endowment were unfolded, the group moved from one area to another in the main assembly room. Concerning this significant event, Joseph Smith recorded:

"I spent the day in the upper part of the store . . . in council with [seven brethren], instructing them in the principles and order of the Priesthood, attending to washings, anointings, endowments and the communication of keys pertaining to the Aaronic Priesthood, and so on to the highest order of the Melchisedek Priesthood, setting forth the order pertaining to the Ancient of Days, and all those plans and principles by which any one is enabled to secure the fullness of those blessings which have been prepared for the Church of the First Born, and come up and abide in the presence of the Eloheim in the eternal worlds. . . . the communications I made to this council were of things spiritual, and to be received only by the spiritual minded: and there was nothing made known to these men but what will be made known to all the Saints of the last days, so soon as they are prepared to receive, and a proper place is prepared to communicate them, even to the weakest of the Saints; therefore let the Saints be diligent in building the Temple."[23]

The Lord had anticipated these blessings and instructions when he spoke of the Saints' "washings" and "anointings" together with other revelations designed for the "glory, honor, and endowment" of Zion. (D&C 124:39.)

About a month after Elder Heber C. Kimball had received his endowment, he wrote of this experience to a colleague in the Twelve, Elder Parley P. Pratt, who was away doing missionary work: "We have received some pressious things through the Prophet on the priesthood that would cause your Soul to rejoice. I can not give them to you on paper fore they are not to be riten."[24] By the time of the Prophet's martyrdom, more than fifty individuals would have received the blessings of the endowment, these instructions being given in the assembly room above Joseph's store or in private homes.

By means of two letters written during the first week of September 1842, the Prophet gave yet further instructions concerning work for the dead. He emphasized the importance of having a recorder present, not only to keep an accurate record but also to assure that each ordinance is done properly. (D&C 127:6; 128:3.) The Prophet linked this keeping of proper records with the power to bind or loose on earth and have this action recognized in heaven. He indicated that in all ages any ordinance that is performed "truly and faithfully" by proper authority and is properly recorded, would be recognized in heaven. (D&C 128:8–9; compare Matthew 16:18–19.) This power to "bind on earth" and in heaven was associated with the keys that Elijah had restored in 1836 just after the dedication of the Kirtland Temple. Because temple baptismal fonts symbolize the grave, the Prophet explained, they should be located "underneath where the living are wont to assemble." (D&C 128:12–13.) Finally, expanding on the writings of Paul (Hebrews 11:40), Joseph Smith declared that "they [the fathers] without us cannot be made perfect—neither can we without our dead be made perfect" and that "their salvation is necessary and essential to our salvation." This is so because in the celestial kingdom we will be organized as God's family according to the patriarchal order. Hence he taught that there must be "a welding link of some kind or other between the fathers and the children." (D&C 128:15, 18.) Vicarious ordinances for the dead, he concluded, were the means of establishing this link.

Among the other blessings unfolded during these years was eternal marriage. During his earthly ministry, the Master had stressed the sanctity of the family. "What therefore God hath joined together," he declared, "let not man put asunder." (Mark 10:9.) The Apostle Paul similarly insisted: "Neither is the man without the woman, neither the woman without the man, in the Lord." (1 Corinthians 11:11.) During the present dispensation a revelation had affirmed that "marriage is ordained of God" as the means of providing earthly tabernacles for the spirits which had lived before the world was made. (D&C 49:15–17.)

Even though the first couple was married for eternity as early as 1841, there were relatively few of these "sealings" at first. In May 1843 the Prophet instructed the Saints that in order to attain the highest degree of the celestial kingdom, one must enter "the new and everlasting covenant of marriage." (D&C 131:1–4.) Two months later he recorded a revelation that among other things declared: "If a man marry him a wife in the world, and he marry her not by me nor by my word, and he covenant with her so long as he is in the world and she with him, their covenant and marriage are not of force when they are dead, and when they are out of the world." (D&C 132:15.) Following these instructions, the number of marriages for eternity increased.

In his 1841 revelation, the Lord had urged the construction of the temple so that he might restore "the fulness of the priesthood." (D&C 124:28.) During the closing year of his life, the Prophet Joseph Smith made sure that the Twelve and others received the highest blessings available through temple ordinances so that the authority necessary to roll forth the Lord's work would remain on the earth. Elder Orson Hyde later recalled that Joseph Smith "conducted us through every ordinance of the holy priesthood, and when he had gone through with all the ordinances he rejoiced very much, and says, now if they kill me you have got all the keys, and all the ordinances and you can confer them upon others, and the hosts of Satan will not be able to tear down the kingdom."[25]

EFFECT OF THE MARTYRDOM

The martyrdom of Joseph and Hyrum Smith on 27 June 1844 caused only a temporary lull in temple construction. Even though the Saints knew they would soon be forced to leave Nauvoo and lose access to the temple, yet they were willing to sacrifice to fulfill their Prophet's dream of erecting the million-dollar House of the Lord. Individual parts of the temple were completed and dedicated piecemeal so that ordinance work could begin as soon as possible.

Endowments were given beginning 10 December. By the end of the month more than a thousand Saints had received these endowment blessings, including 107 who spent Christmas Day in the temple receiving their endowment.

As the year 1846 dawned, pressure on the Saints to leave Illinois mounted. There were rumors that federal troops might be used against them. Hence Church leaders decided to commence the exodus early in February rather than wait until spring. This decision increased the Saints' eagerness to receive temple blessings before leaving Nauvoo, so activity at the temple during January was even greater than during the previous month.

On 12 January Brigham Young recorded: "Such has been the anxiety manifested by the saints to receive the ordinances [of the Temple], and such the anxiety on our part to administer to them, that I have given myself up entirely to the work of the Lord in the Temple night and day, not taking more than four hours sleep, upon an average, per day, and going home but once a week."[26]

During the eight weeks prior to the exodus, approximately 5500 were endowed, fulfilling the Prophet Joseph Smith's compelling desire to make these blessings available to the Saints in Nauvoo.

REFLECTIONS

As I studied the latter-day restoration of temple service, I was struck by the fact that the word *temple* was not always used in reference to these sacred structures. Today we think of these buildings as "temples," but the early Saints more often called them "houses."

The accompanying table summarizes the uses of these terms. From the initial word counts generated by the computer, we had to subtract entries from headings which were added in later years and hence did not reflect the usages at the time under study. We also had to delete the text of Doctrine and Covenants revelations from the *History of the Church*.

	Doctrine and Covenants		*History of the Church*	
	Temple	*House*	*Temple*	*House*
Kirtland	0 0%	40 100%	30 25%	89 75%
Independence	3 50%	3 50%	3 100%	0 0%
Far West	0 0%	7 100%	2 11%	16 89%
Nauvoo	1 12%	7 88%	322 93%	24 7%
Others	9 56%	7 44%	28 46%	33 54%
Totals	13 17%	64 83%	385 70%	162 30%

The Doctrine and Covenants employs the term *temple* about half of the time in referring to the sanctuaries in Jerusalem, in the New Jerusalem, and to temples in general, shown as "Other" on the table. In contrast, almost all references in the revelations to contemporary latter-day temples use the word *house*. The three instances where *temple* is used in connection with Independence, Missouri (D&C 57:3; 58:57; 84:3), all refer to the site where the holy structure was to be built. Hence they may have referred to the great temple of the last days in the New Jerusalem rather than just to the house the Saints were about to build there. On the other hand, the three uses of *house*, all in section 97, deal specifically with the structure the Saints were commanded to erect at that time. The temple in Nauvoo was almost always called a "house" in the revelations, despite the fact that there was a separate building, a hotel or boarding house, specifically named "the Nauvoo House." (D&C 124:60.)

Joseph Smith's *History of the Church* for the Ohio and Missouri period follows the same pattern, but it does employ *temple* part of the time. A dramatic shift is observed, however, when *temple* is used almost consistently in *History of the Church* to refer to the Lord's house in Nauvoo. Perhaps the restoration of sacred ordinances led the Saints increasingly to link the functions of this holy structure with the ancient temples. Interestingly, the only Doctrine and Covenants usage of *temple* in reference to a contemporary building actually is found in an epistle written by the Prophet concerning baptisms for the dead. (D&C 127:4.) Further research into diaries or other documents written at the time may shed greater light on the connection between the Saints' unfolding understand of the functions of temples and their use of that term in reference to these special buildings.

The process of unfolding the Saints' understanding of temples and temple service has continued. Vicarious endowments for the dead were inaugurated with the completion of the St. George Temple in 1877. For the first time the Saints had the privilege of returning to the temple and, while officiating in behalf of others, renewing their own understanding and appreciation of the great teachings contained in the endowment. In 1894 a revelation through President Wilford Woodruff directed the Saints to trace their genealogies and be sealed to their own progenitors as far back as possible. Then, in 1918, President Joseph F. Smith received a remarkable vision, expanding our understanding of how the gospel is being preached in the spirit world. (D&C 138.) Paraphrasing the ninth article of faith, we accept all that God has revealed concerning temples and their ordinances, and we eagerly look forward to whatever more he may yet reveal on this important subject.

NOTES

1. Richard O. Cowan, "The Latter-day Significance of Ancient Temples," in *The Old Testament and the Latter-day Saints: Sperry Symposium 1986* (Salt Lake City: Randall Book Co., 1986), pp. 111–24. For a more complete discussion, see Richard O. Cowan, *Temples to Dot the Earth* (Salt Lake City: Bookcraft, 1989).

2. James E. Talmage, *The House of the Lord* (Salt Lake City: Bookcraft, 1962), p. 17.

3. Sidney B. Sperry, "Some Thoughts Concerning Ancient Temples and Their Functions," *Improvement Era*, Nov. 1955, p. 814.

4. Talmage, *House of the Lord*, p. 110.

5. Orlen C. Peterson, "A History of the Schools and Educational Programs of the Church . . . in Ohio and Missouri, 1831–1839" (Master's thesis, Brigham Young University, 1972), pp. 23–24.

6. Joseph Smith, *History of The Church of Jesus Christ of Latter-day Saints*, ed. B. H. Roberts, 2d ed. rev. (Salt Lake City: The Church of Jesus Christ of Latter-day Saints, 1932–51), 1:358–59.

7. Boyd K. Packer, *The Holy Temple* (Salt Lake City: Bookcraft, 1980), p. 129.

8. Brigham Young, 1 Jan. 1877, in *Journal of Discourses* (London: Latter-day Saints' Book Depot, 1854–86), 18:303.

9. *History of the Church*, 2:379–80.

10. Milton V. Backman, Jr., *The Heavens Resound: A History of the Latter-day Saints in Ohio, 1830–1838* (Salt Lake City: Deseret Book Co., 1983), p. 285.

11. *History of the Church*, 2:415.

12. Harold B. Lee, "Correlation and Priesthood Genealogy," address at Priesthood Genealogical Research Seminar, 1968 (Provo: BYU Press, 1969), p. 60.

13. *History of the Church*, 4:179; see also D&C 124:132.

14. Andrew F. Ehat and Lyndon W. Cook, *The Words of Joseph Smith* (Provo, Utah: Religious Studies Center, Brigham Young University, 1980), p. 49.

15. *History of the Church*, 4:231; Joseph Smith, *Teachings of the Prophet Joseph Smith*, sel. Joseph Fielding Smith (Salt Lake City: Deseret Book Co., 1938), p. 179.

16. *History of the Church*, 4:426.

17. Ibid., 4:186.

18. Brigham Young, 6 Apr. 1853, in *Journal of Discourses*, 2:31.

19. Bruce R. McConkie, *Mormon Doctrine*, 2d ed. (Salt Lake City: Bookcraft, 1966), p. 831.

20. Talmage, *House of the Lord*, pp. 99–100.

21. Lyle G. Brown, "The Sacred Departments for Temple Work in Nauvoo: The Assembly Room and the Council Chamber," *BYU Studies* 19 (Spring 1979): 363.

22. Lucius N. Scovil letter in *Deseret News Semi Weekly*, 15 Feb. 1884, p. 2; quoted in *BYU Studies* 19 (Winter 1979): 159 n.

23. *History of the Church*, 5:1–2.

24. Heber C. Kimball to Parley P. Pratt, 17 June 1842, Parley P. Pratt papers, Archives of The Church of Jesus Christ of Latter-day Saints, Salt Lake City, Utah; quoted in Stanley B. Kimball, *Heber C. Kimball: Mormon Patriarch and Pioneer* (Urbana: University of Illinois Press, 1981), p. 85.

25. *Times and Seasons* 5 (15 September 1844): 651.

26. *History of the Church*, 7:567.

CHAPTER THREE

Light, Truth, and Grace: Three Interrelated Salvation Themes in Doctrine and Covenants 93

Richard D. Draper

Assistant Professor of Ancient Scripture
Brigham Young University

The revelation contained in section 93 of the Doctrine and Covenants was received 6 May 1833. The specific circumstances that generated it are obscure; the general conditions, however, are clear. During the few months before Joseph Smith received this informative masterpiece, the energy of the leaders of the Church was focused on making Kirtland, Ohio, a major stake of Zion. Since March 1833 efforts had been made to buy several farms for Church use.[1] These efforts had met with success and some of the Saints had begun to settle on various pieces of land. During that same period Sidney Rigdon and Frederick G. Williams were ordained to the office of Presidents of the High Priesthood, were given the keys of the kingdom, and became Joseph Smith's counselors.[2] President Williams was assigned to rent one of the pieces of property and to care for it for the benefit of the Church.[3]

At a meeting on 4 May these men presided. The meeting focused on how best to raise funds for a meetinghouse for the School of the Prophets.[4] Rented halls and homes had been used up to this point, but the Lord had instructed the Prophet that the time was right for the school to have its own house in which important instruction on both temporal and spiritual matters could be given. He emphasized individual worthiness to assure the success of the endeavor. Just two months before, the Lord had warned: "Be admonished in all your high-mindedness and pride, for it bringeth a snare upon your souls.

"Set in order your houses; keep slothfulness and uncleanness far from you. . . .

"Search diligently, pray always, and be believing, and all things shall work together for your good, if ye walk uprightly and remember the covenant wherewith ye have covenanted one with another." (D&C 90:17–18, 24.) In this revelation we see concern expressed over pride and slothfulness, and admonitions given for the Saints to pray, to be believing, and to set their homes in order. The latter was needed even at the highest levels of Church leadership. Because this admonition was not followed immediately, circumstances arose that the revelation recorded in Doctrine and Covenants 93 addressed.

During the settling period, rather serious family problems had beset President Williams. Just what these were is unknown, but apparently he had discussed them with the Prophet. The revelation given on 6 May 1833, now recorded in section 93, identified the source of the troubles that were besetting President Williams: "You have not taught your children light and truth, according to the commandments; and that wicked one hath power, as yet, over you, and this is the cause of your affliction." (D&C 93:42.) The revelation then instructed all the members of the First Presidency as well as the bishop of Kirtland, Newel K. Whitney, to set their houses in order. The revelation explained the value and necessity of doing so and in the process provided deeper understanding of certain aspects of salvation, among them, light, truth, and grace. The purpose of this paper is to investigate the contribution this revelation makes to our understanding of the relationship of these concepts in the work of salvation.

THE GLORY OF GOD IS INTELLIGENCE

The Lord commanded President Williams to bring up his children in "light and truth" (D&C 93:42), having already elaborated on the importance of these two elements. In his elaboration the Lord explained, "The glory of God is intelligence, or, in other words, light and truth." (D&C 93:36.) Observe that light and truth are shown to be constituent elements of intelligence, which constitutes the glory of God.

The concept of glory is very prominent in the scriptures, especially as something bestowed on the faithful as part of their final reward. But what is glory? A modern dictionary gives as definitions "fame, honor, distinction, and renown."[5] Over the centuries many Christian theologians, such as Milton, Johnson, and Thomas Aquinas, have felt that this was the sense of the scriptural use. Specifically, glory denoted appreciation or approval from God.[6] Thus, the glory of God was the favor and respect he granted those who met with his divine approbation.

The definition given in section 93 goes beyond such a definition, at least so far as the glory associated with God is concerned. His glory, as defined under inspiration, is something associated with his very nature, not just something he bestows upon others. Moses not only saw but also shared in the glory of God. The account in Moses 1:2 states, "And he saw God face to face, and he talked with him, and the glory of God was upon Moses; therefore Moses could endure his presence." There is no doubt that Moses was in the favor of God, but this revelation shows that God's glory was a capacitating agent that made it possible for Moses to bear God's actual presence. But that was not all. Through that power Moses was endowed with sufficient intellect to understand to a degree the nature of God's work. The Lord stated that he would show Moses the workmanship of his hands, "but not all, for my works are without end, and also my words, for they never cease." He then explained why he would not show Moses all his works: "No man can behold all my works," he said, "except he behold all my glory; . . . and afterwards remain in the flesh on the earth." (Moses 1:4–5.) This scripture suggests that it is God's glory that gives him the capacity to be all seeing. Further, the ability to behold all that glory would require a change in the basic constitution of man that would make him more than mortal.

LIGHT AS AN ASPECT OF GLORY

A modern dictionary gives as a secondary definition of glory as "a ring or spot of light"[7]; *glory* is therefore associated with "radiance." The dictionary gives one the feeling that such association is very limited; that, however, is not the case in a dictionary available to Joseph Smith. According to that dictionary, *glory* is first and foremost "brightness, luster, and splendor." Only in a secondary sense is it fame or praise. That dictionary notes that in a scriptural sense glory is a manifestation of the presence of God.[8] This meaning accords much better with Joseph Smith's use of the term. For example, while recounting his first vision he wrote, "I saw a pillar of light exactly over my head, above the brightness of the sun, which descended gradually until it fell upon me. . . . I saw two Personages, whose brightness and glory defy all description." (Joseph Smith–History 1:16–17.) Writing of this experience on another occasion he stated, "I was enwrapped in heavenly vision, and saw two glorious personages, who exactly resembled each other in features and likeness, surrounded with a brilliant light which eclipsed the sun at noon day."[9] In these passages *glory* is directly associated with "radiance." This association fits nicely with the idea expressed in Doctrine and Covenants 93 that light is a constituent part of glory.

To ancient Israel one of the important aspects of God was his ability to display his power through the manifestation of burning light. Indeed, Israel stood in awe because of the display of a brilliance like a devouring inferno on the top of Sinai. (Exodus 24:17.) Moses proclaimed, "the Lord thy God is a consuming fire." (Deuteronomy 4:24.) His presence was manifest on more than one occasion by a pillar of fire, which gave light to Israel but vexed the Egyptians. (Exodus 13:21; 14:24.) The cloud of his glory dwelt upon the tabernacle while its radiance filled the court. (Exodus 40:34.) That this idea has continued into the present can be seen in the promise to the early Saints that "this generation shall not all pass away until an house shall be built unto the Lord, and a cloud shall rest upon it, which cloud shall be even the glory of the Lord, which shall fill the house." (D&C 84:5.)

Like Moses, Joseph Smith knew well the glory associated with the presence of the Lord. Of His appearance in the Kirtland Temple Joseph Smith reported, "His eyes were as a flame of fire; . . . his countenance shone above the brightness of the sun." (D&C 110:3.) When he comes the second time, we are told that he will be "clothed in the brightness of his glory." (D&C 65:5.) These are only a few of many references suggesting that light and radiance are important aspects of glory.

LIGHT AND THE PROCESS OF SALVATION

Radiance in the normative sense is related to light. But what is light? A careful look at the way the term is used in the scriptures suggests that it is more than mere luminosity. We get a glimpse of the breadth of meaning ascribed to the word when the Lord states, "the light which shineth, which giveth you light, is through him who enlighteneth your eyes, which is the same light that quickeneth your understandings." (D&C 88:11.) This phrase defines light not only as something that makes vision possible but also as that force which activates and stimulates the intellect. Further, light "is in all things," gives "life to all things," and "is the law by which all things are governed." (D&C 88:13.) Thus, a more full definition would make light an ever-present, life- and law-giving power that manifests itself, among other ways, as natural light, intellectual activity, and the living energy in all things. The scriptures declare that this "light proceedeth forth from the presence of God to fill the immensity of space" and that it is "the power of God who sitteth upon his throne, who is in the bosom of eternity, who is in the midst of all things." (D&C 88:12–13.)

These scriptures suggest that the term *light* is used to describe that aspect of the nature of God which radiates out from him expanding with his work and will, enlightening, organizing, capacitating, and quickening as it does.

In sum, light is the ever-present, life- and law-giving, intellectually and spiritually quickening aspect of the power of God. Perhaps the best definition would be living and capacitating energy. Thus, a scripture states, "That which is of God is light; and he that receiveth light, and continueth in God, receiveth more light; and that light groweth brighter and brighter until the perfect day." (D&C 50:24.) This scripture suggests that the continual reception of this living energy endows one with ability. Thus, the Lord states, "if your eye be single to my glory, your whole bodies shall be filled with light and there shall be no darkness in you; and that body which is filled with light comprehendeth all things." (D&C 88:67.) As one increases in light he increases in ability until he is able to comprehend all things.

THE RELATIONSHIP BETWEEN LIGHT AND TRUTH

One is not glorified in light, or as here defined, in power, or energy. Glorification is contingent upon the reception of the other, all-important element. Section 93 teaches us, "He that keepeth [God's] commandments receiveth truth and light, until he is glorified *in truth* and knoweth all things." (D&C 93:28; italics added.) The glorifying principle is truth. Defining truth,[10] the scripture states, "truth is knowledge of things as they are, and as they were, and as they are to come." (D&C 93:24.) In other words, truth is knowledge of what a Latter-day Saint hymn proclaims as "the sum of existence."[11] Truth defined in this way is always associated with light because truth can only be acquired through the power or the capacitating force of light. Without the faculty created by light, a fulness of truth could never be gained.

The acquisition of both light and truth is dependent on obedience. Explaining the need and the reason for obedience, the Lord stated, "You shall live by every word that proceedeth forth from the mouth of God." (D&C 84:44.) The explanation is simple: obedience is requisite for eternal life. Again the Lord explains why: "For the word of the Lord is truth, and whatsoever is truth is light, and whatsoever is light is Spirit, even the Spirit of Jesus Christ." (D&C 84:45.) The factors of life — light and truth — are equated with the Spirit of Christ, because he alone controls their dissemination through the bestowal of his Spirit. Therefore, he can stipulate the means by which they are granted. Thus, obedience to his will is absolutely requisite for those who would gain life.

According to Doctrine and Covenants 131:7–8 all spirit is matter. If this includes the Spirit of Christ, then its bestowal upon an individual would be an imparting of actual celestial substance — actual elements producing higher power, higher capacity, higher life. The result of its infusion would be spiritual and intellectual capacitation, which would allow the individual to progress to the point that he could enjoy eternal life.

But the capacitating force of light would have to precede the possession of this celestial substance. The scripture continues, "And the Spirit giveth light to every man that cometh into the world; and the Spirit enlighteneth every man through the world, that hearkeneth to the voice of the Spirit. And every one that hearkeneth to the voice of the Spirit cometh unto God, even the Father." (D&C 84:46–47.) Light, the capacitating power, and enlightenment, or truth, are received by acquisition of celestial element through the Spirit of Christ to those who obey the word. But, first comes obedience to the word, then light, and finally truth.

Thus, all — word, light, truth, Spirit — become one. They are inseparably welded together so man cannot be touched by one without being touched by all. Accordingly, the scripture states, "My voice is Spirit; my Spirit is truth; truth abideth and hath no end; and if it be in you it shall abound." (D&C 88:66.) As noted already, that body which is filled with light — the power of God — can comprehend all things: truth.

For emphasis, let me say again that truth is the basis of glorification. Section 93 helps us understand why. In verse 30 we read, "All truth is independent in that sphere in which God has placed it, to act for itself, as all intelligence also; otherwise there is no existence." The very essence of existence is the ability of truth and intelligence to act for themselves. But how can truth, which has been defined earlier as knowledge, act? It would be more comprehensible if the scripture stated that truth impels or causes righteous action. But that is not what this verse states. And what does the scripture mean by "all truth"? Is there more than one kind of truth?

Understanding comes from the latter part of verse 30, which states that "all intelligence" is free to act for itself. As noted above, intelligence is equated with the glory of God, i.e. light and truth. But intelligence is also equated with a specific primal substance. Verse 29 of section 93 states, "Intelligence, or the light of truth, was not created or made, neither indeed can be."[12] Thus, intelligence has two scriptural definitions. One is an abstraction designated as "light and truth," conveying the idea of mental acuity by which existence is cognized. The other is more concrete. It designates the primal substance of being, which is called "the light of truth." The context of verse 30 suggests that intelligence should be understood in the latter sense. Thus, all intelligence, or the primal substance from which man is created, is free to act within the bounds in which God has placed it.

Intelligence, then, has two definitions. So may *truth.* The Lord says *all* truth is independent in the sphere in which he has placed it. If truth is the knowledge of the sum of existence then "all truth" would seem to define existence itself.[13] Thus, all existence (or all things that exist — that is, truth) has a measure of independence in which it is free to act. Of this totality, that portion designated as intelligence and associated expressly with man is also free to act. Because it is a portion of the whole of reality, it is designated as the spirit part of truth.

In sum, "all intelligence," as I see it, identifies a component of the spirit aspect of existence. The phrase "all truth" defines the whole of that existence. The condition for glorification is cognition of that whole. Cognition comes only with obedience and the acquisition of light, which allows truth to follow as the capstone and seal. Thus, one is glorified in truth.

Note that God is the one who sets the bounds and conditions that make cognition possible. He has determined that man will be glorified only as he receives truth. But man can receive a fulness of truth only as he receives a fulness of light. Emphasizing this point are the verses that state: "Behold, here is the agency of man, and here is the condemnation of man; because that which was from the beginning is plainly manifest unto them [i.e., truth], and they receive not the light [or capacitating power]. And every man whose spirit receiveth not the light is under condemnation." (D&C 93:31–32.) Intelligence is free to choose or reject light. When it willfully rejects light, it is rejecting truth, and condemnation follows.

WHY MAN CAN RECEIVE LIGHT AND TRUTH

Section 93 explains why man is capable of receiving a fulness of light and truth. The Savior states, "I was in the beginning with the Father." (D&C 93:21.) "I am the Spirit of truth, and John bore record of me, saying: He received a fulness of truth, yea, even of all truth." (D&C 93:26.) Because Christ is of God (I take this to mean that he was the literal Son of God and so was of the genus of the Gods), he had the ability to do what the race of the Gods do and that includes possessing all truth. One purpose of John's record, as preserved in section 93, was to bear testimony that this potential was indeed realized in the Lord.

But the Savior was not the only descendant of the Gods. He tells us that he was but the firstborn of many brethren. (Romans 8:29.) Therefore, concerning mankind, he further explains, "Ye were also in the beginning with the Father; that which is Spirit, even the Spirit of truth." (D&C 93:23.) Here we learn that as Christ was in the beginning with the Father so, too, was man. Further, both man and Christ are the Spirit of truth. They are, therefore, of the same *genus,* their primal nature being identical. Accordingly, what the Savior was able to realize is likewise within the potential of man. This is emphasized in the verses that state, "Verily I say unto you, I was in the beginning with the Father, and am the Firstborn; and all those who are begotten through me are the partakers of the glory of the same, and are the church of the Firstborn." (D&C 93:21–22.) Man can receive glory, even the same glory as the Savior, because he is of the same origin and stock.

CHRIST AS THE SOURCE OF LIGHT AND TRUTH

But what is the process by which mortals receive the glory of Christ? The Savior has answered, "I am the way, the truth, and the life: no man cometh unto the Father, but by me." (John 14:6.) He here emphasizes that the only way is through him, and he explains the reason, stating that he will appoint nothing unto man "except it be by law, even as I and my Father ordained unto you, before the world was." Going on, he states, "I am the Lord thy God; and I give unto you this commandment — that no man shall come unto the Father but by me or by my word, which is my law, saith the Lord." (D&C 132:11–12.)

Here we see the central place that the word of Christ plays in the process of salvation. Man can only come to know God through the word of the Lord. But we have already seen that his "word" is equated with Spirit, light, and truth. Therefore, the reception of the word is the reception of light and truth. The Savior's objective is to bring obedient souls to a fulness of glory. He knows how, for he followed the way set down by the Father. And if man receives glory, it will be in the same way through which Christ received it.

God's glory consists in a fulness of light and truth. Christ was glorified as he, too, came to possess a fulness of light and truth. It did not happen all at once. Section 93 states: "I, John, saw that he received not of the fulness at the first, but received grace for grace;

"And he received not the fulness at the first, but continued from grace to grace, until he received a fulness." (D&C 93:12–13.)

THE ROLE OF GRACE

The role played by grace in the process through which the Lord received a fulness of the glory of the Father was twofold: he received grace for grace, and he went from grace to grace. But what does it mean to receive grace for grace and to go from grace to grace? The answer lies in the very nature of grace. The word denotes favor, kindness, and goodwill. Out of this comes the theological definition: "the free unmerited love and favor of God," which brings divine assistance to his chosen ones.[14] The key expressions here are love and favor, and unmerited assistance. To receive grace for grace is to receive assistance on the condition of giving assistance. But not just any kind of assistance can be given. What transforms assistance into grace is the kindness and favor felt by the giver which is extended to the receiver, when such service is totally unmerited. But grace does not have to be given without condition. Indeed, an important aspect of the word is reciprocity. The scripture states specifically that man receives "grace for grace." (D&C 93:20.) Thus, the extension of favor is meant to obligate the recipient so that he will extend the same. As he meets this condition, more grace is extended to him, which further obligates him to greater assistance of others.

Apparently, it was necessary for the Lord to grow through this process. In order to do so, he first received grace, or divine assistance, from the Father. This grace he extended to his brethren. As he did so he received even more grace. The process continued until he eventually received a fulness of the glory of the Father. The implication of this process is interesting: in a very real way Christ himself was saved by grace.

Such a concept sheds light on certain aspects of the Savior's teachings. "The Father hath not left me alone," he stated, "for I do always those things that please him." (John 8:29.) Here he acknowledged the contingent relationship that existed between him and his Father. He was totally dependent upon the Father for power and knowledge. By doing God's will, the Savior enjoyed communion with the Father through which God gave grace to the Son. This association anchored the Savior's profound abilities to teach and to do. He insisted, "The Son can do nothing of himself," but "the Father that dwelleth in me, he doeth the works." (John 5:19; 14:10.) Thus, the grace of God was, of necessity, upon the Son. But note that it was truly grace, for the Atonement did not effect the Father's salvation. Otherwise, any assistance God rendered could not be considered an act of grace but of necessity.

In a very real way, the Savior has the same relation to the Father as we have to Christ. He stated, "As the branch cannot bear fruit of itself, except it abide in the vine; no more can ye, except ye abide in me. I am the vine, ye are the branches: He that abideth in me, and I in him, the same bringeth forth much fruit: for without me ye can do nothing." (John 15:4–5.)

These verses suggest another important aspect of grace, that of impartation. Whenever grace is extended, something is imparted. This imparting results in increased ability in the recipient. In the scriptures the reception of grace is expressed in two ways: a loss of the very propensity for sin and the accompanying ability to live God's laws. Paul taught this concept, saying, "What shall we say then? Shall we continue in sin, that grace may abound? God forbid. How shall we, that are dead to sin, live any longer therein? . . . For sin shall not have dominion over you: for ye are not under the law, but under grace." (Romans 6:1–2, 14.)

The Savior himself had to have power to live his Father's law. According to Joseph Smith, "None ever were perfect but Jesus; and why was He perfect? Because He was the Son of God, and had the fullness of the Spirit, and greater power than any man."[15] This power came through grace, even the grace of God.

Just what was imparted to Christ and, by inference, to man? Doctrine and Covenants 93 makes clear that it is light and truth. The possession of light and truth allows one to forsake the evil one and to be protected against his machinations. Further, light and truth enable their recipient to progress toward a fulness of the glory of God. This was the case with the Lord. Through his benevolence he received grace. Additional powers of light and truth were continually being extended to him such that he went from grace to grace. In other words, he went from one power level to another, from one capacity to a greater, until he received a fulness of the Father.

Receiving these life-giving principles of God allowed the Lord to become the spiritual Son of the Father.[16] John seems to have been communicating this idea when he stated, "And *thus* he was called the Son of God, because he received not of the fulness at the first." (D&C 93:14; italics added.) The Father confirmed that sonship had been accomplished when he stated: "This is my beloved Son." (D&C 93:15.) The fulness of sonship was contingent upon receiving the fulness of grace or, in other words, light and truth. The Savior did receive this fulness, and John testified, "He received a fulness of the glory of the Father; And he received all power, both in heaven and on earth, and the glory of the Father was with him, for he dwelt in him." (D&C 93:16–17.) Thus, section 93 is clear about the way the Savior gained the glory of the Father. Since he is the way, the course he pursued must be the way all must follow. Section 93 is emphatic that this is the case. The Savior states, "I give unto you these sayings that you many understand . . . that you may come unto the Father in my name, and in due time receive of his fulness.

"For if you keep my commandments you shall receive of his fulness, and be glorified in me as I am in the Father; therefore, I say unto you, you shall receive grace for grace." (D&C 93:19–20.)

Expressing the same thought, Joseph Smith stated, "You have got to learn how to be Gods yourselves, and to be kings and priests to God, the same as all Gods have done before you, namely, by going from one small degree to another, and from a small capacity to a great one; from grace to grace, from exaltation to exaltation, until you attain to the resurrection of the dead, and are able to dwell in everlasting burnings, and to sit in glory, as do those who sit enthroned in everlasting power." [17]

CONCLUSION

An essential part of the glory of God is light, or living, life-giving energy. Light is a capacitating power through which man is given the faculty to receive truth. Possession of truth is the condition that must be met for glorification. A fulness of truth, or the knowledge of the sum of existence, requires the acquisition of the fulness of light. The grace of God plays a direct part in the reception of light and truth. Grace expresses itself through impartation. That which is imparted is light. The agency of man is expressed in choosing or rejecting light. But he is not free to choose or reject grace. Grace comes to all men freely, as it is the unmerited favor that God holds for all his children. Grace allows light to flow unto man. Thus, light, through grace, is freely manifest unto man. When man rejects light, he rejects God's favor and cuts himself off from truth. Thus, he stands under condemnation. When he accepts grace by choosing light he is capacitated to receive truth. As he continues from grace to grace by giving grace for grace, he receives more light and truth until he is eventually glorified in truth.

NOTES

1. Joseph Smith, *History of The Church of Jesus Christ of Latter-day Saints,* ed. B. H. Roberts (Salt Lake City: The Church of Jesus Christ of Latter-day Saints, 1932–51), 1:335.

2. Ibid., p. 334.

3. Ibid., p. 336.

4. Ibid., pp. 342–43.

5. *Webster's New Collegiate Dictionary* (Springfield, Mass.: G. & C. Merriam Co., 1973), s.v. "glory."

6. C. S. Lewis, *The Weight of Glory* (Grand Rapids: William B. Eerdmans Publishing Co., 1949), pp. 8–9.

7. *Webster's,* s.v. "glory."

8. Noah Webster, *American Dictionary of the English Language,* 3d ed. of the reprint of the 1829 ed. (San Francisco: Foundation of American Christian Education, 1983), s.v., "glory."

9. *History of the Church,* 4:536.

10. *American Dictionary*, in standard use during Joseph Smith's lifetime, defines *truth* as "conformity to fact or reality; exact accordance with that which is, or has been, or shall be." (S.v. "truth.")

11. John Jaques, "Oh Say, What Is Truth?" *Hymns* (Salt Lake City: The Church of Jesus Christ of Latter-day Saints, 1985), no. 272.

12. The Prophet Joseph Smith elaborated on this thought, stating, "Intelligence is eternal and exists upon a self-existent principle. It is a spirit from age to age, and there is no creation about it." (*Teachings of the Prophet Joseph Smith*, sel. Joseph Fielding Smith [Salt Lake City: Deseret Book, 1939], p. 354.) B. H. Roberts believed this referred to the primal substance from which man's spirit was organized. (See Smith, *Teachings*, p. 354 n. 9; see also p. 158 n. 5.)

13. This is the definition in "Oh Say, What Is Truth?" (*Hymns*, 1985, no. 272.) This hymn, as a piece of poetry, was once a part of the Pearl of Great Price. It was set to music and placed in the LDS hymnal.

14. *American Dictionary*, s.v. "grace."

15. Smith, *Teachings*, pp. 187–88.

16. The Savior was already the spirit Son of God. He was also the physical Son. But it was the reception of the divine attributes of light and truth by which he was glorified and gained eternal life. Accordingly, he became the spiritual or eternal Son of God when he received of the fulness of the Father.

17. Smith, *Teachings*, pp. 346–47.

CHAPTER FOUR

The Oath and Covenant of the Priesthood

S. Brent Farley

Instructor, Logan Institute of Religion
Logan, Utah

"When we receive the Melchizedek Priesthood, we enter into a covenant with the Lord. It is the covenant of exaltation. . . .

" . . . There neither is nor can be a covenant more wondrous and great."[1] Thus testified Elder Bruce R. McConkie.

The core of revelation focusing upon the oath and covenant of the priesthood is found in Doctrine and Covenants 84:33–48. This nucleus of information is rich with doctrine which, like the hub of a great wheel, is connected with and extends out to the very circumference of the entire gospel. It is the purpose of this paper to examine that hub, or nucleus, in a verse-by-verse analysis so that we may achieve a greater and clearer understanding of this pivotal covenant that affects the eternities.

DOCTRINE AND COVENANTS 84:33

"For whoso is faithful unto the obtaining these two priesthoods of which I have spoken, and the magnifying their calling, are sanctified by the Spirit unto the renewing of their bodies."

The two priesthoods are the Aaronic and Melchizedek, and *obtaining* means "to be ordained to." The key word that precedes *obtaining* is *faithful*. One must live so as to be judged worthy of receiving each of these priesthoods. President Joseph Fielding Smith explained that "the Aaronic Priesthood is a preparatory priesthood to qualify us to make the covenant and receive the oath that attends this higher priesthood."[2]

In the course of personal priesthood development, men are to magnify their callings. To what are they called? Alma repeatedly associates the word *called* or *calling* with the priesthood itself (as contrasted with particular priesthood assignments), teaching that men are "called by this holy calling, and ordained unto the high priesthood of the holy order of God." (Alma 13:6.) The way to magnify that calling to priesthood authority is beautifully illustrated by the Lord as he explains why "there are many *called*, but few are chosen." (D&C 121:34; italics added.) One who magnifies his calling to the priesthood will understand that "the rights of the priesthood are inseparably connected with the powers of heaven, and that the powers of heaven cannot be controlled nor handled only upon the principles of righteousness." He will know that "no power or influence can or ought to be maintained by virtue of the priesthood, only by persuasion, by long-suffering, by gentleness and meekness, and by love unfeigned; by kindness, and pure knowledge, which shall greatly enlarge the soul without hypocrisy, and without guile." (D&C 121:36, 41–42.)

One whose service is characterized by those qualities is magnifying his calling to the priesthood, and he has the foundation for success for the varied priesthood tasks and offices he may hold throughout his life. He will also use these principles in his home, for, President Harold B. Lee stated, "Remember that the most important of the Lord's work that you will ever do will be the work you do within the walls of your own home. . . . God will never ask any man to sacrifice his family in order to carry out his other duties in the kingdom."[3]

What does it mean to magnify a calling? Elder McConkie explained: "Now, to magnify as here used means to enlarge or increase, to improve upon, to hold up to honor and dignity, to make the calling noble and respectable in the eyes of all men by performing the mission which appertains to the calling in an admirable and successful manner."[4]

Elder Carlos E. Asay listed ways that one magnifies a priesthood calling: "By learning one's duty and executing it fully. (See D&C 107:99–100.)

"By giving one's best effort in assigned fields of labor.

"By consecrating one's time, talents, and means to the Lord's work as called upon by our leaders and the whisperings of the Spirit. . . .

"By teaching and exemplifying truth."[5]

In referring to magnifying one's calling, Elder Marion G. Romney said: "I am persuaded that it requires at least the following three things: 1. That we obtain a knowledge of the gospel. 2. That we comply in our personal living with the standards of the gospel. 3. That we give dedicated service."[6]

Faithful priesthood holders are "sanctified by the Spirit unto the renewing of their bodies." (D&C 84:33.) To be sanctified is to be made clean through the power of the Holy Ghost and then to have its operative power giving guidance for life's activities. Such influence has a positive effect upon the body. *Renew* is defined as something that restores to a good state, rebuilds, repairs, confirms, revives, makes fresh and vigorous, transforms, implants holy affections, etc.[7] It is not necessarily that the body is visibly transformed (though this could be the case at times), but the positive effects of the Spirit support and invigorate physical and mental well-being. In connection with the oath and covenant of the priesthood, the renewal of the body refers to an eternal effect as well as a mortal one. Ultimately, the one who is faithful to the oath and covenant will have the body renewed in celestial glory in the resurrection. (See D&C 88:28–29.)

DOCTRINE AND COVENANTS 84:34

"They become the sons of Moses and of Aaron and the seed of Abraham, and the church and kingdom, and the elect of God."

Sonship denotes belonging to a family and having certain rights as a member and as an heir. We speak of becoming sons and daughters of Jesus Christ when we are converted, or born again, to the things of the Spirit. In this gospel conversion sense, becoming a son implies the acceptance of the person and principles of the one designated as the father. To become a son of Moses and Aaron, then, would imply accepting them and their principles so that we would have a relationship and as heirs, receive certain rights, including the rights of the priesthood.

Moses was called of God as the prophet to gather Israel, lead them from Egyptian bondage, and establish them as an independent and strong people. (Exodus 3:10–17.) He was the prophet, the mouthpiece of the Lord to Israel; by following his inspired direction the people could obtain exaltation. Those who become sons of Moses today are those who accept the mouthpiece of the Lord who has been called to deliver modern Israel from the bondage of worldliness in order to become established as a strong and independent people and be led toward exaltation. They too participate in the gathering of Israel, the keys of which Moses committed to Joseph Smith and Oliver Cowdery in the latter-day restoration. (D&C 110:11.)

The sons of Moses have a right "to the Holy Priesthood," "which priesthood continueth in the church of God in all generations, and is without beginning of days or end of years." (D&C 84:6, 17.) Moses sought diligently to prepare his people for this right to be worthy of the presence of God through the authority, ordinances, and power of the priesthood. (D&C 84:19–23.) The sons of Moses today hearken to the one called of God to guide them in their preparation to behold His presence.

Aaron was a spokesman for Moses and an assistant to him, Moses having the greater calling and Aaron the lesser. The lesser, or preparatory, priesthood was named after Aaron. (D&C 84:18, 26–27.) The sons of Aaron today are those who accept the preparatory, or Aaronic, Priesthood and live its principles, thus proving worthy of greater blessings as they enter the Order of the Melchizedek Priesthood. They learn to accept all who are called as spokesmen (those other local and general authorities who help accomplish the Lord's work) under the direction of the prophet. They are also willing themselves to serve as spokesmen in priesthood capacities when called to do so.

Thus, the sons of Moses and of Aaron today are faithful priesthood holders. In the course of their progress, they will become worthy temple recommend holders. They will "offer an acceptable offering and sacrifice in the house of the Lord" (D&C 84:31) by receiving their own temple endowment and performing work for the dead. "And the sons of Moses and of Aaron shall be filled with the glory of the Lord, upon Mount Zion in the Lord's house, whose sons are ye; and also many whom I have called and sent forth to build up my church." (D&C 84:32.)

The mention of the temple is most significant, for it is through the ordinances of the Lord's house that we prepare to achieve the goal sought by Moses for his people: to enter the Lord's presence. Elder McConkie noted that "the greatest blessings are reserved for those who obtain 'the fulness of the priesthood,' meaning the fullness of the blessings of the priesthood. These blessings are found only in the temples of God."[8] The oath and covenant of the priesthood includes all of the covenants made in the temple.

In similitude to the mission of Moses to gather Israel and establish them as a people, the Lord revealed a latter-day mission of the "sons of Moses:" "Yea, the word of the Lord concerning his church, established in the last days for the restoration of his people, as he has spoken by the mouth of his prophets, and for the gathering of his saints." (D&C 84:2.) The corollary between the mission of Moses in ancient Israel and the mission of the sons of Moses in modern Israel is not coincidental.

Doctrine and Covenants 84:34 specifies that "they become . . . the seed of Abraham." The literal house of Israel all descended from Abraham, but as Paul explained, "they are not all Israel, which are of Israel: Neither, because they are all children of Abraham, are they the seed. . . . but the children of the promise are counted for the seed." (JST Romans 9:6–8.) In other words, faithfulness to the principles the patriarch taught (the gospel) determines heirship and acceptance— literal descent is not enough. Abraham became a model for all Saints, eventually achieving godhood. (See D&C 132:37.) The blessings of the gospel are often referred to in connection with the Abrahamic covenant, which is, as explained by Elder McConkie, "that Abraham and his seed (including those adopted into his family) shall have all of the blessings of the gospel, of the priesthood, and of eternal life,"[9] including eternal increase. The Lord revealed that "this promise is yours also, because ye are of Abraham" and that we should "go . . . therefore, and do the works of Abraham." (D&C 132:31–32.)

Elder McConkie noted that "what we say for Abraham, Isaac, and Jacob we say also for Sarah, Rebekah, and Rachel, the wives . . . who with them were true and faithful in all things,"[10] for, as President Joseph Fielding Smith taught, "the Lord offers to his daughters every spiritual gift and blessing that can be obtained by his sons."[11]

In order to enjoy the full blessings of the oath and covenant of the priesthood, a man must marry for time and eternity in the house of the Lord. (See D&C 131:1–3.) Elder McConkie explained that "this covenant, made when the priesthood is received, is renewed when the recipient enters the order of eternal marriage."[12] Further, "when he is married in the temple for time and for all eternity, each worthy member of the Church enters personally into the same covenant the Lord made with Abraham. This is the occasion when the promises of eternal increase are made, and it is then specified that those who keep the covenants made there shall be inheritors of all the blessings of Abraham, Isaac, and Jacob."[13]

Those taking the covenant of the priesthood are included in "the church and kingdom of God." (D&C 84:34.) They are members of "the only true and living church upon the face of the whole earth." (D&C 1:30.) Their king is the Savior, and the church and kingdom upon the earth is a type for the heavenly kingdom yet to be obtained.

Elder Harold B. Lee referred to "the church and kingdom of God" as "the church of the firstborn."[14] Not all members of The Church of Jesus Christ of Latter-day Saints are members of the Church of the Firstborn, however, for as Elder McConkie explained, "the Church of the Firstborn is made up of . . . those who are destined to be joint-heirs with Christ in receiving all that the Father hath."[15] Hence, that church membership includes those who are now proving or who will in the future prove themselves worthy of that exalted society.

Those upon earth who are living worthy of such future attainment are also called "the elect of God." (D&C 84:34.) Elder McConkie defined these as "the portion of church members who are striving with all their hearts to keep the fulness of the gospel law in this life so that they can become inheritors of the fulness of gospel rewards in the life to come.

"As far as the male sex is concerned, they are the ones, the Lord says, who have the Melchizedek Priesthood conferred upon them and who thereafter magnify their callings and are sanctified by the Spirit."[16]

Those who receive the Lord's priesthood and his servants are accepting both the Lord and the Father who sent him (D&C 84:35–37), for the Father and Son are one in purpose and mission. Such unity was the Savior's desire when he prayed: "Holy Father, keep through thine own name those whom thou hast given me, that they may be one, as we are. . . . Father, I will that they also, whom thou hast given me, be with me where I am; that they may behold my glory, which thou hast given me." (John 17:11, 24.) The oath and covenant of the priesthood is the means for the fulfillment of that prayer.

DOCTRINE AND COVENANTS 84:38

"And he that receiveth my Father receiveth my Father's kingdom; therefore all that my Father hath shall be given unto him."

Herein is the fulfillment of heirship: "Wherefore, all things are theirs. . . . These shall dwell in the presence of God and his Christ forever and ever. . . . They who dwell in his presence are the church of the Firstborn; . . . and he makes them equal in power, and in might, and in dominion." (D&C 76:59, 62, 94–95.)

Elder Asay said of this promise of heirship: "Few of us, I suppose, can comprehend all that this promise means. Even though we know that it includes eternal life, or the inheritance of exaltation, still it is so great and so wonderful that it defies proper explanation."[17] Of this the scripture testifies, "Eye hath not seen, nor ear heard, neither have entered into the heart of man, the things which God hath prepared for them that love him." (1 Corinthians 2:9.)

Two key words mentioned in the oath and covenant serve as a foreshadowing of this great blessing of eternal life: *calling* (D&C 84:33) and *elect* (D&C 84:34). Elder McConkie testified that "brethren whose calling and election is made sure always hold the holy Melchizedek Priesthood. Without this delegation of power and authority they cannot be sealed up unto eternal life."[18] President Marion G. Romney also gave witness that "we talk about making our callings and elections sure. The only way we can do this is to get the priesthood and magnify it."[19]

Joseph Smith taught that "Abraham, Isaac, and Jacob had the promise of eternal life confirmed to them by an oath of the Lord, but that promise or oath was no assurance to them of their salvation. But they could, by walking in the footsteps and continuing in the faith of their fathers, obtain for themselves an oath for confirmation that they were meet to be partakers of the inheritance with the saints in light.

"If the saints in the days of the Apostles were privileged to take the saints for example and lay hold of the same promises and attain to the same exalted privileges of knowing that their names were written in the Lamb's book of life and that they were sealed there as a perpetual memorial before the face of the Most High, will not the same faith bring the same assurance of eternal life and that in the same manner to the children of men now in this age of the world?"[20]

Thus, those priesthood holders accounted as the seed of Abraham may receive the same blessings as their faithful forebears.

DOCTRINE AND COVENANTS 84:39–40

"And this is according to the oath and covenant which belongeth to the priesthood. Therefore, all those who receive the priesthood, receive this oath and covenant of my Father, which he cannot break, neither can it be moved."

Who makes the oath? What is the oath? Who makes the covenant, and what are the terms?

Elder Marion G. Romney defined an oath as "a sworn attestation to the inviolability of the promises in the agreement."[21] President Joseph Fielding Smith explained that "to swear with an oath is the most solemn and binding form of speech known to the human tongue."[22] In the oath and covenant of the priesthood, it is the Father who makes the oath. Elder McConkie taught that the oath is "that everyone who keeps the covenant made in connection with the Melchizedek Priesthood shall inherit, receive, and possess all things in his everlasting kingdom, and shall be a joint-heir with that Lord who is his Only Begotten. . . .

"God swore with an oath that Christ would be exalted, and he swears anew, at the time each of us receives the Melchizedek Priesthood, that we will have a like exaltation if we are true and faithful in all things."[23] This oath is as eternal as the priesthood, and always accompanies it, signifying its validity in providing for the exaltation of God's faithful children.

Elder Romney explained that "a covenant is an agreement between two or more parties. . . . In the covenant of the priesthood the parties are the Father and the receiver of the priesthood."[24]

For the preparatory Aaronic Priesthood, Elder McConkie stated: "Those who receive the Aaronic Priesthood covenant and promise to magnify their callings, to serve in the ministry of the Master, to forsake the world, and to live as becometh Saints.

"In return, the Lord covenants and promises to enlarge the standing and station of all who keep their Aaronic covenant. He promises to give them the Melchizedek Priesthood, out of which eternal life comes. [The oath from God accompanies the higher, or Melchizedek Priesthood.]

"Those who receive the Melchizedek Priesthood covenant and promise, before God and angels, to magnify their callings, to 'live by every word that proceedeth forth from the mouth of God' (D&C 84:44), to marry for time and all eternity in the patriarchal order, and to live and serve as the Lord Jesus did in his life and ministry."[25]

Elder Asay noted that God's covenant to faithful priesthood holders includes the following promises: "Promise 1: We Will Be Sanctified by the Spirit. . . .

"Promise 2: We Will Be Numbered with the Elect of God. . . .

"Promise 3: We Will Be Given All That God Has."[26] Elder McConkie explained that to be given all that God has includes exaltation and godhood and admittance to "his eternal patriarchal order, an order that prevails in the highest heaven of the celestial world, an order that assures its members of eternal increase, or in other words of spirit children in the resurrection. (See D&C 131:1–4)."[27]

DOCTRINE AND COVENANTS 84:41

"But whoso breaketh this covenant after he hath received it, and altogether turneth therefrom, shall not have forgiveness of sins in this world nor in the world to come."

This is a solemn declaration. According to Elder McConkie, "this has never been interpreted by the Brethren to mean that those who forsake their priesthood duties, altogether turning therefrom, shall be sons of perdition; rather, the meaning seems to be that they shall be denied the exaltation that otherwise might have been theirs."[28]

Joseph Fielding Smith explained that there is a chance to repent if a man has not altogether turned from the priesthood. If he does altogether turn from it, however, there is no forgiveness. "That does *not* mean that man is going to become a son of perdition, but the meaning is that *he will never again have the opportunity of exercising the priesthood and reaching exaltation.* That is where his forgiveness ends. He will not again have the priesthood conferred upon him, because he has trampled it under his feet; but as far as other things are concerned, he may be forgiven."[29]

DOCTRINE AND COVENANTS 84:42

"And wo unto all those who come not unto this priesthood."

As the priesthood is the only source and channel through which exaltation may be obtained from the Lord, it follows that those who avoid it also avoid their only chance for eternal happiness in the celestial kingdom.

"And even I have given the heavenly hosts and mine angels charge concerning you." (D&C 84:42.) Worthy priesthood holders have the right to the ministering of angels (D&C 13), which may come as direct visitations or as communications via the Holy Ghost, for "angels speak by the power of the Holy Ghost" (2 Nephi 32:3; see also 1 Nephi 17:45). Worthy priesthood holders also have the rights of fellowship and communion "with the general assembly and church of the Firstborn" (D&C 107:19), meaning those faithful members whose names "are written in heaven" (Hebrews 12:23), referring to Saints on both sides of the veil.

DOCTRINE AND COVENANTS 84:43

"And I now give unto you a commandment to beware concerning yourselves, to give diligent heed to the words of eternal life."

This verse is a key verse within the oath and covenant of the priesthood. It leads one to an understanding of how to obtain the fulness of the oath and covenant of the priesthood.

DOCTRINE AND COVENANTS 84:44

"For you shall live by every word that proceedeth forth from the mouth of God."

The words of eternal life have God as their source; how one receives these words is next explained in a chain of logic.

DOCTRINE AND COVENANTS 84:45

"For the word of the Lord is truth, and whatsoever is truth is light, and whatsoever is light is Spirit, even the Spirit of Jesus Christ."

DOCTRINE AND COVENANTS 84:46

"And the Spirit giveth light to every man that cometh into the world; and the Spirit enlighteneth every man through the world, that hearkeneth to the voice of the Spirit." Elder McConkie explained that the light of Christ "is the instrumentality and agency by which Deity keeps in touch and communes with all his children, both the righteous and the wicked. It has an edifying, enlightening, and uplifting influence on men. One of its manifestations is called conscience, through which all men know right from wrong.

"It is the means by which the Lord invites and entices all men to improve their lot and to come unto him and receive his gospel."[30]

DOCTRINE AND COVENANTS 84:47

"And every one that hearkeneth to the voice of the Spirit cometh unto God, even the Father."

Elder McConkie explained: "By following the light of Christ, men are led to the gospel covenant, to the baptismal covenant, to the church and kingdom. There they receive the Holy Ghost."[31] Those who are sensitive to the Holy Ghost continue to learn the words of God and direct their lives according to his counsel. Faithful brethren are led by this process to the oath and covenant of the priesthood.

DOCTRINE AND COVENANTS 84:48

"And the Father teacheth him of the covenant which he has renewed and confirmed upon you."

This is the apex, the grandest key in understanding the oath and covenant of the priesthood: a man who holds and honors the Melchizedek Priesthood will be taught of that holy covenant by revelation from God.

Elder McConkie testified: "This doctrine, this doctrine of the priesthood — unknown in the world and but little known even in the Church — cannot be learned out of the scriptures alone. It is not set forth in the sermons and teachings of the prophets and Apostles, except in small measure.

"The doctrine of the priesthood is known only by personal revelation. It comes, line upon line and precept upon precept, by the power of the Holy Ghost to those who love and serve God with all their heart, might, mind, and strength."[32]

In revealing the proper use of the priesthood, the Lord directed: "Let thy bowels also be full of charity towards all men, and to the household of faith, and let virtue garnish thy thoughts unceasingly; then shall thy confidence wax strong in the presence of God; *and the doctrine of the priesthood shall distil upon thy soul as the dews from heaven.*" (D&C 121:45; italics added.) By this means one progresses within the oath and covenant of the priesthood.

Sufficient scriptural information is given to place a brother upon the pathway of exaltation, but the printed word in the standard works is not the culmination point. It is an aid in helping one to progress to the point where revelation is the key in magnifying a calling and in learning more about the oath and covenant of the priesthood. And one may progress through this medium to a certain point where he is considered to have received sufficient light and knowledge from God that to turn away would incur the awful penalty of no forgiveness. (D&C 84:41.) This opens the very real possibility that some might indeed suffer the fate of sons of perdition, having progressed to such a degree in tutelage from God that then to turn away would condemn them to that eternal fate.

The concept of worthiness to be directed by God through personal revelation also relates to Joseph Smith's teaching regarding one's knowing that his calling and election is sure. Elder Romney testified: "To do this one must receive a divine witness that he will inherit eternal life."[33] Alma recorded a similar witness from God: "And whosoever doeth this, and keepeth the commandments of God from thenceforth, the same will remember that I say unto him, yea, he will remember that I have said unto him, he shall have eternal life, according to the testimony of the Holy Spirit, which testifieth in me." (Alma 7:16.)

Another illustration is the following revelation to Joseph Smith: "For I am the Lord thy God, and will be with thee even unto the end of the world, and through all eternity; for verily I seal upon you your exaltation, and prepare a throne for you in the kingdom of my Father, with Abraham your father." (D&C 132:49).[34] As the Lord confirmed the priesthood by his own voice out of the heavens to his servants (D&C 84:42), so may he confirm the promise of eternal life, whether in this life or the next.

The fulfillment of that promise of eternal life is the grand purpose of the oath and covenant of the priesthood. Every worthy priesthood holder may qualify if he will keep the covenants of the priesthood. President Joseph Fielding Smith said: "It is perfectly clear that there are no more glorious promises that have or could be made than those that came to us when we accepted the privilege and assumed the responsibility of holding the holy priesthood and of standing as ministers of Christ."[35] Herein is brought to pass the most noble goal of existence: "For behold, this is my work and my glory—to bring to pass the immortality and eternal life of man." (Moses 1:39.)

NOTES

1. Bruce R. McConkie, *A New Witness for the Articles of Faith* (Salt Lake City: Deseret Book Co., 1985), pp. 312–13.

2. Joseph Fielding Smith, in Conference Report, Oct. 1970, p. 92.

3. Harold B. Lee, as cited in *Prepare Ye the Way of the Lord: Melchizedek Priesthood Study Guide, 1978–79* (Salt Lake City: The Church of Jesus Christ of Latter-day Saints, 1978), p. 127.

4. Bruce R. McConkie, *Mormon Doctrine*, 2d ed. (Salt Lake City: Bookcraft, 1966), pp. 481–82.

5. Carlos E. Asay, in Conference Report, Oct. 1985, p. 57.

6. Marion G. Romney, in Conference Report, Oct. 1980, p. 64.

7. See *American Dictionary of the English Language* (San Francisco: The Foundation for American Christian Education, 1985).

8. McConkie, *Mormon Doctrine*, p. 482.

9. McConkie, *New Witness*, p. 505.

10. Bruce R. McConkie, *New Era*, May 1978, p. 37.

11. Joseph Fielding Smith, in Conference Report, Apr. 1970, p. 59.

12. McConkie, *New Witness*, p. 313.

13. Ibid., p. 508.

14. Harold B. Lee, in Conference Report, Apr. 1950, p. 99.

15. McConkie, *Mormon Doctrine*, p. 139.

16. Ibid., p. 217.

17. Asay, in Conference Report, Oct. 1985, p. 59.

18. Bruce R. McConkie, *The Promised Messiah* (Salt Lake City: Deseret Book Co., 1978), p. 587.

19. Marion G. Romney, in Conference Report, Apr. 1974, p. 115.

20. *The Personal Writings of Joseph Smith*, comp. Dean C. Jessee (Salt Lake City: Deseret Book Co., 1984), p. 300; spelling and punctuation standardized.

21. Marion G. Romney, in Conference Report, Apr. 1962, p. 17.

22. Joseph Fielding Smith, in Conference Report, Oct. 1970, p. 92.

23. Bruce R. McConkie, in Conference Report, Apr. 1982, p. 49.

24. Romney, in Conference Report, Apr. 1962, p. 17.

25. McConkie, in Conference Report, Apr. 1982, p. 49.

26. Asay, in Conference Report, Oct. 1985, pp. 58–59.

27. McConkie, in Conference Report, Apr. 1982, p. 49.

28. McConkie, *New Witness*, p. 232.

29. Joseph Fielding Smith, *Doctrines of Salvation*, comp. Bruce R. McConkie (Salt Lake City: Bookcraft, 1954–56), 3:141–42.

30. McConkie, *New Witness*, p. 259.

31. Ibid., p. 260.

32. McConkie, in Conference Report, Apr. 1982, p. 47.

33. Marion G. Romney, in Conference Report, Oct. 1965, p. 20.

34. Elder Bruce R. McConkie cited this as a classic example for our day of one who was sealed up unto eternal life. See *Doctrinal New Testament Commentary* (Salt Lake City: Bookcraft, 1981), 3:348.

35. Joseph Fielding Smith, in Conference Report, Oct. 1970, p. 92.

CHAPTER FIVE

God, Natural Law, and the Doctrine and Covenants

LaMar E. Garrard

Professor of Church History and Doctrine
Brigham Young University

Which came first, natural law or God? It is my thesis that God came first, for natural law in our universe has its origin in the mind of our God:[1] he thinks and plans ahead according to his wisdom as to how he wants the elements to behave and then has the power to command them to behave in that prescribed orderly and consistent manner. That prescription is a natural law. The orderly and consistent manner in which the elements obey these commandments is not natural law itself but the product of God's wisdom and power. Sometimes God commands the elements to change their behavior from that which they have consistently done in the past to a new behavior which we are not used to observing. We call that a miracle. Sometimes Christ intentionally performed these miracles during his earthly ministry as evidence to the Jews that he had power over the elements, that he was indeed the Lord God over the universe.[2]

Some have taken the position that natural laws existed before any God. If such were the case, these natural laws would be self-existing: they would not have originated in the mind of a God according to his wisdom and knowledge and would not have depended upon his power for their enforcement. Proponents of this theory feel that because God would then not be the author these self-existing laws, he would not have the power to change or revoke them. His role then would have been similar to that of a scientist who merely discovers these self-existing natural laws and then works with them rather than creating them. Miracles would be explained away as God's manipulating the elements in a manner with which we are not familiar: he would be using higher natural laws that he had discovered and worked with but of which man was not yet aware. It is proposed that such views have risen in the minds of some because they have unwittingly accepted some of the premises of the philosophy of naturalism without critically examining this philosophy itself and what it implies. To understand why some began to believe in natural laws that are self-existing, it is necessary to trace historically the rise of this philosophy, as science also rose and developed. Of necessity, our discussion will cover such subjects as God, man, physical matter, and spirit matter, since they are all interrelated with the subject of natural law.

HISTORICAL PERSPECTIVE

A better understanding of the rise of the philosophy of naturalism can be gained by discussing some of the beliefs adopted by the Christian church before the advent of naturalism, since the naturalistic way of looking at the universe emerged partially as a reaction against these doctrines and beliefs. These adopted doctrines and beliefs came from the teachings of Saint Augustine (350–430) and Saint Thomas Aquinas (1227–74) and became part of the Christian outlook on the nature of the universe. These two men based many of their teachings on certain statements made in the Bible, but they were also greatly influenced by the Greek philosophers. They both taught that God is eternal (self-existent) and is all-powerful and all-knowing. According to Augustine, God created matter out of nothing (ex nihilo); he also created all other things in the universe, including time, space, and the laws governing matter in time and space. "Thus everything that is or ever shall be is a creation of God and must follow His laws and will."[3] Later, Aquinas taught much the same thing concerning the origin of the universe.[4] Augustine taught that man is a union of soul and body and that the soul, although immaterial, directs the body. The soul did not exist before the body in which it dwells.[5] Later, Aquinas taught that God created the soul which was added to the body at birth.[6] Both men taught that the soul of man, once created, was immortal and continued to exist after the death of the body.

Man's views of the nature of the universe began to change some-what in relation to the Christian outlook — which had been greatly influenced by the teachings of Augustine and Aquinas — during the eighteenth, nineteenth, and twentieth centuries. Influenced by scientific methodology and discoveries, some tended to take a more "naturalistic" view of the nature of the universe. Some of the early areas of investigation were astronomy and physics. The scientists soon learned to base their conclusions only upon observations that could be made by man through the use of his physical senses or through the use of instruments that aided or extended the physical senses – the telescope, for example. This method became necessary because the scientists' observations of nature did not always agree with what the philosophers and church authorities had said or were saying. Since the scientists' observations could be verified by any competent observer, there was a tendency by some to look at the scientists as newer and more reliable authorities than the philosophers and theologians.

Another feature of the scientific method gave the scientists still more influence. When they repeated their observations under similar conditions, they obtained the same results as before. After many repeated observations with identical results, they were able to accurately predict events in the future, based on the conformity and order of these past observations.[7] Nevertheless, the assumption that nature will behave the same way in the future as it has done in the past is an "induction" that is not deductively valid, even though it works.[8] The power to predict (or control)[9] and be accurate in those predictions brought remarkable success to science and made it an even greater authority in the minds of many.

But science has another goal besides prediction and control, and that goal is to explain reasonably why things happen as they do. Since induction does not reasonably explain why the universe is consistent and orderly (which gives the scientist this power to predict), another approach was needed. For Robert Boyle (1627–91) and Isaac Newton (1642–1727) the explanation was simple: the elements were merely obeying the laws prescribed by God and therefore were acting in a consistent and orderly manner.[10] For other scientists, however, those who were reacting against the church men and who wanted to eliminate God from the picture by basing all their explanations on a physical, or natural, foundation, there had to be an alternate explanation: they felt that matter was conforming to self-existent and unchangeable natural laws. From a metaphysical point of view, they were substituting one hypothetical construct (self-existing natural laws) for another (God) in order to account for order and consistency in the universe. Now, they could give a reasonable and logical explanation for why they were able to predict (and later on to control) and get the same results in the future that they had obtained in the past under the same experimental conditions – *without giving credit to God's wisdom and power.*

As time went on and science became more credible, Boyle's and

Newton's explanations of why the universe was consistent and orderly became less popular and the explanations based on the theory of self-existing natural laws became more popular. Even today, the reason given for the scientist's ability to reliably predict the occurrence of future events (which also gives him the ability to control), is to imply that matter will (or must) conform to, or act in accordance with, certain "self-existent natural laws." For example, we take physical measurements with our instruments, represent them as points on a system of coordinates, and then draw a graph or smooth curve through the points. Or, we may represent the measurements by a mathematical equation or a formula of some sort. We then call the curve, the equation, or the formula the "law," of such-and-such. As soon as we use the word "law" we are implying that matter must act in the future in accordance with these curves, equations, or formulas. We are not just describing events that occurred in the past, but we are implying that there is some sort of enforcement agency that we can rely on to give consistency and order in the universe: that enforcement agency is self-existing natural laws. A philosopher of science, John G. Kemeny, points out the predicament of the scientists: when they use the word *law* they have become philosophers. They are no longer objective scientists who report only what they physically observe but are delving into metaphysics, whether they realize it or not.

"It is a great pity for the Philosophy of Science that the word 'law' was ever introduced. The usage of 'law' carries the connotation that it can somehow be disobeyed. The idea of obeying or disobeying should not have entered these discussions at all. I am afraid this is part of our tendency to try to recreate the universe in our own image. It may perhaps date back to the primitive idea of God. To primitive people, God is but a very large and powerful human being. . . . In mythology we find examples where the gods are endowed with human strength and human weaknesses. It is perhaps a remnant from these days that we associate the idea of a law with nature. Presumably the laws of nature were passed by God. They were laid down on a heavenly piece of paper. . . . These are the things that nature must obey. There are even recorded examples of violations of the laws of nature, and these are called miracles.

"We must realize that nature is not like a human being. Nature cannot obey or disobey. The laws of nature do not prescribe but, rather describe what happens. A law of nature is but a description of what actually takes place."[11]

One advocate of naturalism in our day was the noted philosopher and mathematician Bertrand Russell. He pointed out that "before Galileo [1564–1642] it had been thought that a lifeless body will not move of itself. . . . Only living beings, it was thought, could move without help of some external agency."[12] The heavenly bodies were kept in motion by some supernatural power. As long as these views prevailed, "physics as an independent science was impossible, since the physical world was thought to be not casually self-contained. But Galileo and Newton [1642–1727] between them proved that all the movement of the planets, and of dead matter on the earth, proceed according to the law of physics, and once started, will continue indefinitely. There is no need of mind in this process."[13]

The philosopher and mathematician René Descartes (1596–1650) went one step further in the acceptance of the metaphysical concept that all things that happen in the universe can be attributed to the operation of self-existing natural law: he proposed that animals did not have spirits but were mere machines subject to natural law.[14] Later, the physician and philosopher Julien de La Mettrie (1709–51) proposed that even humans have no spirits. At one time he fell ill with a fever. "It was during this fever and his realization that his mental powers were diminished along with his physical powers that the conviction came to him with the force of conversion that thought is after all nothing but the result of mechanical action of the brain and nervous system. . . . Being unable to distinguish between thought and the soul, his new belief meant to him that the soul is as mortal as the brain and that man is but a machine — as much so as Descartes believed the animals to be."[15]

Further discoveries in science seemed to contradict even more the teachings of Augustine and Aquinas and to call the reliability of their teachings increasingly into question. The scientists were discovering that matter could be transformed from one state to another but that there were no examples of it ever being created or destroyed. J. P. Joule (1818–89) demonstrated in his classical experiment that heat or energy can be converted to work, and work converted to heat or energy, but neither could be destroyed. In this climate of scientific discoveries and ideas in 1847 in Berlin the scientist and physician Hermann von Helmholtz (1821–94) presented his famous paper on the law of conservation of energy. "Nobody ever 'discovered' the law of conservation of energy. The idea had been developing since Newton. Joule a few years earlier had demonstrated the fact that heat has a mechanical equivalent. Helmholtz brought together much of the previous work and gave the theory mathematical formulation. He was still being the physicist within physiology, for one of his motives was to show that this principle works within the bodily machine, that the living organism is no exception to the laws of physics. This paper aroused vigorous discussion."[16] It was the aim of Helmholtz and others to eliminate the idea that man has a spirit inside of him (vitalism) that directs his physical body and accounts for his behavior. They were eventually successful in promoting the idea that man is a physical machine and his behavior results solely from the interaction of self-existing natural laws with physical matter.

"In 1845, . . . four young, enthusiastic and idealistic physiologists, all pupils of the great Johannes Müller, all later to be very famous, met together and formed a pact. . . . They were . . . Carl Ludwig, . . . Emil du Bois-Reymond, Ernst Brücke and Hermann Von Helmholtz. . . . They were joining forces to fight vitalism, the view that life involves forces other than those found in the interaction of inorganic bodies. The great Johannes Müller was a vitalist, but these men were of the next generation. Du Bois and Brücke even pledged between them a solemn oath that they would establish and compel the acceptance of this truth: 'No other forces than the common physical chemical ones are active within the organism.' . . . Thirty-five years later, Helmholtz and du Bois in Berlin, Ludwig at Leipzig and Brücke at Vienna saw their aspiration well on its way to complete acceptance."[17]

Helmholtz and his associates were not the only ones who promoted the idea that life itself involves only the operation of self-existing natural laws on physical matter. Russell pointed out that Charles Darwin (1809–82) helped place the capstone on the disbelief that man has a spirit within him to account for his behavior. According to the evolutionists, the origin of life did not involve the placing of an organized spirit into an already organized physical body; rather, life originated by chance operation of natural laws on physical matter. According to Charles Darwin, the various species (with no spirit in them) then developed by the operation of self-existing natural law on physical matter in terms of mutation and survival of the fittest. According to this theory, it took millions of years to develop the various species by these naturalistic methods. Furthermore, Russell pointed out, these theories helped to bring about a disbelief in "purpose" being involved in the origin and continued existence of the universe, for such laws do not think, do not plan ahead, or for that manner, do not have body, parts, or passions. This, of course, eliminated a need for a God who thinks (has all wisdom and knowledge), who planned ahead the creation of the world with all its forms of life, who planned ahead the events that would take place on this planet from beginning to end, and who is concerned and very much involved in what takes place on this earth.

"We know of 'purpose' in human affairs, and we may suppose that there are cosmic purposes, but in science it is the past that determines the future, not the future the past. 'Final' causes, therefore, do not occur in the scientific account of the world.

"In this connection Darwin's work was decisive. What Galileo and Newton had done for astronomy, Darwin did for biology. . . .

"It was not the fact of evolution, but the Darwinian mechanism of the struggle for existence and the survival of the fittest that made it possible to explain adaptation without bringing in 'purpose.' Random variation and *natural* selection use only *efficient* causes. . . .

"Darwinism has had many effects upon man's outlook on life and the world, in addition to the extrusion of purpose of which I have already spoken. The absence of any sharp line between men and apes is very awkward for theology. When did men get souls? Was the Missing Link capable of sin and therefore worthy of hell? Did Pithecanthropus Erectus have moral responsibility? Was Homo Pekinienis damned? Did Piltdown Man go to heaven?"[18]

In summary, we see that during the eighteenth, nineteenth, and twentieth centuries, a "naturalistic" philosophy accompanied the rise of science, wherein some men advocated contrasting views to those of Augustine and Aquinas. They claimed there is no self-existing, all-powerful, and all-knowing God who with a mind and with a divine power created, *ex nihilo*, man with his spirit, matter, space, time, and all the laws governing matter in space and time. Rather, the naturalistic philosophers held, matter, space, and time are self-existent, and the laws governing matter in space and time are self-existent. These laws replace God, for it is through them that our universe, including life on this planet, came into existence by chance and will probably also go out of existence by chance. Since the events that have happened in the past and those that will occur in the future are not the result of God's wisdom and power but rather the operation of self-existent laws over matter, God has been replaced by self-existing natural law, which has no mind or purpose, as the sovereign power over this universe.

The philosophy of naturalism not only eliminates God from the picture but also eliminates the spirit in man to account for his thinking and resultant behavior. Man becomes then a machine composed only of physical matter acting in accordance with self-existing natural laws. Russell felt, however, that man can become a sort of a "god," not by acquiring faith in God but by acquiring a knowledge of all self-existing natural laws and then manipulating and controlling the environment by use of them. According to this view, a "god" is nothing more than a super engineer.

"In the pre-scientific world, power was God's. There was not much that man could do even in the most favorable circumstances, and the circumstances were liable to become unfavorable if men incurred the divine displeasure. . . .

"In the scientific world, all this is different. It is not by prayer and humility that you cause things to go as you wish, but by acquiring a knowledge of natural laws. . . . The power of science has no known limits. We were told that faith could remove mountains, but no one believed it; we are told that the atomic bomb can remove mountains, and everyone believes it.

"It is true that if we ever did stop to think about the cosmos we might find it uncomfortable. The sun may grow cold or blow up; the earth may lose its atmosphere and become uninhabitable. Life is a brief, small, and transitory phenomenon in an obscure corner, not at all the sort of thing that one would make a fuss about if one were not personally concerned. . . . Let us get on with the job of fertilizing the desert, melting Arctic ice, killing each other with perpetually improving techniques. Some of our activities will do good, some harm, but all alike will show our power. And so, in this godless universe, we shall become gods."[19]

THE DOCTRINE AND COVENANTS AND NATURAL LAW

The Doctrine and Covenants reveals to us that God is a thinking, intelligent being, for he knows all things (D&C 38:2; 93:26) and is all powerful (D&C 61:1). All things are present before his eyes (D&C 38:2) so that he can comprehend all things.

"He comprehendeth all things, and all things are before him, and all things are round about him; and he is above all things, and in all things, and is through all things, and is round about all things; and all things are by him, and of him, even God, forever and ever." (D&C 88:41.)

Furthermore, the Doctrine and Covenants states that God plans ahead what he is going to do,[20] for he tells us that his "designs, and . . . purposes . . . cannot be frustrated, neither can they come to naught." (D&C 3:1.) Then when God commands the elements,[21] they obey him. (D&C 133:23.) In this manner, he tells us, "the world was made, and all things came by me." (D&C 38:3.) God is able to speak to the elements by the power of his Spirit: "As the words have gone forth out of my mouth even so shall they be fulfilled, . . . in all things whatsoever I have created by the word of my power, which is the power of my Spirit. For by the power of my Spirit created I them." (D&C 29:30–31.)

It is through his Spirit—the Light of Christ, which proceeds from his presence to fill the immensity of space—that God's commands or power are relayed to the elements so that not only the earth, but also the sun, the moon, and the stars were created.

"Which truth shineth. This is the light of Christ. As also he is in the sun, and the light of the sun, and the power thereof by which it was made.

"As also he is in the moon, and is the light of the moon, and the power thereof by which it was made;

"As also the light of the stars, and the power thereof by which they were made;

"And the earth also, and the power thereof, even the earth upon which you stand. . . .

"Which light proceedeth forth from the presence of God to fill the immensity of space." (D&C 88:7–10, 12.)

Furthermore, the Doctrine and Covenants depicts Christ as a divine monarch sitting upon his throne, who not only created the universe but continues to command or govern the elements through the Light of Christ: "The light which is in all things, which giveth life to all things, which is the law by which all things are governed, even the power of God who sitteth upon his throne, who is in the bosom of eternity, who is in the midst of all things." (D&C 88:13.)

God is depicted as the author of natural law for he is the one who has given the commandment or law to the heavenly bodies that causes them to move in definite orbits, thereby resulting in conformity and order. We should give God credit for this conformity and order, for it is a result of his majesty and power.

"And again, verily I say unto you, *he hath given a law* unto all things, by which they move in their times and their seasons;

"And *their courses are fixed,* even the courses of the heavens and the earth, which comprehendeth the earth and all the planets.

"And they give light to each other in their times and in their seasons. . . .

"The earth rolls upon her wings, and the sun giveth his light by day, and the moon giveth her light by night, and the stars also give their light, as they roll upon their wings in their glory, in the midst of the power of God. . . .

"Behold, all these are kingdoms, and any man who hath seen any or the least of these hath seen God moving in his majesty and power." (D&C 88:42–45, 47; italics added.)

Joseph Smith emphasized that the universe did not come into existence by chance but was created by God. God is a thinking, intelligent person whose purpose and wisdom were used to formulate natural laws and whose power is now used to govern the elements, resulting in such regularity and order. Without these laws of God and his power, the universe would fall into chaos:

"If man has grown to wisdom and is capable of discerning the propriety of laws to govern nations, what less can be expected from the Ruler and Upholder of the universe? . . . He is perfect intelligence, and . . . His wisdom is alone sufficient to govern and regulate the mighty creations and worlds which shine and blaze with such magnificence and splendor over our heads, as though touched with His finger and moved by His Almighty word. And if so, it is done and regulated by law; for without law all must certainly fall into chaos. . . .

"Think for a moment, of the greatness of the Being who created the Universe. . . . the voice of *reason,* the language of *inspiration,* and the Spirit of the living God, our Creator, teaches us . . . [and] the heavens declare the glory of a God, and the firmament showeth His handiwork; and a moment's reflection is sufficient to teach every man of common intelligence, that all these are not the mere productions of *chance,* nor could they be supported by any power less than an Almighty hand."[22]

Joseph Smith did not give self-existing law—which does not think,

plan, or have purpose and also does not have body, parts, or passions —
credit for the uniformity and order in the universe. Rather, he taught
that the universe is governed and upheld by a powerful God who has
body, parts, and passions and who is in the form of man. "If the veil
were rent today, and the great God who holds this world in its orbit,
and who upholds all worlds and all things by his power, was to make
himself visible . . . you would see him like a man in form — like yourselves."[23]

God takes credit not only for the movement of the heavenly bodies
but also for the physical changes that take place above the earth in the
atmosphere, on the earth, and in the earth itself. For example, since
he is responsible for creating natural law, he is ultimately responsible
for the rain and snow and for the budding and blossoming of plants.
He told William Marks and Newel K. Whitney to "settle up their business speedily and journey from the land of Kirtland, before I, the Lord,
send again the snows upon the earth." He also told them, "will I not
make solitary places to bud and blossom, and to bring forth in abundance? saith the Lord." (D&C 117:1, 7.)

Joseph Smith explained that physical matter must obey the decrees
or commandments of God (natural laws) until these laws are changed
or revoked by a different commandment from God: "God has made
certain decrees which are fixed and immovable; for instance, God set
the sun, the moon, and the stars in the heavens, and gave them their
laws, conditions and bounds, which they cannot pass, except by His
commandments; they all move in perfect harmony in their sphere and
order, and are as lights, wonders, and signs unto us. The sea also has
its bounds which it cannot pass."[24]

God can revoke a former commandment or law given to the
elements[25] for he tells us that at a future time he "shall command the
great deep [sea], and it shall be driven back into the north countries,
and the islands shall become one land." (D&C 133:23.) He also will
utter his voice "which shall break down the mountains, and the valleys
shall not be found" (D&C 133:22) so that the earth will be renewed
and transfigured. (D&C 63:20–21.) These scriptures imply that when
these great physical and geological changes take place, they will not
take thousands of years to occur, because the elements will be obeying
God.[26] If we were to restrict such changes to the operation of self-
existing natural laws according to the modern geological theory of

uniformitarianism, the usual assumption is that such changes would take millions of years to occur.

The earth itself first existed as a plan in the mind of God. Then, according to that plan, God commanded the elements to come together in a prescribed manner and they did.[27] Later, the physical structure and composition of the earth, as well as its location in reference to God's residence, was changed by God's power to a telestial sphere when Adam and Eve fell. Furthermore, its structure and composition will be changed to a terrestrial sphere at the second coming of Christ. Finally, through the power of God, after the Millennium it will be changed to a celestial sphere and rolled back into the presence of God.[28] The scriptures indicate the last three changes would not take thousands of years to occur, because they result from a decree or commandment of God.[29] This would seem to indicate that the first change (the Creation) did not necessarily have to take place over a period of thousands of years of time, because it too resulted from decrees or commandments of God rather than from the operation of self-existent natural laws.

Even though God can command physical matter to undergo certain changes, even to the point of changing water to wine or water to earth (John 2:1–11; 1 Nephi 17:50), he tells us that he cannot create physical matter ex nihilo. Contrary to what Augustine and Aquinas taught, the Doctrine and Covenants reveals that the fundamental particles of physical matter (element) are eternal (D&C 93:33) or self-existent: God cannot command matter to come into existence, neither can he destroy matter or cause it to cease to exist. Joseph Smith elaborated that fundamental matter or "element" was not created ex nihilo, for "anything created cannot be eternal; and earth, water, etc., had their existence in an elementary state, from eternity."[30] He further explained that the word *created* as used in the scriptures "should be formed, or organized."[31] God organized the world out of chaotic matter or element by his wisdom and power, but the basic matter itself is eternal or self-existent and has always coexisted with God.

Joseph Smith stated: "Now, the word create came from the word *baurau*, which does not mean to create out of nothing; it means to organize; the same as a man would organize materials and build a ship. Hence, we infer that God had materials to organize the world out of chaos—chaotic matter, which is element, and in which dwells all the glory. Element had an existence from the time he had. The pure principles of element are principles which can never be destroyed. . . . They had no beginning, and can have no end."[32]

So far as man's physical body is concerned, God first organized the earth from these fundamental particles of physical matter called element, which are eternal or self-existent. He later organized, or formed, man from the dust of this same earth. (Genesis 2:7.) Therefore, it is through the wisdom and power of God that these elementary particles of matter eventually became organized into the intricate and complex machine we call the human body. This organization of man's physical body from the dust of the earth did not necessarily have to take place over a long period of time, for God reorganized the body of Lazarus, who had been dead for four days,[33] and will also reorganize the physical bodies of the dead, which have decayed to dust, in the resurrection in a relatively short period of time.[34]

In a sense, man's body can be considered to be eternal and have no end, even though it can go through various states of organization and reorganization. It is essentially composed of self-existing elements, which are eternal and have no end, even though they existed at first in an unorganized state.[35]

The Doctrine and Covenants also teaches that besides fundamental physical matter, or element, there also exists spirit matter, which at the present time we cannot see:

"There is no such thing as immaterial matter. All spirit is matter, but it is more fine or pure, and can only be discerned by purer eyes;

"We cannot see it; but when our bodies are purified we shall see that it is all matter." (D&C 131:7–8.)

Man's spirit, which resembles his physical body,[36] is composed of this spirit matter and can exist either separately or combined with the physical body. (D&C 93:33–34.) The Prophet wrote: "In tracing the thing to the foundation, and looking at it philosophically, we shall find a very material difference between the body and the spirit; the body is supposed to be organized matter, and the spirit, by many, is thought to be immaterial, without substance. With this latter statement we should beg to differ, and state the spirit is a substance; that it is material, but that it is more pure, elastic and refined matter than the body; that it existed before the body, can exist in the body; and will exist separate from the body, when the body will be mouldering in the dust; and will in the resurrection, be again united with it."[37]

The spirit of man was organized by God, to be in God's likeness and image,[38] from elementary spirit matter, or "intelligence," which "was not created or made, neither indeed can be." (D&C 93:29.) Like fundamental physical matter, fundamental spirit matter did not come about through the wisdom and power of God. Hence, the spirit of man is eternal[39] — having no beginning or having no end — in the sense that "the intelligence of spirits had no beginning, neither will it have an end. . . . That which has a beginning may have an end."[40] It should be emphasized, however, that through the wisdom and creative power of God this intelligence becomes organized as spirit offspring of God the Father to be in his likeness and image.[41] Besides the spirits of men, God was also responsible for the organization of the spirits of the animals before their physical bodies were organized upon the earth.[42] Rather than life beginning on this earth as a result of the chance operation of self-existing natural laws upon physical matter, it began when God placed a previously organized spirit into a physical body that he had organized to be in the image or likeness of that spirit.[43] The spirit then animated that body (vitalism) and this was the beginning of mortal life for that kind of animal.[44] Thereafter, according to God's prescriptions or commands, these "classes of beings" reproduced after their own kind[45] in their "destined order or sphere of creation." (D&C 77:3.)

Even though both elementary physical matter and elementary spirit matter are self-existent, without the wisdom and power of God, neither the physical body nor the spirit body would exist in its organized state but would have remained forever in that eternal but unorganized state. The existence of the spirit and physical bodies of man and the animals is explained on the basis of a law created by God: evidently God designed and planned what their spirits as well as what their physical bodies should look like[46] and then, with his power, he prescribed that the "intelligence" and "element" be organized according to that design. Therefore, each birth process — which produces a spirit or a physical body — produces a body of that previously planned design. Even plant life came about through a law created by God.[47] The tree, the herb, and the fruit also were organized into particular shapes and textures from fundamental matter as a result of a decree or commandment of God. The Prophet Joseph Smith taught: "God has set many signs on the earth, as well as in the heavens; for instance, the oak of the forest, the fruit of the tree, the herb of the field, all bear a sign that seed hath been planted there; for it is a decree of the Lord that every tree, plant, and herb bearing seed should bring forth of its kind, and cannot come forth after any other law."[48]

God organized man's spirit from uncreated intelligence, gave him agency, and then held him accountable for his actions in the premortal state.[49] He next placed man's spirit in an organized physical body to activate his body (vitalism), continued to give him agency, and also continued to hold him accountable for his actions in this mortal state.[50] On the other hand, if man had come into existence as a result of chance operation of self-existing laws acting upon physical matter (a physical body with no spirit), he would have been a robot, a physical machine acting according to these laws. If such were the case, he could not act independently with agency but could only be acted upon by outside forces or powers. In such a universe, there would be no need for moral laws, for man would not be responsible for his actions any more than an automobile is morally responsible for what it does when rolling down a hill without a driver.[51]

CONCLUSION

An examination of the Doctrine and Covenants and the teachings of Joseph Smith indicates that natural law is not self-existent. It is eternal only in the sense that "Eternal Law" is God's law for he created it and "Eternal" is his name:[52] it has a beginning and it may have an end, depending upon the circumstances. It is a command, or prescription, that has its origin in the mind of our God, who is motivated by certain purposes and goals. (Moses 1:39.) He is a thinking, planning, and intelligent being who has the power to cause that prescription to be fulfilled and later to be changed or revoked. Natural law in our universe, or realm, did not exist before our God, it is not above our God, and is not the sovereign power in our universe. In the sense that it is a created thing (since God originated, or created, it) without body, parts, or passions, we should be careful not to worship it, the "created," but instead worship God, the "Creator."[53]

In the teachings of Augustine and Aquinas, physical matter, the spirit of man, and natural law were all considered to be in the same category in the sense that they were all brought into existence ex nihilo through the power of God. When the discoveries in science gave evidence that matter cannot be created nor destroyed and when the Prophet Joseph Smith revealed that fundamental physical matter (element) and fundamental spirit matter (intelligence) coexisted with God and are self-existent, some have assumed that "natural law" was in this same category and was therefore also self-existent. Once we begin to believe in the self-existence of natural law, however, to be logical and consistent we begin to accept many other beliefs associated with the philosophy of naturalism that are contrary to the revelations in the scriptures and the teachings of the Prophet Joseph Smith.[54] E. A. Burtt, in his book *The Metaphysical Foundations of Modern Science,* traced historically the rise of naturalism from medieval to modern times. He points out that many in our day — even though they are not philosophers or scientists — have unwittingly accepted a "naturalistic" outlook that has affected their thinking and outlook on life:

"How curious, after all, is the way in which our moderns think about our world! And it is so novel, too. The cosmology underlying our mental processes is but three centuries old — a mere infant in the history of thought — and yet we cling to it with the same embarrassed zeal with which a young father fondles his new-born baby. Like him, we are ignorant enough of its precise nature; like him, we nevertheless take it piously to be ours and allow it a subtly pervasive and unhindered control over our thinking."[55]

Joseph Smith explained that "happiness is the object and design of our existence," and it is God who has planned and "designed our happiness — and the happiness of all His creatures."[56] But "the great principle of happiness consists in having a body," and life is not possible without a body.[57] If God had not planned and then used his power, unorganized spirit matter or intelligence would have remained in that state forever and there would have been no premortal life and, consequently, no happiness there with spirit bodies.[58] Similarly, without the wisdom and power of God, unorganized physical matter or element would have remained in that state forever and there would have been no mortal life and happiness here without physical bodies to house our spirit bodies. So also, without the wisdom and power of God, all the physical bodies of dead animals and men would remain in that corrupt state forever, and there would be no happiness, which results from obtaining immortal bodies in the resurrection. The Doctrine and Covenants summarizes this concept by indicating that "the happiness of man, and of beasts, and of creeping things, and of the fowls of the air" in their spirit, mortal (temporal), and spiritual (resurrected) states and "the glory of the classes of beings in their destined order or sphere of creation" is made possible by the wisdom and power of God, so that eventually all living things will share "in the enjoyment of their eternal felicity." (D&C 77:2–3.)[59]

The revelations in the Doctrine and Covenants and the teachings of the Prophet Joseph Smith indicate that all things exist as they are now as a result of two things: one, the self-existence of matter and the wisdom of God, and two, God's power acting upon self-existent matter. There may be other self-existent qualities or principles associated with matter of which we are not yet aware because they have not yet been revealed.[60] Nevertheless, that does not justify our taking the "naturalistic" position by saying that if we knew them and understood them, then God's wisdom and power would not be needed to account for things as they are now and as they will be in the future. To do so would not fit the scriptures, for God has said that he made the spirits and physical bodies of men, animals, and plants.[61] He also said that he organized, or created, the earth, sun, moon, and stars, and he takes credit for the existence of all these things as they are now and as they will be in the future.[62]

Let us not deny the wisdom and power of God, by attributing things as they were, as they are now, and as they will be, to the operation of self-existent natural laws. Rather, let us acknowledge that God organized this earth and all things upon its face through his wisdom and power. Even though God has given man enough agency to hold him accountable for his actions,[63] let us acknowledge that He still ultimately controls what has happened, what is happening, and what will happen on this earth.[64] Let us not offend him or kindle his wrath against us by not acknowledging his hand in all things.[65] "And in nothing doth man offend God, or against none is his wrath kindled, save those who confess not his hand in all things, and obey not his commandments." (D&C 59:21.)

NOTES

1. In the Doctrine and Covenants, it is Christ who is speaking (D&C 18:47; 88:1), who acts according to the will of the Father (D&C 19:24), and who is "one" with him (D&C 35:2).

2. John 9:1–41. The blind man did not ask to be healed, but Christ healed him "that the works of God should be made manifest in him" (John 9:3), or in other words, to show His power over the physical elements. See also John 11:1–

48, where Christ brought Lazarus back from the dead "for the glory of God, that the Son of God might be glorified thereby." (John 11:4.)

3. S. E. Frost, *The Basic Teachings of the Great Philosophers* (New York: The New Home Library, 1942), p. 18.

4. Ibid., p. 22.

5. Ibid., p. 179.

6. Ibid., p. 180.

7. When repeated observations are made under the same initial conditions (the independent variable) and the same results are always obtained (the dependent variable or variables), that consistency in relationship between the two variables (natural law) is represented by the scientist as a curve on a system of coordinates, a mathematical equation, or a formula of some sort. The power and reliability of science increased when the scientist was able to make accurate future predictions under different initial conditions but based on the same original relationship (natural law) found previously to exist between the independent and dependent variables.

8. In deduction, a proposition or conclusion must necessarily follow from certain given premises and certain agreed upon rules. In induction, however, the general statement or proposition is assumed to be true on the basis of examining only a sample of the whole population. In science it is usually impossible to examine the whole population of events in question, for to do so would require the scientist to examine all possible past, present, and future occurrences of that event. Hence, when a scientist predicts that a certain event will occur in the future, he is assuming that the relationship between the independent variable and dependent variables (natural law) which are part of the event, will be the same in the future as that observed in the past. In other words, he is assuming that natural law will not change but will be consistent and uniform over time and space.

9. When a causal relationship is discovered between two variables (natural law), control is only possible when scientists have power to vary one variable (called the independent variable), thereby causing the other variable (called the dependent variable) to vary in a predicted manner. In the early days of science such as in astronomy, the scientists did not have the power to vary the forces which would result in changing the movement of a heavenly body. Therefore, they were restricted to merely observing and predicting the movement of one heavenly body in relation to another. Today, however, scientists can manipulate or vary the forces which result in the movement of a satellite in a predicted manner. Hence, as science progressed—on a small scale at least—the scientist became capable of not only predicting, but controlling the movement of a heavenly body such as a satellite.

10. Both Robert Boyle and Isaac Newton held theistic beliefs: they believed that God was the author of natural law. See Edwin Arthur Burtt, *The Metaphysical Foundation of Modern Physical Science* (London: Routledge and Kegan Paul Ltd., 1950), pp. 289–90.

11. John G. Kemeny, *A Philosopher Looks at Science* (Princeton, New Jersey: D. Van Nostrand Co., 1963), pp. 37–38.

12. Bertrand Russell, *The Impact of Science on Society* (New York: Simon and Schuster, 1953), p. 9.

13. Ibid., p. 10.

14. Edwin G. Boring, *A History of Experimental Psychology* (New York City: Appleton-Century-Crofts, 1957), p. 162.

15. Ibid., p. 213.

16. Ibid., p. 299.

17. Ibid., p. 708.

18. Russell, *Impact of Science,* pp. 11–12, 15–16.

19. Ibid., pp. 14–15.

20. Before the earth and all living things on it were actually created (Abraham 5:4–9, 20), God planned ahead that creation (Abraham 3:24; 5:1–3) and saw that his plan was good (Abraham 4:21).

21. Abraham 2:7; 4:6–7, 9–12, 18, 21, 25; Helaman 12:7–17. Sometimes God even gives this power temporarily to men to command the elements (through their faith), and the elements obey. (Moses 1:25; 6:34; 7:13; Jacob 4:6; Helaman 10:3–10, 16; 11:4–6; Ether 12:30.)

22. Joseph Smith, *Teachings of the Prophet Joseph Smith,* sel. Joseph Fielding Smith (Salt Lake City: Deseret Book Co., 1938), pp. 55–56.

23. Smith, *Teachings of the Prophet Joseph Smith,* p. 345.

24. Ibid., pp. 197–98.

25. In the days of Joshua, God revoked a former law given to the earth (D&C 88:42–45) by commanding that it cease to rotate for several hours and then go back to its normal rotation. (Helaman 12:14–15; Joshua 10:12–14; see also 2 Kings 20:8–11.)

26. Since the temporal or mortal existence of the earth (from the fall of Adam to the celestialization of the earth) is only seven thousand years (D&C 77:6–7), these single events would not take thousands of years to occur. See also Abraham 2:7; 1 Nephi 17:26, 46.

27. See n. 20.

28. A more detailed discussion of the whole earth's having its physical structure and composition changed as well as its physical location changed in relation to God's residence, is given by the author in nn. 81 and 82 of "The Fall of Man," *Principles of the Gospel in Practice: Sperry Symposium 1985* (Salt Lake City, Utah: Randall Book Co., 1985), pp. 64–65.

29. See n. 26.

30. Smith, *Teachings of the Prophet Joseph Smith,* p. 158.

31. Ibid., p. 181.

32. Ibid., pp. 350–52.

33. John 11:1–46.

34. Moses 4:25; D&C 29:24–26; 45:45–46; 88:97–98.

35. Smith, *Teachings of the Prophet Joseph Smith,* pp. 158, 181, 350–52.

36. The spirit of Christ resembled a physical body so much that the brother of Jared mistook Christ's spirit for his physical body. (Ether 3:6–9, 16.)

37. Smith, *Teachings of the Prophet Joseph Smith,* p. 207.

38. The premortal Christ told the brother of Jared that "all men were created in the beginning after mine own image." (Ether 3:15.) A comparison of this statement with the one in which the Lord says that "every spirit of man was innocent in the beginning" (D&C 93:38) seems to indicate that all spirits of men were organized in their premortal state to be in the image and likeness of God.

39. Abraham referred to the spirits of men as having "no beginning" and having "no end . . . for they are gnolaum or eternal." (Abraham 3:18.) But he also referred to spirits or souls as "intelligences that were organized before the world was." (Abraham 3:22–23.) So also did Joseph Smith refer to the spirit or soul of man as eternal and "not a created being." (*Teachings of the Prophet Joseph Smith,* p. 158; see also pp. 181, 351–53.)

40. Smith, *Teachings of the Prophet Joseph Smith,* p. 353.

41. The scriptures teach that God "made the world, and men before they were in the flesh" (Moses 6:51), "for in heaven created I them" (Moses 3:5), and that the inhabitants of the worlds "are begotten sons and daughters unto God" (D&C 76:24). Joseph Smith referred to God the Father as the "Father of our spirits," "our Great Parent," and "our Father." (*Teachings of the Prophet Joseph Smith,* pp. 48, 55, 56.)

42. Moses 3:5; D&C 45:1; 77:2.

43. The physical or temporal bodies of the animals are organized to be "in the likeness" of their spirits. (D&C 77:2.) Man, animals, and plants became "living souls" when God took their previously organized spirits and put them into their organized physical bodies (breathed into them the breath of life). See Abraham 5:7–8; Smith, *Teachings of the Prophet Joseph Smith,* pp. 352–53; cf. Moses 3:7, 9, 19; 6:59; D&C 77:2.

44. There are some species of animals which God has created but which he never placed here on this earth. See Smith, *Teachings of the Prophet Joseph Smith,* pp. 291–92; D&C 77:2–3.

45. Moses 2:21, 24–26; Abraham 4:24–26.

46. See nn. 38, 42, and 43.

47. Moses 2:11–12; 3:5, 9; Abraham 4:11–12; 5:5, 8–9.

48. Smith, *Teachings of the Prophet Joseph Smith,* p. 198.

49. D&C 93:29–33; 29:36; Moses 4:3. A further explanation of why man is responsible for his own actions because his basic "intelligence" is uncreated, is given by the author in "What Is Man?" *Hearken O Ye People* (Sandy, Utah: Randall Book Co., 1984), pp. 133–37, 142; "The Origin and Destiny of Man," *Studies in Scripture, Vol. 1: The Doctrine and Covenants,* ed. Robert L. Millet and Kent P. Jackson (Sandy, Utah: Randall Book Co., 1984), pp. 370–72.

50. D&C 98:8; 101:78; Moses 7:32. Mortal man must have a spirit as well as a physical body in order to be a "compound being" and therefore be subject to moral law authored by God. See 2 Nephi 2:11–14, 26. Further explanations on this subject are given by the author in "Creation, Fall, and Atonement," *Studies in Scripture, Vol. 7: 1 Nephi to Alma 29,* ed. Kent P. Jackson (Salt Lake City: Deseret Book Co., 1987), pp. 87–90.

51. Lehi explained that if mortal man was composed only of a physical body

("one body") rather than a spirit within a body ("compound in one") he could not "act" for himself but could only be "acted upon" (be a robot or machine). In such a universe there would be no God, no moral law, and no sin. (2 Nephi 2:11–16; see also 2 Nephi 9:25; Alma 42:17.)

52. Similar reasoning was used by God to explain that "eternal punishment" or "endless punishment" did not mean that there was no beginning or end, but merely that it was God's punishment, for "Eternal" and "Endless" are two of his names. See D&C 19:6–12; Moses 7:35.

53. Some consider God to be nothing more than the order and uniformity found in the universe. This is worshiping the "created" rather than the "Creator." Paul warned the people in his day of worshiping the created rather than the Creator (Romans 1:16–25) and the results which follow from accepting such beliefs (Romans 1:26–32). The results of worshiping the "created" in his day are strikingly similar to the conditions found in the world today.

54. The implications resulting from accepting the premises of naturalism are discussed in more detail by the author in "What Is Man?" pp. 133–42; "Creation, Fall, and Atonement," pp. 87–102; "Korihor the Anti-Christ," *Studies in Scripture, Vol. 8: Alma 30 to Moroni,* ed. Kent P. Jackson (Salt Lake City: Deseret Book Co., 1988), pp. 1–15.

55. Burtt, *Metaphysical Foundation,* p. 1.

56. Smith, *Teachings of the Prophet Joseph Smith,* pp. 255–56.

57. Ibid., p. 181. See n. 43; death occurs when the spirit leaves the body. (John 19:30–33.)

58. The Doctrine and Covenants seems to indicate that the spirit began its existence (even though the basic intelligence was uncreated) when it was organized by God and placed by God in a sphere where it could act for itself. (D&C 93:29–31.) The scriptures seem to indicate that in order for there to be happiness, there must also be the freedom to act with the resultant consequences of misery as well as happiness. (2 Nephi 2:13.) For a more detailed discussion on this subject, see "What Is Man?" pp. 140–44.

59. Joseph Smith taught that there were and will be beasts in heaven "giving glory to God." He said that those who did not believe in the salvation of beasts "would tell you that the revelations are not true." (*Teachings of the Prophet Joseph Smith,* p. 291).

60. The power of the priesthood is a self-existent principle, for, Joseph Smith said, "the Priesthood is an everlasting principle, and existed with God from eternity, and will to eternity, without beginning of days or end of years." (*Teachings of the Prophet Joseph Smith,* p. 157; cf. Alma 13:7–8.) The scriptures imply that it is a self-existent principle that matter is subject to the power of God. (Helaman 12:7–17; Moses 1:25; Abraham 2:7.)

61. Moses 3:5; 7:32, 59; D&C 45:1.

62. D&C 45:1; Moses 7:36. In rebutting Korihor (who was an advocate of naturalism), Alma said the following: "The scriptures are laid before thee; yea, and all things denote there is a God; yea, even the earth, and all things that are upon the face of it, yea, and its motion, yea, and also all the planets which move

in their regular form do witness that there is a Supreme Creator." (Alma 30:44; see also Psalm 19:1.)

63. See nn. 49 and 50.

64. For the naturalist, there is no God, and self-existent natural laws determine all things that happen in our universe. For the deist, God creates the natural laws at first but then withdraws and never interferes thereafter, allowing the universe to run by itself according to these natural laws like a big mechanical machine. In such a universe, there would be no miracles, for God would never change his commands to the elements and there would be no revelation or commandments given by God to man. For the theist, however, God creates the natural laws (D&C 88:13, 42) but can later change his commands to the elements, thereby causing a catastrophic flood (Moses 8:17), catastrophic changes in weather (Helaman 10:4–11:17), catastrophic changes in the movement of heavenly bodies (Helaman 12:13–15), exerting the powers of heaven (D&C 84:119), catastrophic geological changes on and in the earth (Helaman 12:6–12; 16–17; 3 Nephi 8:5–19), etc. He can also cause changes in events among men on earth by influencing them by his spirit (1 Nephi 13:10–15), by giving them revelations and commanding them to do certain things (D&C 1:17–23), and by destroying them if they become too wicked (Moses 8:24; Genesis 19:24–25; 3 Nephi 9:1–15). Hence, God depicts himself as a divine monarch (D&C 88:13; 106:6; 132:54; 133:61) who rules over our universe (Abraham 3:21; 2 Nephi 29:7), who controls the destinies of armies and nations (D&C 49:10; 60:4; 117:6; 124:1–10), and whose designs and purposes cannot be frustrated (D&C 3:1; 121:33). A short historical discussion on the progression from theism to naturalism is given by the author in "What Is Man?" pp. 134–38.

65. Just because we cannot comprehend the wisdom and power and workings of God does not mean that they do not exist. (Mosiah 4:9.)

Chapter Six

Redemption for the Dead

Leland Gentry

Instructor, Salt Lake Institute of Religion
Salt Lake City, Utah

MORONI'S VISIT

Moroni visited Joseph Smith three times on the night and early morning of September 21, 1823. During these encounters he quoted a number of Old Testament passages of scripture to the seventeen-year-old prophet. One of the more significant passages was taken from the writings of the prophet Malachi. Almost every sentence is filled with great significance for us who live today. This is what Moroni quoted from Malachi:

"For behold, the day cometh that shall burn as an oven, and all the proud, yea, and all that do wickedly shall burn as stubble; for they that come shall burn them, saith the Lord of hosts, that it shall leave them neither root nor branch.

" . . . Behold, I will reveal unto you the Priesthood, by the hand of Elijah the prophet, before the coming of the great and dreadful day of the Lord.

" . . . And he [Elijah] shall plant in the hearts of the children the promises made to the fathers, and the hearts of the children shall turn to their fathers. If it were not so, the whole earth would be utterly wasted at his [Christ's] coming."[1]

The last two verses of this prophecy are also found in section 2 of the Doctrine and Covenants. We will examine and explicate these scriptural passages as they relate to the doctrine of the redemption of the dead. We shall do this by asking and then trying to answer certain questions raised by this passage of scripture.

First, what is meant by the phrase "the great and dreadful day of the Lord," a day that will burn like an oven and leave the wicked with neither root nor branch? Latter-day Saints recognize this phrase as an allusion to the second coming of our Savior, a day that will be great for the righteous and dreadful for the wicked. Every corruptible thing on earth shall be consumed by the brightness of our Savior's coming, and to be left with neither root nor branch means to be bereft of both ancestry (roots) and posterity (children) inasmuch as the wicked will be unsealed either to their children or to those from whom they descend. It is difficult to think of a more appropriate figure to describe this condition than a tree with neither roots nor branches. The whole earth would be utterly wasted at Christ's second coming.[2]

Second, what is meant by Moroni's phrase of planting in the hearts of the children the "promises made to their fathers," thus causing the "hearts of children" to "turn to their fathers"? The fathers are the ancient patriarchs, such as Adam, Enoch, Noah, Abraham, Isaac, Jacob, and Joseph. God made unique promises to these men because of their faithfulness. President Joseph Fielding Smith once said: "What was the promise made to the fathers that was to be fulfilled in the latter-days by the turning of the hearts of the children to their fathers? It was the promise of the Lord made through Enoch, Isaiah, and the prophets, to the nations of the earth, that the time should come when the dead should be redeemed. And the turning of the hearts of the children is fulfilled in the performing of the vicarious temple work and in the preparation of their genealogies. . . .

"Some of these promises made to the fathers are found in the scriptures. For instance, Isaiah said in reference to our Savior: 'I the Lord have called thee in righteousness, and will hold thine hand, and will keep thee, and give thee for a covenant of the people, for a light of the Gentiles; To open the blind eyes, to bring out the prisoners from the prison, and them that sit in darkness out of the prison house.' [Isaiah 24:21–22.] . . .

"Again, he says: 'The Spirit of the Lord God is upon me; because the Lord hath anointed me to preach good tidings unto the meek; he hath sent me to bind up the brokenhearted, to proclaim liberty to the captives, and the opening of the prison to them that are bound.' [Isaiah 61:1.] This was spoken of as the mission of the Redeemer, both his work for the living and the dead, who were prisoners that were bound."[3]

Thus the promises made to the fathers in ancient times included not only a covenant that their descendants' temple work would be performed in the latter days but also a promise that Christ would come, open the eyes of the spiritually blind, enlighten the Gentiles, preach the gospel to those in the spirit prison, and liberate the righteous dead who were handicapped by lack of opportunity. God also made a special covenant with Father Abraham that he would make of him "a great nation," bless him "above measure," and make him a blessing to his seed by giving them "the blessings of the Gospel, which are the blessings of salvation, even of life eternal."[4]

Our Father in heaven is at the head of one vast family. This grand system of things he has organized on earth under the direction of Adam, our first earthly father, and given title to as the patriarchal order in which all of the aforementioned blessings are passed from father to son. Patterned after the heavenly arrangement, Adam, often referred to in scripture and elsewhere as the Ancient of days,[5] stands at the head of this holy order over which he will yet sit in formal judgment as "ten thousand times ten thousands" pass before to acknowledge him as their grand patriarch, the "father of all." He will preside at the great council at Adam-ondi-Ahman to be held at a future date and eventually "reign over his righteous posterity in the Patriarchal Order to all eternity."[6]

Third, Why would the earth be utterly wasted at our Savior's second coming if the work of salvation for the dead were not performed? This question has already been answered in part. Interestingly enough, Malachi in his original prophecy used the word *cursed,* whereas the angel Moroni used the phrase "utterly wasted." God created this earth as a home for man to work out his eternal life and salvation. Were all men to be left with neither ancestry or posterity, there would be no eternal family of God to inherit the earth. Were those in the spirit prison waiting for their temple work to be done never to realize that great blessing (they, too, once lived on this mortal earth), that would be one of the greatest catastrophes imaginable. To answer the question succinctly, we must view the eternal family organization from Adam and Eve to the present time as one grand unit and realize that God desires the salvation and even the exaltation of all his children. Hear these words of scripture: "The earth will be smitten with a curse unless there is a welding link of some kind or other between the fathers and the children. . . . For we without them cannot be made perfect; neither can they without us be made perfect. Neither can they nor we be made perfect without those who have died in the gospel also."[7] Were this not the case, each person would exist "separately and singly, without exaltation, in their saved condition [that is, with some degree of glory], to all eternity; and from henceforth are not gods, but are angels of God forever and ever."[8] I love the thought of a welding link — the very thing that holds me to my wife and children for time and all eternity, if we live worthy lives.

Fourth, and finally, What about the promise to reveal the priesthood by the hand of Elijah the prophet? The Prophet Joseph Smith said: "Elijah was the last Prophet that held the keys of the Priesthood, and who will, before the last dispensation, restore the authority and deliver the keys of the Priesthood, in order that all the ordinances may be attended to in righteousness. It is true that the Savior had authority and power to bestow this blessing; but the sons of Levi were too prejudiced. 'And I will send Elijah the Prophet before the great and terrible day of the Lord,' etc., etc. Why send Elijah? Because he holds the keys of the authority to administer in all the ordinances of the Priesthood; and without the authority is given, the ordinances could not be administered in righteousness."[9]

Elijah did come as promised. Shortly after the Kirtland Temple was dedicated, Moses, Elias, Elijah, and the Savior himself visited there. Elijah bestowed on Joseph Smith and Oliver Cowdery the sealing keys of the Melchizedek Priesthood,[10] the very powers that today in modern temples join couples together and commit to them the powers of eternal increase.

Fortunately for us, Joseph Smith made at least two other interesting observations on the work of Elijah: "Now comes the point. What is this office and work of Elijah? It is one of the greatest and most important subjects that God has revealed. He should send Elijah to seal the children to the fathers, and the fathers to the children.

"Now was this merely confined to the living, to settle difficulties with families on earth? By no means. It was a far greater work. Elijah! what would you do if you were here? Would you confine your work to the living alone? No: I would refer you to the Scriptures, where the subject is manifest: that is, without us, they could not be made perfect, nor we without them; the fathers without the children, nor the children without the fathers.

"I wish you to understand this subject, for it is important; and if you receive it, this is the spirit of Elijah, that we redeem our dead, and connect ourselves with our fathers which are in heaven, and seal up our dead to come forth in the first resurrection; and here we want the power of Elijah to seal those who dwell on earth to those who dwell in heaven. This is the power of Elijah and the keys of the kingdom of Jehovah."[11]

How appropriate for the great prophet of the latter days to refer to Elijah's work as "one of the greatest and most important subjects that God has revealed." The Prophet also said this: "The spirit, power, and calling of Elijah is, that ye have power to hold the key of the revelations, ordinances, oracles, powers and endowments of the fulness of the Melchizedek Priesthood and of the kingdom of God on the earth; and to receive, obtain, and perform all the ordinances belonging to the kingdom of God, even unto the turning of the hearts of the fathers unto the children, and the hearts of the children unto the fathers, even those who are in heaven."[12]

We could scarcely overemphasize the role of Elijah where redemption for the dead is concerned. But the inquiring student might ask, "What evidence do you have that Elijah ever truly held the sealing powers of the holy priesthood?" For the answer, we have only to examine the life and activities of Elijah as they are recorded in the pages of the Old Testament. A careful reading of 1 Kings 17–18 shows that it was Elijah who, in the days of Ahab, king of Israel, sealed up the heavens so that it did not rain for three years, unsealed those same heavens so that the earth received its needed moisture, sealed up a widow woman's flour barrel and cruse of oil against depletion during the famine, raised her only son from the dead, called down fire upon the priests of Baal to impress them with the true god's power, and finally was taken into heaven in a chariot of fire without tasting death.[13] He, as a translated being, appeared with Moses to Peter, James, and John on the Mount of Transfiguration and in the presence of the Savior of the world delivered his sealing keys that they, too, might bind on earth what is bound in heaven.[14]

REDEMPTION FOR THE DEAD REVEALED

As with most principles of the gospel, the doctrine of redemption for the dead came to the Church gradually, literally "line upon line, precept upon precept, here a little and there a little."[15] This appears to be the usual process by which our Heavenly Father works. How much of the doctrine the young prophet understood as a result of Moroni's first three visits we are not prepared to say, but it seems safe to assume that it was abundantly clear in Moroni's mind. He knew that temple work would be one of the glorious truths introduced by Joseph Smith in these latter days.

As new revelation was added, Joseph Smith and other prophets grew progressively expansive in their expressions about temple work. The following are some of their comments:

"It is sufficient to know in this case, that the earth will be smitten with a curse unless there is a welding link of some kind or other between the fathers and the children."[16]

"I will give you a quotation from one of the prophets, who had his eye fixed on the restoration of the priesthood, the glories to be revealed in the last days, and in an especial manner this most glorious of all subjects belonging to the everlasting gospel, namely, the baptism for the dead."[17]

"For we without them cannot be made perfect: neither can they without us be made perfect."[18]

"And now, my dearly beloved brethren and sisters, let me assure you that these are principles in relation to the dead and the living that cannot be lightly passed over, as pertaining to our salvation. For their salvation is necessary and essential to our salvation, as Paul says concerning the fathers—that they without us cannot be made perfect—neither can we without our dead be made perfect."[19]

"The saints have not too much time to save and redeem *their* dead. . . . if the whole Church should go to with all their might to save *their* dead . . . and spend none of their time in behalf of the world, they would hardly get through."[20]

"What kind of characters are those who can be saved although their bodies are decaying in the grave? When his [God's] commandments teach us, it is in view of eternity. The greatest responsibility in this world that God has laid upon us, is to seek after our dead.—The apostle [Paul] says, they without us cannot be made perfect. Now I will speak of them:—I say to you Paul, you cannot be perfect without us: it is necessary that those who are gone before, and those who come after us should have salvation in common with us, and thus hath God made it obligatory to man."[21]

"President Joseph Smith, by request of some of the Twelve, gave instructions on the doctrine of Baptism for the Dead. . . . The speaker presented 'Baptism for the Dead' as the only way that men can appear as saviors on mount Zion. The proclamation of the first principles of the gospel was a means of salvation to men individually, and it was the truth, not men that saved them; but men, by actively engaging in rites of salvation substitutionally, became instrumental in bringing multitudes of their kin into the kingdom of God. . . .

"This doctrine [salvation for the dead] he said, presented in a clear light, the wisdom and mercy of God in preparing an ordinance for the salvation of the dead, being baptised by proxy, their names recorded in heaven, and they judged according to the deeds done in the body. This doctrine was the burden of the scriptures. Those saints who neglect it, in behalf of *their* deceased relatives, do it at the peril of their own salvation."[22]

"In 1894, the Lord re-emphasized in a revelation through his prophet, Wilford Woodruff, that it was necessary, in the completion of temple work, to have children sealed to their parents and the parents in turn to their parents in all generations. The saints were told to trace their genealogies and run this chain of generations back into the past as far as it was possible to do so. 'This,' said Pres. Woodruff, 'is the will of the Lord to His people.' "[23]

The first temple completed in this dispensation was built in Kirtland, Ohio. Although a full complement of temple ordinances was never performed therein, small inklings of future events did emerge. Shortly before Elijah restored his keys, the School of the Prophets met in the attic of the printing office and there attended to "the ordinance of washing our bodies in pure water." That same evening, Joseph Smith and others took oil in their hands, blessed it, and "consecrated it in the name of Jesus Christ," and anointed the head of Joseph's father with the holy oil and pronounced upon him "many blessings," and those present blessed him to be their patriarch. Each in his turn then received a blessing and an anointing from the hands of the new patriarch. Joseph then reports that the heavens were opened and he "beheld the celestial kingdom of God, and the glory thereof," the Father and the Son, Adam and Abraham, and Joseph Smith's own mother, father, and brother Alvin. It was this view of Alvin that caused Joseph to marvel, since the older brother had never been baptized. The revelation recorded in section 137 of our Doctrine and Covenants was then given. From this Joseph learned the great doctrinal truth that "all who have died without a knowledge of this Gospel, who would have received it if they had been permitted to tarry shall be heirs of the celestial kingdom of God."[24]

From this point on, the Prophet began to use the term *endowment* with greater and greater frequency, and the word soon became well known throughout the Church.[25] Practically nothing was known about the endowment, however, as we know it today. Not until the fulness of the priesthood was revealed in Nauvoo, Illinois, was the Church to have a clearer understanding of the higher ordinances.

The first real reference to temple work as we know it occurred in a revelation given at Nauvoo on 14 January 1841, while the temple was still under construction. The Lord speaks in section 124 of "your anointings, and your washings, and your baptisms for the dead" and said these were to be attended to in that place. Among much else, the revelation states: "And verily I say unto you, let this house be built unto my name, that I may reveal mine ordinances therein unto my people;

"For I deign to reveal unto my church things which have been kept hid from before the foundation of the world, things that pertain to the dispensation of the fulness of times.

"And I will show unto my servant Joseph all things pertaining to this house, and the priesthood thereof, and the place whereon it shall be built."[26]

Baptisms for the dead began shortly after Joseph Smith preached about them on 16 August 1840, at the funeral of Seymour Brunson.[27] From that time, although careful records were not always kept, the Saints commenced to think about the necessity for this ordinance and began to attend to it. Jane Nyman appears to have been among the first. After consultation with her husband, she entered the waters of the Mississippi River on 13 September 1840 and was baptized in behalf of her deceased son.[28] One month later, on 15 October, residents on the Iowa side of the Mississippi commenced to do the same.[29] One year later, at the October conference, the Prophet brought the baptisms for the dead outside the temple to a halt: "There shall be no more baptisms for the dead, until the ordinance can be attended to in the Lord's House."[30] The first baptisms for the dead performed in the temple took place on 21 November 1841.[31]

Many of the ordinances required for salvation cannot be attended to in person by those in need of the ordinances. Like Joseph's brother Alvin, they died before the fulness of the priesthood was restored, or they never heard the gospel message while in life. Thus, we learn from President Joseph F. Smith's vision of the redemption of the dead that the Savior visited the spirits in prison, organized his missionary forces, and sent them forth to preach the gospel to the dead:

"These were taught faith in God, repentance from sin, vicarious baptism for the remission of sins, the gift of the Holy Ghost by the laying on of hands,

"And all other principles of the gospel that were necessary for them to know in order to qualify themselves that they might be judged according to men in the flesh, but live according to God in the Spirit. . . .

"Thus it was made known that our Redeemer spent his time during his sojourn in the world of spirits, instructing and preparing the faithful spirits of the prophets who had testified of him in the flesh;

"That they might carry the message of redemption unto all the dead, unto whom he could not go personally, because of their rebellion and transgression, that they through the ministration of his servants might also hear his words."[32]

CONCLUSION

Vicarious, or proxy, work is the very heart of the gospel of Jesus Christ. Our Savior's atonement in our behalf was a vicarious act, the strong doing for the weak that which they cannot do for themselves if they would only comply with His principles and ordinances. It is the same in the spirit world. Water and the laying on of hands are elements of this physical world and are essential features of redemption. They must be complied with here. It is an act of purest love to make it possible for the living to comply with earthly ordinances in behalf of those who never had that opportunity. May I commend all faithful temple workers who unselfishly devote hours of loving service in behalf of the worthy deceased. May I also compliment those untiring servants of the Lord who spend countless hours researching to locate names, dates, places, and relationships that make temple work the blessed work it is. Small wonder that the Prophet Joseph Smith should issue his fervent appeal to those of us who live today, to us whose hearts have turned to our fathers in the world of spirits, who never had the chance to comply with the ordinances of salvation:

"Brethren, shall we not go on in so great a cause? Go forward and not backward. Courage, brethren; on, on to the victory! Let your hearts rejoice, and be exceedingly glad. Let the earth break forth into singing. Let the dead speak forth anthems of eternal praise to the King Immanuel, who hath ordained, before the world was, that which would enable us to redeem them out of their prison; for the prisoners shall go free."[33]

NOTES

1. Joseph Smith–History 1:37–39.
2. D&C 2:1–3.
3. Joseph Fielding Smith, *Doctrines of Salvation*, comp. Bruce R. McConkie, 3 vols. (Salt Lake City: Bookcraft, 1954–6), 2:154–55.
4. Abraham 2:9–11.
5. Daniel 7:9–14; Joseph Smith, *Teachings of the Prophet Joseph Smith*, sel. Joseph Fielding Smith (Salt Lake City: Deseret Book Co., 1938), pp. 157–59, 167–69.
6. Bruce R. McConkie, *Mormon Doctrine* (Salt Lake City: Bookcraft, 1966), pp. 17–18.
7. D&C 128:18.
8. D&C 132:17.
9. Joseph Smith, *History of The Church of Jesus Christ of Latter-day Saints*, ed. B. H. Roberts, 7 vols., 2d ed. rev. (Salt Lake City: Deseret Book Co., 1932–51), 4:211.
10. D&C 110:15–16.
11. Smith, *Teachings of the Prophet Joseph Smith*, pp. 337–38.
12. Ibid., p. 337.
13. 1 Kings 17:1; 18:32–35; 17:14, 21–24; 18:36–39; 2 Kings 3:9–12.
14. Matthew 17:1–13; Smith, *Teachings of the Prophet Joseph Smith*, p. 158.
15. 2 Nephi 28:30.
16. D&C 128:18.
17. D&C 128:17.
18. D&C 128:18.
19. D&C 128:15.
20. History of Joseph Smith, 21 Jan. 1844, Historical Department, The Church of Jesus Christ of Latter-day Saints, Salt Lake City, Utah.
21. Conference minutes for Apr. 1844, *Times and Seasons*, 5:616.
22. Conference minutes for 1 Oct. 1841, *Times and Seasons*, 2:577–78.
23. *Handbook for Genealogy and Temple Work*, 1956 ed., p. 2.
24. *History of the Church*, 2:379–80.
25. D&C 32:32, 38; 95:8; 105:11–12; 110:9; 124:39; 132:59.
26. D&C 124:39–42.
27. Joseph Smith's Letter Book, 6 Nov. 1838 to 9 Feb. 1843, pp. 191–96, Historical Department.
28. Letter of George A. Smith, n.p., n.d., Historical Department.
29. John Smith Diary, Thursday, 15 Oct. 1840, Historical Department.
30. *History of the Church*, 4:426.
31. Ibid., 4:454.
32. D&C 138:33–37.
33. D&C 128:22.

CHAPTER SEVEN

Salvation Cannot Come without Revelation

Richard Neitzel Holzapfel

Instructor, Irvine Institute of Religion
Irvine, California

"Salvation cannot come," said the Prophet Joseph Smith, "without revelation."[1] This is one of the grand keys revealed to a modern world through the restoration of the Gospel of Jesus Christ. Without modern revelation, the Saints' situation would be very similar to that of the Jews of Jesus' day. They believed in the dead prophets of Israel and their writings but did not accept revelation in their own time. Thus they denied Christ's proclamation of the Good News to themselves and their children. In a modern setting, without their belief in modern revelation the Latter-day Saints would be like all other churches, denominations, and sects. Their beliefs are based on the writings of Old and New Testament prophets, written thousands of years ago. Joseph Smith said that the sectarian churches were "buil[t] [with] hay, wood and stubble on the old revelations without the spirit of revelation."[2]

Sectarian Christianity has splintered because of many interpretations of the scriptures. Where can one find the truth in the midst of such diversity of interpretation and opinion? Joseph Smith said "that it was impossible for a person young as [he] was, and so unacquainted with men and things, to come to any certain conclusion who was right and who was wrong." (Joseph Smith–History 1:8.)

Why was the Bible not enough revelation for Joseph? "For the teachers of religion of the different sects," he recorded, "understood the same passages of scripture so differently as to destroy all confidence in settling the question by an appeal to the Bible." He wrote, "Unless I could get more wisdom than I then had, I would never know." (Joseph Smith–History 1:12.)

Joseph began to receive the spirit of revelation from the Lord while reading the New Testament book of James. It was not a vision, nor an angel, but the voice of the Spirit that spoke to him that day:

"I was one day reading the Epistle of James, first chapter and fifth verse, which reads: If any of you lack wisdom, let him ask of God, that giveth to all men liberally, and upbraideth not; and it shall be given him.

"Never did any passage of scripture come with more power to the heart of man than this did at this time to mine. It seemed to enter with great force into every feeling of my heart." (Joseph Smith–History 1:11–12.)

Obedient to the first dictates of the Spirit, Joseph determined to ask God for more wisdom on the subject. As a result, he went into the woods near his home to pray for further guidance. He received one of the greatest revelations in world history. The Father, the Son, and many angels appeared to young Joseph, and he received the assurance that his sins were forgiven.[3] This revelation signaled the beginning of Joseph's own personal salvation and the salvation of a dark world, a world that had forgotten that salvation comes only upon the principle of continued revelation. Later the Prophet taught John Taylor the importance of cultivating the Spirit. He said, "Now listen to the dictates of that spirit and cultivate it, and it will become a spirit of revelation."[4]

The Prophet often expressed difficulty revealing God's will because of false traditions (false interpretations of scripture). He claimed that the inhabitants of a modern world were "differently situated from any other people that ever existed upon this Earth. Consequently those former revelations cannot be suited to our condition, because they were given to other people who were before us." He concluded that if the revelations and the Book of Mormon were taken away, "Where is our religion? We have none."[5]

The Lord announced to the inhabitants of the earth, "This generation [dispensation] shall have my word through you [Joseph Smith]." (D&C 5:10.) Joseph is not only the spokesman of God but is an example of a disciple of the Lord in this time. An analogy could be made between one who seeks salvation and Joseph Smith, although some may think it inappropriate to use Joseph as a model to receive revelation. They reason that Joseph was in some way special and therefore different from others seeking answers. Remember Joseph was a seeker of truth before he was a prophet. His story teaches universal principles that apply to every honest and sincere individual. Joseph taught that he had no "corner on the market" for revelation. To the brethren of the Church the Prophet said, "God hath not revealed anything to Joseph, but what he will make known unto the Twelve and even the least Saint may know all things as fast as he is able to bear them."[6]

REVELATION PROMISED IN THE LATTER DAYS

Revelation is promised in the latter days by ancient scripture. The fulfillment of the prophecy of Joel is occurring today. Joseph learned this from Moroni on September 23, 1827: "He also quoted the second chapter of Joel, from the twenty-eighth verse to the last. He also said that this was not yet fulfilled, but was soon to be." (Joseph Smith–History 1:41.)

The Lord's preface to the Doctrine and Covenants states, "The voice of the Lord is unto all men," for "all that will hear may hear." (D&C 1:2, 11.) The Lord makes several special promises of continued revelation in this new dispensation of the gospel. One such promise is found in Doctrine and Covenants 5:16: "Whosoever believeth on my words [in reference to the Book of Mormon], them will I visit with the manifestation of my Spirit." Another promise is found in Doctrine and Covenants 84:64: "I say unto you again, that every soul who believeth on your words [referring to Joseph Smith in particular], and is baptized by water for the remission of sins, shall receive the Holy Ghost." We must accept revelation through the Lord's anointed to receive the promise of more individual revelation. The Lord made this promise in Doctrine and Covenants 42:61: "If thou shalt ask, thou shalt receive revelation upon revelation, knowledge upon knowledge, that thou mayest know the mysteries and peaceable things — that which bringeth joy, that which bringeth life eternal."

Since Joseph's life is a model of the life of a true disciple, then the Doctrine and Covenants is our handbook on revelation. There the day-to-day revelatory experience of the Prophet unfolds. In the Doctrine and Covenants one can witness the spiritual growth and maturity of Joseph Smith as he receives inspiration and revelation from the Lord.

REVELATION COMES IN DIVERSE WAYS

A careful study of the Doctrine and Covenants shows that revelation comes in diverse manners. During the Church's organizational meeting of April 6, 1830, Joseph said that the "revelations of God . . . shall come hereafter by the gift and power of the Holy Ghost, the voice of God, or the ministering of angels." (D&C 20:35.) While recording a later revelation, the Prophet wrote, "Thus saith the still small voice, which whispereth through and pierceth all things, and often times it maketh my bones to quake while it maketh manifest." (D&C 85:6.) This statement implies that there were times when Joseph's bones did not quake.

As a young man I served my mission in Italy. Naively I believed and taught that the Prophet had a personal priesthood interview with the Lord each day. I thought it was a common experience for the Lord's anointed to speak face to face with Him. Showing a picture of the modern Church Presidency and Quorum of the Twelve, I said, "This man is our prophet. He is just like Moses and speaks with the Lord face to face." When President S. Dilworth Young of the First Quorum of Seventy visited our mission and met with us in a zone conference, he specifically asked us to stop saying that the prophet regularly talked with the Lord face to face. He then explained that those occurrences over the last four or five thousand years are actually quite rare. He also said: "All revelation comes by the Holy Ghost. . . . Only a few times does God the Father or Jesus Christ appear. They go through the Holy Ghost, and they are one. Just as the First Presidency signs three names at the bottom of their message it is still only one message. When Pres. Romney refers to a letter he says, 'President Kimball said . . .' not himself, and so it is with our Father in Heaven. He operates like that by way of the Holy Ghost."[7]

Examining the Doctrine and Covenants, I learned that President Young was right. Like Isaiah of old, I discovered that the Lord speaks to his modern servants by the same "still small voice." It was the same small still voice that spoke to me. (See 1 Kings 19:12.)

THE DOCTRINE AND COVENANTS AS A GUIDE TO REVELATION

There are a few examples in the Doctrine and Covenants when revelation came to Joseph Smith through a messenger. These include sections 2, 13, 27, and 110. Section 128, an epistle, mentions the appearance of several other angelic ministers who came to Joseph.

Revelation also comes by vision. There are only two examples of revelations received in this way in the Doctrine and Covenants during the lifetime of the Prophet. They are sections 76 and 137.

Several revelations came through the use of divine instruments. Usually it was the seer stone, or Urim and Thummim. Sections 3, 6–7, 10–11, and 14–17 came in that way.

Doctrine and Covenants 130:14–15 is an account of Joseph's hearing a voice speak to him. This seems to be the only revelation recorded in the Doctrine and Covenants that was received in this way.

Of all the 135 sections of the Doctrine and Covenants recorded during Joseph's lifetime, only 16 came in these special ways. They were truly unusual events in Joseph's revelatory experience. An examination of all ancient scripture seems to show this to be true. Modern and ancient scriptures testify that the "holy prophets . . . spake as they were inspired by the gift of the Holy Ghost." (D&C 20:26.) This was the usual way of communicating the mind and will of the Lord. Latter-day Saints as individuals should expect that the general law of revelation is the still small voice instead of bright lights and loud voices.

REVELATION THROUGH THE SPIRIT

Most of the Doctrine and Covenants consists of revelations given by the Holy Ghost. These revelations were given by the Spirit clothed in language by the Prophet. The Lord says that the voice Joseph heard "[was] as the voice of one crying in the wilderness — in the wilderness, because you cannot see him — my voice, because my voice is Spirit; my Spirit is truth; truth abideth and hath no end; and if it be in you it shall abound." (D&C 88:66.) Revelations given by the voice of the Spirit may include: Doctrine and Covenants 1, 4–5, 8–9, 12, 18–26, 28–64, 66–73, 75, 78–101, 103–8, 111–12, 114–20, 122, 124–26, 129, and 132–33.

Doctrine and Covenants 65, 109, and 121 are prayers, but the Prophet says in his record that they are revealed prayers.[8] Several other sections are Spirit-inspired letters (D&C 123; 127–28), minutes of a Church meeting (D&C 102), instructions (D&C 130–31), and questions and answers (D&C 77; 113). The total of Spirit-directed scriptures is thus 124 of the 135 sections of the Doctrine and Covenants recorded during the Prophet's lifetime. By far the most scripture came by the Spirit of the Lord, nearly 88 percent of the Doctrine and Covenants. The Lord announced who he was and how he spoke to his servants when he said, "Behold, I, Jesus Christ, your Lord and your God, and your Redeemer, by the power of my Spirit have spoken it." (D&C 18:47.)

There are several differences between Joseph's reception of revelation and the individual Saint's reception of revelation. First, Joseph clothed his impressions in words and wrote them down. Orson Pratt said, "Joseph the Prophet, in writing the Doctrine and Covenants, received the ideas from God, but clothed those ideas with such words as came to his mind." Elder Pratt continued: "Had [modern scripture] been through Orson Pratt or John Taylor, probably different words would have been used by each one to convey the same meaning."[9] A possible sign of this procedure is found in Doctrine and Covenants 104:81, where the Lord commanded Joseph to write a letter to New York. "Therefore write speedily," said the Lord, "and write according to that which shall be dictated by my Spirit."

This principle is involved today in the Church through patriarchal blessings. The patriarch receives the promptings of the Spirit. A patriarch could receive revelation in another way, maybe hearing a voice or seeing a vision, but this would probably be the exception. He then clothes these impressions in his own words to convey the meaning of the ideas. Different patriarchs use different words to convey the same meaning, depending upon the patriarch's education and culture. The patriarch's words are recorded and a written copy is given to the individual receiving the blessing. The individual can take that revelation and include it in his own "doctrine and covenants" for his own use and edification.

Brigham Young made the following observation concerning language and revelation:

"When God speaks to the people, he does it in a manner to suit their circumstances and capacities. He spoke to the children of Jacob through Moses, as a blind, stiff-necked people, and when Jesus and his Apostles came they talked with the Jews as a benighted, wicked, selfish people. They would not receive the Gospel, though presented to them by the Son of God in all its righteousness, beauty and glory. Should the Lord Almighty send an angel to re-write the Bible, it would in many places be very different from what it now is. And I will even venture to say that if the Book of Mormon were now to be re-written, in many instances it would materially differ from the present translation."[10]

The Lord uses the language of the individual to reveal his mind and will. (D&C 1:24.) In early Church history there were men who had more formal education than the Prophet. Some of them were concerned with the language Joseph used in the revelations. The Lord said, "Your eyes have been upon my servant Joseph Smith, Jun., and his language you have known, and his imperfections you have known; and you have sought in your hearts knowledge that you might express beyond his language." (D&C 67:5.) They were concerned with the Church leader's language and grammar, not necessarily with gospel messages revealed. The Lord's Spirit gave knowledge to Joseph, and he put that knowledge into his own language so others could read it.

Another difference between Joseph Smith and the individual Latter-day Saint is that Joseph's revelations not only were personal revelations or stewardship revelations but also were institutional revelations for the entire Church. (D&C 21:1–4; 28.)

HOW TO GET REVELATION

"By learning the Spirit of God and understanding it," the modern seer taught, "you may grow into the principle of revelation, until you become perfect in Christ Jesus."[11] Learning the Spirit of God may mean that one must "notic[e] the first intimation of the Spirit of Revelation." This first intimation occurs when you "feel pure Intelligence flowing unto you it may give you sudden strokes of ideas."[12] By noticing these strokes of ideas an individual will find the spirit of revelation. To Oliver Cowdery the Lord said, "Yea, behold, I will tell you in your mind and in your heart, by the Holy Ghost. . . . Now, behold, this is the spirit of revelation." (D&C 8:2–3.) He told Oliver that the answer would come not by a voice or in a vision, but as a feeling.

Christ has promised revelation to all who "serve [him] in righteousness and in truth unto the end." (D&C 76:5–7.) Joseph Smith emphasized: "No man can be called to fill any office in the ministry without it [the gift of the Holy Ghost]; we also believe in prophecy, in tongues, in visions, and in revelations, in gifts, and in healings; and that these things cannot be enjoyed without the gift of the Holy Ghost. We believe that the holy men of old spake as they were moved by the Holy Ghost, and that holy men in these days speak by the same principle; we believe in its being a comforter and a witness bearer, that it brings things past to our remembrance, leads us into all truth, and shows us of things to come; we believe that 'no man can know that Jesus is the Christ, but by the Holy Ghost.' "[13]

After his death, Joseph appeared to Brigham Young in a dream. Brigham had several questions to ask him on important Church doctrines and practices. Instead of answering Brigham Young directly, Joseph Smith responded with this advice: "Be sure and tell the people one thing. Do you be sure and tell the brethren that it is all important for them to keep the spirit of the Lord, to keep the quiet spirit of Jesus . . . which always brings peace and makes one happy and takes away every other spirit. When the still small voice speaks, always receive it."[14] The Spirit is the general way for the Saints to receive guidance.

BEGINNING TO RECEIVE REVELATION

The scriptures are the best place to begin to feel and hear the still small voice of the Spirit. This was Joseph's pattern, starting with his reading of James 1:5. The next step in this process is found in Doctrine and Covenants 18. Every person who hears or reads the revelations and receives the Spirit's witness to them can "testify that [they] have heard [the Lord's] voice, and know [the Lord's] words." (D&C 18:34–36.) Jesus said to the young prophet, "What I say unto one I say unto all." (D&C 93:49.) Individuals can get the spirit of revelation by reading and studying the scriptures. The scriptures become personal revelation. Once these revelations are accepted as God's word, God may be asked for the continuous revelation he has promised. The Holy Spirit can give individuals the personal revelation so necessary for meeting the problems and situations of a modern day. If God does not reveal himself, he cannot be known. Without such divine communication, therefore, an individual remains forever ignorant of the process of salvation. Continued personal revelation becomes scripture. "And whatsoever they shall speak," said the Lord, "when moved upon by the Holy Ghost shall be scripture, shall be the will of the Lord, shall be the mind of the Lord, shall be the word of the Lord, shall be the voice of the Lord, and the power of God unto salvation." (D&C 68:4.)

SUMMARY

These are the days spoken of by Joel the prophet. Through him the Lord said: "I will pour out my spirit upon all flesh; and your sons and your daughters shall prophesy, your old men shall dream dreams, your young men shall see visions:

"And also upon the servants and upon the handmaids in those days will I pour out my spirit." (Joel 2:28–29.)

As with Joseph's first revelation after reading James 1:5, a new convert reads the Book of Mormon and then asks God for wisdom, after which the Holy Ghost manifests the truth to him. Revelation comes by the Spirit, which if followed, brings salvation to the sincere believer in Christ.

The Lord has given a pattern that will help an individual to know whether the revelation is from Him or some other spirit:

"And now, verily, verily, I say unto thee, put your trust in that Spirit which leadeth to do good — yea, to do justly, to walk humbly, to judge righteously; and this is my Spirit.

"Verily, verily, I say unto you, I will impart unto you of my Spirit, which shall enlighten your mind, which shall fill your soul with joy;

"And then shall ye know, or by this shall you know, all things whatsoever you desire of me, which are pertaining unto things of righteousness, in faith believing in me that you shall receive." (D&C 11:12–14.)

The Lord made known his intentions concerning all his faithful Saints, "As well might man stretch forth his puny arm to stop the Missouri river in its decreed course, or to turn it up stream, as to hinder the Almighty from pouring down knowledge from heaven upon the heads of the Latter-day Saints." (D&C 121:33.)

With the Doctrine and Covenants as a guide, each of us can begin to understand and learn how to gain revelation. Revelation comes by the Holy Ghost. The Lord said to Oliver Cowdery, "Blessed art thou . . . ; thou hast inquired of me, and behold, as often as thou hast inquired thou hast received instruction of my Spirit. . . .

"Behold, thou knowest that thou hast inquired of me and I did enlighten thy mind; and now I tell thee these things that thou mayest know that thou hast been enlightened by the Spirit of truth. . . .

"Did I not speak peace to your mind concerning the matter? What greater witness can you have than from God?" (D&C 6:14–15, 23.) This witness of the Spirit is the guide to salvation. The Lord said, "For they that are wise and have received the truth, and have taken the Holy Spirit for their guide, and have not been deceived — verily I say unto you, they shall not be hewn down and cast into the fire, but shall abide the day." (D&C 45:57.)

Revelation is an important part of salvation for the whole earth and all its inhabitants. The Prophet Joseph Smith said at the conference where the Doctrine and Covenants was approved for publication that modern revelation was the "foundation of the Church and the salvation of the world."[15]

NOTES

1. Joseph Smith, *History of The Church of Jesus Christ of Latter-day Saints*, ed. B. H. Roberts, 2d ed. rev. (Salt Lake City, Utah: The Church of Jesus Christ of Latter-day Saints, 1932–51), 3:389.

2. Andrew F. Ehat and Lyndon W. Cook, eds., *The Words of Joseph Smith* (Provo, Utah: Religious Studies Center, Brigham Young University, 1980), p. 212.

3. Dean C. Jessee, "The Early Accounts of Joseph Smith's First Vision," *BYU Studies* 19 (Spring 1979): 280.

4. L. John Nuttall Diary, 3 Aug. 1881, Special Collections, Harold B. Lee Library, Brigham Young University, Provo, Utah.

5. Kirtland Council Minute Book, pp. 43–44, Historical Department, The Church of Jesus Christ of Latter-day Saints, Salt Lake City, Utah.

6. Ehat and Cook, *Words of Joseph Smith*, p. 4.

7. Richard Neitzel Holzapfel Missionary Journal, 23 Apr. 1974, pp. 126–27. This journal is in private possession.

8. *Times and Seasons* 5 (1 April 1844): 482; *History of the Church*, 2:420.

9. Minutes of the School of the Prophets, Salt Lake Stake, 9 Dec. 1872, p. 3, Historical Department, The Church of Jesus Christ of Latter-day Saints, Salt Lake City, Utah.

10. Brigham Young, in *Journal of Discourses* (London: Latter-day Saints' Book Depot, 1855–86), 9:311.

11. *History of the Church*, 3:381.

12. Ehat and Cook, *Words of Joseph Smith*, p. 5.

13. Joseph Smith, *Teachings of the Prophet Joseph Smith*, sel. Joseph Fielding Smith (Salt Lake City: Deseret Book Co., 1938), p. 243.

14. Juanita Brooks, ed., *On the Mormon Frontier: The Diary of Hosea Stout* (Salt Lake City: University of Utah Press, 1982), 1:238.

15. Donald Q. Cannon and Lyndon W. Cook, eds., *Far West Record: Minutes of The Church of Jesus Christ of Latter-day Saints* (Salt Lake City: Deseret Book Co., 1983), p. 32.

CHAPTER EIGHT

The Law of Consecration: The Covenant That Requires All and Gives Everything

Clark V. Johnson

Associate Professor of Church History and Doctrine
Brigham Young University

In December 1830 and January 1831, the Prophet Joseph Smith received two revelations commanding him to move the Church to Ohio. (D&C 37; 38.) The Lord promised to reveal his law and to endow Church members with "power from on high" once the Prophet arrived in Ohio. (D&C 38:32.) On 1 February 1831 Joseph arrived at the Gilbert and Whitney store in Kirtland, Ohio. Leaving his sleigh, he entered the establishment where he greeted the "junior partner" with "Newel K. Whitney! Thou art the man!" Newel responded, "You have the advantage of me, . . . I could not call you by name as you have me." The Prophet replied, "I am Joseph the Prophet. . . . You've prayed me here, now what do you want of me?"[1] Thus began a lasting friendship between Newel K. Whitney and the Prophet Joseph Smith. Joseph and Emma boarded with the Whitneys for several weeks.

Joseph's arrival in 1831 in Ohio began one of the most fruitful revelatory periods in the history of the Church. Through 1838, the Prophet received sixty-one revelations in Ohio and twenty-one in Missouri as well as others in sundry places, such as New York and Massachusetts. Many of these revelations are now part of the Doctrine and Covenants. The subjects of these revelations are broad, embracing the law of the Church, the personal conduct of members, Church organization, the law of consecration, the united order, prophecy, life after death, war, health laws, visions, temples, and missionary work. Almost all of these topics are an outgrowth of section 42 (the law of the Church), in which the Savior prescribed the required conduct for his people.

Much research has already been done concerning the law of consecration and stewardship. Milton V. Backman, in *The Heavens Resound,*

Leonard Arrington, in *Great Basin Kingdom* and *Building the City of God,* and Lyndon Cook, in *Joseph Smith and the Law of Consecration,* discuss the doctrine of consecration and stewardship during the Kirtland-Missouri and the Western periods of Church history. This paper discusses the principles of consecration and the organization of the united order as revealed through Joseph Smith between 1831 and 1838 and recorded in the Doctrine and Covenants.

The law of consecration is the covenant of consecration as defined in the scriptures, the temple, and in the writings of Joseph Smith. The united order is the attempt made by the early Saints to apply that covenant. I will discuss three points in relation to the law of consecration and the united order: first, the covenant of consecration and the principles that undergird it; second, the implementation of the law of consecration given in the Doctrine and Covenants; third, the challenges faced by the Prophet when he attempted to implement this law in Kirtland and Missouri.

THE PRINCIPLES OF CONSECRATION

On 9 February 1831, eight days after the Prophet's arrival in Ohio, in the presence of twelve elders the Lord revealed to his prophet the law of the Church,[2] now recorded in Doctrine and Covenants 42. In this revelation the Lord called upon his disciples to teach by the Spirit and to preach the gospel found in the New Testament and the Book of Mormon. (D&C 42:4–5, 7–8, 12.) The Savior instructed his followers not to kill, steal, lie, commit adultery or lust, or speak evil of others, and he warned them to beware of pride and to avoid idleness. (D&C 42:18–29, 41–42, 74–93.)

He also commanded them to take care of the poor and the sick. With these instructions, the Lord began to lay down those principles upon which the law of consecration rests. "And whosoever among you are sick, and have not faith to be healed, but believe, shall be nourished with all tenderness, with herbs and mild food, and that not by the hand of an enemy.

"And the elders of the church, two or more, shall be called, and shall pray for and lay their hands upon them in my name; and if they die they shall die unto me, and if they live they shall live unto me.

"Thou shalt live together in love . . .

"And it shall come to pass that those that die in me shall not taste of death, for it shall be sweet unto them;

" . . . And again, it shall come to pass that he that hath faith in me to be healed, and is not appointed unto death, shall be healed." (D&C 42:43–51.)

At least four points are made in these verses. First, the Lord expects his disciples to sustain and help one another. Second, the priesthood is used to benefit those who are ill. Third, a person can be healed by the power of the priesthood if that individual has faith and is "not appointed unto death"—information that gives confidence to the person as he realizes that the Lord has given him time to work out his exaltation. (D&C 121:25; 42:61; Alma 34:32.) Fourth, the Lord expects his disciples to love one another. These principles—mutual assistance, proper use of priesthood, the need for faith, and reciprocal love—are the cornerstones of the covenant.

Continuing, the Lord said to remember the poor and "consecrate of thy properties for their support that which thou hast to impart unto them, with a covenant and a deed which cannot be broken.

"And inasmuch as ye impart of your substance unto the poor, ye will do it unto me; and they shall be laid before the bishop of my church and his counselors, two of the elders, or high priests, such as he shall appoint or has appointed and set apart for that purpose." (D&C 42:30–31.)

Here we see that the Lord's intent is not just to take care of the immediate needs of the poor so that the poor can sustain themselves. Rather, the Church members were to willingly set aside some of their properties for the poor and "impart unto them, with a covenant and a deed which cannot be broken." Thus we see that a person was to lay freely his properties before the bishop of the Church. Joseph Smith taught that the consecration of properties must be done by mutual consent. The bishop could not dictate in matters of consecration or he would have "more power than a king." The Prophet further explained that there must be a balance of power between the bishop and the people in order to preserve "harmony and good-will."[3]

Through giving of his income, the donor received a stewardship from the bishop for his support and for the support of his family. In the scriptures the stewardship is also called an inheritance. (D&C 42:32; 51:4.) After the initial donation was made, the person was expected to contribute to the program by giving to the bishop what he earned in excess of the needs of his stewardship. (D&C 42:33.) The properties cannot be taken back from the Church once they have been given to

it, and the stewardship, or inheritance, received from the Lord must
be sufficient to support the steward and his family. (D&C 42:32.)

According to Joseph Smith, the amount of the inheritance depended
upon the properties consecrated and the means provided for the poor.[4]
The more wealth given to the storehouse, the larger the stewardship.
Thus the living standard of everyone, including the poor, rose according
to the selfless dedication of members of the united order. Every person
was accountable to the Lord for his stewardship. The Savior reminded
his people that there were two kinds of stewardship—temporal and
spiritual. For example, the bishop, who is charged with operating a
storehouse, receiving consecrations, and managing the Lord's properties, has a spiritual stewardship; however, because he also draws
from the storehouse the goods he needs to provide for himself he
enjoys a temporal stewardship. (D&C 42:33, 71.) Thus Church leaders
claimed goods from the storehouse for their support or to be reimbursed
for their expenses. (D&C 42:71–72; 51:14.) In the Lord's eyes, both
temporal and spiritual stewardships serve to build his kingdom. (D&C
70:12.) Each stewardship was suited to the gifts and needs of the
individual to give him or her the maximum opportunity for growth in
the kingdom of God, with the result, Joseph Smith said, "many of our
brethren are wise in . . . their labors, and have rid their garments of
the blood of this generation and are approved before the Lord."[5]

The Lord reminded his prophet, who subsequently reminded
Church members, that they were the Lord's stewards and therefore,
had to account for their stewardship "both in time and in eternity."
(D&C 72:3; see also 70:4, 9.) The accounting procedures were quite
clear. First, members accounted to the bishop for their stewardship as
well as for their personal conduct. (D&C 72:5, 16–17; 104:12–13.)[6] And
second, they will ultimately account to their Father in heaven.

The Lord reminded members of the Church that when they had
enough to satisfy their needs, they were to give the surplus to the
storehouse. (D&C 70:7–9; 82:18.) Excess gained in the operation of
the stewardship was to be used to administer to those who were in
need. (D&C 42:33–34.) Every person developed and improved his stewardship according to his talent. (D&C 82:18.)

The bishop kept all surplus donated from the stewardships in a
storehouse he organized. (D&C 51:13.) Once the poor were taken care
of, the residue was to be used for purchasing lands and for building
houses of worship and temples. (D&C 42:34–35.)

The Lord recognized that as the Church grew more than one united order would need to be organized. Hence, different organizations of the united order operated independently from one another: "If another church [branch] would receive money of this church [branch], let them pay into this church [branch] again according as they shall agree." (D&C 51:11.) The bishop or his agent represented the Lord in all donations and surpluses received into the storehouse, and they also negotiated the agreements between separate united orders. (D&C 51:10–12.)

The Savior also revealed that inheritances, or stewardships, are secured in writing and that even though a person might transgress the law of the Church, he continued to hold the property deeded to him by the bishop but he had no claim on previous donations or help from the storehouse. (D&C 51:5.)

The Lord also required the bishop of the Church to give every man an inheritance. He explained that Church members were equal according to their family, circumstances, wants, and needs. (D&C 51:4, 7.) The Lord does not desire his people to have everything the same or all things in common, but to have "all things common among them." (4 Nephi 1:3; see also Moses 7:18.) To have "all things common among them" is to understand that everything a person has is a gift from God, which God has given to bless his children. This attitude does away with superiority complexes and class structure and allows people to reach a level of equality in which there are no "rich and poor, bond and free," but all are "made free, and partakers of the heavenly gift," or life eternal. (4 Nephi 1:3; see also D&C 42:61.) Joseph Smith taught that this same attitude must exist on the part of the destitute, "He that hath not, and cannot obtain, but saith in his heart, if I had, I would give freely, is accepted as freely as he that gives of his abundance."[7]

In accordance with the principle of equality, the Prophet taught Church members, two fundamental attitudes had to exist for a person to live the law of consecration: First, the earth and everything on it is God's. He created it; therefore, he owns it. Second, the individual is the Lord's steward, and "whatsoever man possesses in it, he holds as a stewardship."[8]

Recognizing that differences of opinion and personality clashes might occur among Church members, the Lord also revealed the law of offense to his followers. If someone were offended, he was to go to the person who had offended him and settle the differences. If the differences could not be resolved between the two parties, then the matter was to be taken before the elders. Thus, violators of the commandments and covenants were to be tried by the Church, subject to the "law of God." (D&C 42:81.) The principle set forth by the Savior in this situation is this: "And if thy brother or sister offend many, he or she shall be chastened before many.

"And if any one offend openly, he or she shall be rebuked openly. . . .

"If any shall offend in secret, he or she shall be rebuked in secret, that he or she may have opportunity to confess in secret to him or her whom he or she has offended, and to God, that the church may not speak reproachfully of him or her." (D&C 42:90–92.)

While the Lord continued to direct his servants in the operation of the law of consecration, the principles set forth in Doctrine and Covenants 42 and 51 outlined the basic premises for the organization of the storehouse and the united order. In subsequent revelations, Joseph learned that the united order existed "for the benefit of my church, and for the salvation of men," until the Lord comes. (D&C 104:1.) Joseph Smith wrote: "The cause of God is one common cause, in which the Saints are . . . all interested. . . . The advancement of the cause of God and the building up of Zion is as much one man's business as another's." He noted that the only differences are between the duties individuals are asked to perform: "One is called to fulfill one duty, and another another duty."[9] By November 1831 Joseph said that no one was exempt from living the law of consecration or from giving the surplus from his stewardship to the storehouse. (D&C 70:10–11.)

ORGANIZATION OF THE UNITED ORDER

On 4 February 1831, just three days after the Prophet's arrival in Kirtland, the Savior through his prophet called Edward Partridge to be bishop and referred to him as "Nathanael of old, in whom there is no guile." (D&C 41:9–11.) Some time later the Lord explained to Bishop Partridge that he had been chosen to organize the people according to God's laws. (D&C 51:2–3.)

By 1 August 1831 the Colesville Saints had arrived in Missouri, and Joseph wrote to Bishop Partridge, giving him instructions concerning the inheritances they were to receive. He warned Bishop Partridge not to "condescend to very great particulars in taking inventories." Joseph taught that a person is bound by the covenant to consecrate his property. Because a man is his own judge, he needed to decide what he gave to the storehouse as well as what he received for an inheritance; however, the Prophet cautioned Bishop Partridge about those who tended to keep more than they needed for their support.[10] As individuals entered the united order, deeds and leases were used to receive consecrated properties and to give inheritances. (This principle was not always complied with while the Saints resided in Jackson County, Missouri. The property in Jackson County was held by Bishop Edward Partridge.)

The forms used to exchange and secure property between Bishop Edward Partridge and Titus Billings[11] serve as examples of the type of instruments used:

> BE IT KNOWN, THAT I, Titus Billings of Jackson county, and the state of Missouri, having become a member of the Church of Christ, organized according to law, and established by the revelations of the Lord, on the 6th day of April, 1830, do, of my own free will and accord, having first paid my just debts, grant and hereby give unto Edward Partridge of Jackson county, and state of Missouri, Bishop of said Church, the following described property, viz.: — sundry articles of furniture valued fifty-five dollars twenty-seven cents; also two beds, bedding and extra clothing valued seventy-three dollars twenty-five cents; also farming utensils valued forty-one dollars; also one horse, two wagons, two cows and two calves, valued one hundred forty-seven dollars.
>
> For the purpose of purchasing lands in Jackson county, Mo., and building up the New Jerusalem, even Zion, and for relieving the wants of the poor and needy. For which I, the said Titus Billings, do covenant and bind myself and my heirs forever, to release all my right and interest to the above described property, unto him, the said Edward Partridge, Bishop of said Church.
>
> And I, the said Edward Partridge, Bishop of said Church, having received the above described property, of the said Titus Billings, do bind myself, that I will cause the same to be expended for the above mentioned purposes of the said Titus Billings to the satisfaction of said Church; and in case I should be removed from the office of Bishop of said Church, by death or otherwise, I hereby bind myself and my heirs forever, to make over to my successor in office, for the benefit of said Church, all the above described property, which may then be in my possession.
>
> IN TESTIMONY WHEREOF, we have hereunto set our hands and seals this _____ day of _____, in the year of our Lord, one thousand, eight hundred and thirty _____
>
> In the presence of _____,
>
> _____
>
> Signed, TITUS BILLINGS.
> EDWARD PARTRIDGE

BE IT KNOWN, THAT I, Edward Partridge, of Jackson county, state of Missouri, Bishop of the Church of Christ, organized according to law, and established by the revelations of the Lord, on the 6th day of April, 1830, have leased and by these presents do lease unto Titus Billings, of Jackson county, and state of Missouri, a member of said Church, the following described piece or parcel of land, being a part of section No. three, township No. forty-nine, range No. thirty-two, situated in Jackson county, and state of Missouri, and is bounded as follows, viz: — Beginning eighty rods E. from the S. W. corner of said section; thence N. one hundred and sixty rods; thence E. twenty-seven rods, twenty-five links; thence S. one hundred and sixty rods; thence W. twenty-seven rods, twenty-five links, to the place of beginning, containing twenty-seven and one-half acres, be the same more or less, subject to roads and highways. And also have loaned the following described property, viz: — Sundry articles of furniture, valued fifty-five dollars twenty-five cents; also two beds, bedding and clothing, valued seventy-three dollars twenty-seven cents; also sundry farming utensils, valued forty-one dollars; also one horse, two cows, two calves, and two wagons, valued one hundred forty-seven dollars, to have and to hold the above described property, by him, the said Titus Billings, to be used and occupied as to him shall seem meet and proper.

And as a consideration for the use of the above described property, I, the said Titus Billings, do bind myself to pay the taxes, and also to pay yearly unto the said Edward Partridge, Bishop of said Church, or his successor in office, for the benefit of said Church, all that I shall make or accumulate more than is needful for the support and comfort of myself and family. And it is agreed by the parties that this lease and loan shall be binding during the life of the said Titus Billings, unless he transgresses and is not deemed worthy by the authority of the Church, according to its laws, to belong to the Church. And in that case I, the said Titus Billings, do acknowledge that I forfeit all claim to the above described leased and loaned property, and hereby bind myself to give back the lease, and also pay an equivalent, for the loaned [articles] for the benefit of said Church, unto the said Edward Partridge, Bishop of said Church, or his successor in office. And further, in case of said Titus Billings' or family's inability in consequence of infirmity or old age to provide for themselves while members of this Church, I, the said Edward Partridge, Bishop of said Church, do bind myself to administer to their necessities out of any fund in my hands appropriated for that purpose, not otherwise disposed of, to the satisfaction of the Church. And further, in case of the death of the said Titus Billings, his wife or widow, being at the time a member of said Church, has claim upon the above described leased and loaned property, upon precisely the same conditions that her said husband had them, as above described; and the children of the said Titus Billings, in case of the death of both their parents, also have claim upon the above described property, for their support, until they shall become of age, and no longer; subject to the same conditions yearly that their parents were; provided, however, should the parents not be members of said Church, and in possession of the above described property at the time of their deaths, the claim of the children as above described, is null and void.

IN TESTIMONY WHEREOF we have hereunto set our hands and seals this _____ day of _____, in the year of our Lord, one thousand eight hundred and thirty _____

In presence of _____,

_____

Signed, EDWARD PARTRIDGE
TITUS BILLINGS

A clerk was appointed and a history was kept of "all things" that happened in "Zion." This history included writings of the faith and the works of the Saints, the stewardships received, and the names of people consecrating property; however, the names of those who apostatized were not recorded.[12]

Church members who gathered to Zion were instructed to avoid disorder and haste in purchasing lands in order not to alarm the local citizens. They were cautioned to prepare temporally and spiritually — meaning they had to settle their debts and be prepared to give "all to the Lord."[13] Joseph Smith instructed the Saints to account to the bishop in the east, Bishop Newel K. Whitney, and receive a certificate of recommendation from him. (D&C 72:17.) With this recommend a person was eligible to receive an inheritance from Bishop Partridge and to become a steward in Zion. Without the certificate a man was not acceptable. (D&C 72:18.) These instructions were published in *The Evening and the Morning Star* as an "extra" and made available to Church members as a handbill. Finally, a call was sent to the membership of the Church throughout the east to send money to the bishop in Zion to purchase lands for inheritances. (D&C 58:51.)

In addition to the storehouse, two treasuries were organized to receive monies donated to the order. One treasury worked in harmony with the storehouse and was used to take care of the poor, to purchase lands, to build buildings, and to satisfy the needs of the Saints. All monies received from stewardship improvements were placed in this treasury as fast as they were received. (D&C 104:68.) The other treasury, the "sacred treasury," contained those things most holy and money earned from the sale of scriptures, holy and sacred writings, and other sacred things. Monies in this treasury were used for printing the scriptures and were consecrated to the Lord for his work. (D&C

104:63, 65–66.) Treasurers were appointed to handle the accounts in each treasury. No one person could take items or monies from the storehouse or treasuries. Access to the treasuries was only by voice of the order's members or by commandment of the Lord. (D&C 104:64, 71–72.) Thus, the storehouse and treasuries belonged to members of the order, and a worthy steward had claim on the storehouse and treasury. (D&C 104:62, 72.)

Through revelation the Lord instructed his servants to honor requests from the treasury and storehouse made by the steward regardless of the sum as long as there were goods in the storehouse or money in the treasury. Hence, the items or money was not to accumulate but was to be used by the steward to improve and operate his stewardship. (D&C 104:73.) The only reason to deny access was lack of personal worthiness. (D&C 104:75.)

The Church in Kirtland and Zion operated mercantile and literary firms. The Prophet wrote that "all members of the United Firm [united order] are considered one. The order of the Literary Firm is a matter of stewardship, . . . and the mercantile establishment God commanded to be devoted to the support thereof."[14] Historically, the united order at Kirtland was dissolved temporarily and then quickly reorganized. From 1831 through 1833 the united order in Kirtland and Zion had operated together, but as Church membership and problems increased in Missouri, it became necessary to separate the orders. (D&C 104:47–49, 51.)[15]

Inheritances were given according to the individual's needs and talents. W. W. Phelps was congratulated by the Prophet for the improvement he made in his stewardship, which was publishing *The Evening and the Morning Star.* Sidney Rigdon received a home and a tannery. (D&C 104:20.) The Lord called Martin Harris to lay his monies before the bishop and then gave him a lot owned by John Johnson in exchange for his former inheritance.[16] (D&C 58:35; 104:24.) Newel K. Whitney received the mercantile establishment he owned in Kirtland as his inheritance. (D&C 104:40–41.) Parley P. Pratt's stewardship called upon him to preach the gospel and promised him that when his work was done, God would take him to Himself. Pratt was also warned to beware of pride, strife, and vainglory and to avoid evil. In addition, Oliver Cowdery prophesied that Parley Pratt would experience persecution and imprisonment as he sought to fulfill his responsibilities as a steward.[17] During the Nauvoo period Robert B. Thompson was called to write for the Prophet Joseph Smith. (D&C 124:12.)

THE CHALLENGES OF LIVING THE LAW OF CONSECRATION

The problems that arose when Church members embraced the covenant of consecration and attempted to live the united order in Kirtland and Missouri during the 1830s proved to be insurmountable.

Prior to the Prophet's arrival in Ohio, more than one thousand people had been converted to the Church. The membership at Kirtland proved to be about one hundred saints organized into a "Family."[18] Their desire to live the gospel as purely as possible existed previous to their baptism into the Church, and they had adopted an organization that held all things in common in the manner they believed the ancient Saints in the New Testament had used. (Acts 4:32, 34–35.) Joseph Smith observed that "strange notions and false spirits had crept in among them." He further explained that "with a little caution and some wisdom I soon assisted the brethren and sisters to overcome them. The plan of 'common stock,' . . . was readily abandoned for the more perfect law of the Lord; and the false spirits were easily discerned and rejected by the light of revelation."[19]

In a revelation given to Joseph Smith on 16 December 1833 after the Saints' expulsion from Jackson County, Missouri, the Lord said, "I, the Lord, have suffered the affliction [their expulsion] to come upon them, wherewith they have been afflicted, in consequence of their transgressions." (D&C 101:2.) He specified the nature of their transgressions: "there were jarrings, and contentions, and envyings, and strifes, and lustful and covetous desires among them; therefore by these things they polluted their inheritances.

"They were slow to hearken unto the voice of the Lord their God; therefore, the Lord their God is slow to hearken unto their prayers, to answer them in the day of their trouble.

"In the day of their peace they esteemed lightly my counsel; but, in the day of their trouble, of necessity they feel after me." (D&C 101:6–8.)

During the early Kirtland-Missouri period the Prophet faced at least three problems while he tried to implement the law of consecration among the Saints. First, personal greed was exhibited on the part of some of the members. Second, a few Church members attempted to receive revelation for the Church. Third, the unrighteous conduct of some Church leaders caused problems. In spite of these problems and the weaknesses displayed by the Saints, the Lord said, "I will own them, and they shall be mine in that day when I shall come to make up my jewels." (D&C 101:3.)

Shortly after the law of the church was received, Leman Copley, a member, consecrated his farm located in Thompson, a few miles east of Kirtland, to the united order to be used as stewardships for those who wished to enter the covenant. Joseph Smith sent for the Colesville, New York, branch to come to Kirtland to receive their inheritance. After the Colesville Saints arrived in Kirtland, the Prophet received another revelation in May 1831 and the New Yorkers settled on the Copley farm in Thompson.[20] According to Newel Knight, they "commenced work in good faith" and made improvements on the land.[21]

At this same time Copley, Sidney Rigdon, and Parley P. Pratt were called to serve a proselyting mission to the Quaker community near Cleveland. (D&C 49, headnote.) These brethren proclaimed the gospel in obedience to the revelation, but the Shakers failed to accept their teachings. Apparently Leman Copley, once a Quaker, still retained some of his earlier beliefs. He became disillusioned with the Church, broke his covenant, withdrew his farm from the order, and demanded that the recent arrivals leave. Commenting upon the Copley incident, Milton V. Backman noted that, "While the precise reasons for the conflict are not known selfishness and greed no doubt played a part."[22] The *History of the Church* indicates that Ezra Thayre also played a part in the dislocation of the Colesville Saints. Evidence indicates that his entanglement at Thompson prevented him from fulfilling the obligations of the covenant he had made. (D&C 56:8–10; headnote.)

During the 1830s some embraced the Church only to become disillusioned with it and its prophet a short time later. The reasons were as varied as the personalities of the individuals involved. When Norman A. Brown's horse died on his way to Zion, he reasoned, "If this had been the work of God, my horse would not have died." Joseph H. Wakefield withdrew from the Church after seeing Joseph emerge from his translating room and begin playing with some children. Simonds Ryder left the Church because the Prophet misspelled his name in a revelation. Ezra Booth withdrew his membership when it appeared to him that Joseph had too many revelations of convenience. And Philastus Hurlburt was excommunicated for adultery.[23] The Hulet brothers were censured for teaching the false doctrine that the devil, his angels, and the sons of perdition would be restored after they repented. Others were cut off from the Church for receiving revelations for the Church.[24]

In Zion during the summer of 1833 the people lived in peace. There were no lawsuits, thieves, robbers, or murderers; few or no idlers; "all seemed to worship God with a ready heart." In August they received a revelation from Joseph Smith, who resided in Kirtland. In the revelation the Lord asked his people to build a temple "like unto the pattern which I have given you." According to Pratt the Saints never complied with the revelation, which failure led to their expulsion from Jackson County by Missouri mobs during the winter of 1833–34.[25] Other problems also contributed to the failure of Zion. The Lord had asked his people to send monies to Zion to purchase land, specified the order for gathering to Zion, and required that the poor be cared for. Unfortunately many did not follow the requirements issued by the Prophet. For example, as more people joined the Church, the rules were often ignored as converts gathered faster with "irrational enthusiasm," the rich were afraid to send money to purchase lands, and the poor migrated "in numbers, without having any places provided."[26]

In Zion petty jealousies developed among the leading brethren. Joseph wrote to the stake presidency in Missouri, reprimanding them for their failure to share with Bishop Partridge the information he had sent. "We were not a little surprised to hear that some of our letters of a public nature, which we sent for the good of Zion, have been kept back from the Bishop. This is conduct which we highly disapprobate." This was the result of the bishop's complaint that information from the Prophet was being withheld from him. Joseph continued to counsel the brethren in Zion, indicating that letters directing the affairs of the Church "should be laid before the Bishop, so as to enable him to perform his duty." Then the Prophet cautioned the brethren to "be careful of one another's feelings."[27]

As contention increased among Church members, the mobs in Jackson County gained power by playing upon the disunity among the Saints, finally driving them from their homes and the land of their inheritance. A mob that broke into the storehouse managed by A. S. Gilbert destroyed and threw much of the merchandise in the street.[28] Gilbert was forced to abandon the storehouse as he fled from Jackson County. When the question arose as to the sale of the store, the Lord commanded Sidney Gilbert not to sell it. (D&C 101:96.) During the months that followed, Gilbert engineered a correspondence with Governor Dunklin of Missouri. He tried to secure the Saints' rights to the property they had previously owned in Jackson County. On 29 June 1834 he was attacked by cholera and died.[29]

In June 1835 the Prophet Joseph Smith wrote a letter "To the Saints Scattered Abroad," which he published in the *Messenger and Advocate*. He reminded the elders in Zion that the high council had been organized to administer in the spiritual affairs of the Church, whereas the bishop and his counselors presided over temporal matters. In addition he stated that "the Elders in Zion, or in her immediate region, have no authority or right to meddle with her spiritual affairs, to regulate her concerns, or hold councils."[30] In vain he tried to teach Church members that revelation for the Church had to come from the constituted authorities of the Church.

In April 1837, the Presidency and the high council at Far West met and organized a committee to build a temple in the city. The committee consisted of Jacob Whitmer, Elisha H. Groves, and George M. Hinkle with Bishop Partridge appointed as treasurer and Isaac Morley named as secretary. In addition the committee decided that "no store" be "connected with building the house, but that every firm or individual that embarks in that business have, own, and claim such property as their own private individual property and stewardship."[31] One year later, on 10 March 1838 at a high council meeting, charges were brought against W. W. Phelps and John Whitmer by the high council in Zion. The minutes of the meeting included complaints of everything from unchristian conduct to the most serious accusation, fraudulent use of Church funds.[32] These men were found guilty and excommunicated from the Church.

By the end of 1838 the Missouri Militia had taken control of Far West, and during the winter and spring of 1838–39, the Mormons were forced to leave Missouri. In March 1840 in an address given to the Iowa High Council assembled at Montrose, Joseph instructed its members that "the law of consecration could not be kept here, and that it was the will of the Lord that we should desist from trying to keep it." During this meeting Joseph assumed full responsibility for the Saints' not living it.[33] This closed almost a decade of struggle on the part of the Prophet to prepare a Zion people, a people prepared to build the New Jerusalem. Even though temples had not been built and Zion redeemed in the 1830s, the Prophet prophetically explained that the Lord would "open the way and deliver Zion in the appointed time."[34]

Once the Saints were driven from their inheritances in Jackson County, Missouri, they never successfully reinstated the united order again. The Lord revealed to them instead the law of tithing. Prior to 8 July 1838 the term *tithing* included not only one-tenth, but all donations made. (D&C 64:23; 85:3; 97:11.) The headnote to Doctrine and Covenants 119 states that "because of failure on the part of many to abide by this covenant [consecration], the Lord withdrew it for a time, and gave instead the law of tithing to the whole Church." The Lord required that surplus properties be placed in the hands of the bishop and thereafter that people be tithed on their increase. (D&C 119:1, 3–4.)

CONCLUSIONS

As early Church members sought to comply with God's will concerning them, they learned that the "work" and "glory" of God was their "immortality and eternal life." (Moses 1:39.) As revealed in Doctrine and Covenants 42 they learned that while the law of consecration promised them eternal life, it required that they give everything, both temporally and spiritually. They began to understand that they had to have personal integrity when dealing with one another, and they had to be concerned about others' welfare. They learned that the commitment had to be total and included material things as well as spiritual. The attitude they had to develop went beyond mere lip service. They had to internalize the principles of the law. (D&C 42.) They had to embrace the ideals that the earth is the Lord's and that men are the Lord's stewards.

While they attempted to establish the ideal, history shows they fell short because of contentions among themselves, personal unrighteousness, and failure to understand the operations of the Spirit because of their lack of knowledge and overzealous nature toward establishing the kingdom of God according to their own design rather than following the leadership of the Prophet and other officers appointed by the Savior to direct his Church. After their effort failed, Jesus promised them that Zion would still be redeemed but gave them the law of tithing to prepare them and their children to live the law of consecration.

The Church today is still living the law of tithing, and yet, there are subtle indications that the Lord's prophets would like to move us from a strict tithe to a more liberal attitude of giving that would be in harmony with the principles of consecration. President Spencer W. Kimball challenged us to "give, instead of the amount saved by our two meals of fasting, perhaps much much more—ten times more where we are in a position to do it."[35] President Thomas S. Monson also asked us to increase our fast offerings so that the needs of the poor might be totally satisfied from them.[36] If we cloaked his words in the vernacular spoken about consecration in the 1830s, he would have said bring your surplus to the storehouse or treasury and take care of the poor and receive your inheritance from the Lord. With this accomplished then all the tithes in the sacred treasury can be used for sacred things— meaning missionary work, publishing the scriptures, organizing missions, building temples, and extracting names for temple work.

As we change from donating what we are required to give to giving all we can, then we will find ourselves living the law of consecration, which we have promised to live when we are "endowed with power from on high" in the temple. Then members of our family, our ward, our stake, and finally, the Church will have all things common among them; therefore there are no rich and poor, bond and free, but all are free, and partakers of eternal life. (See 4 Nephi 1:3.)

NOTES

1. Joseph Smith, *History of The Church of Jesus Christ of Latter-day Saints*, 2d ed. rev., ed. B. H. Roberts (Salt Lake City: The Church of Jesus Christ of Latter-day Saints, 1932–51), 1:146 n.

2. Ibid., 1:148–54.

3. Joseph Smith, *Teachings of the Prophet Joseph Smith*, sel. Joseph Fielding Smith (Salt Lake City: Deseret Book Co., 1938), p. 23.

4. Joseph Smith, *The Personal Writings of Joseph Smith*, ed. Dean C. Jessee (Salt Lake City: Deseret Book Co., 1984), p. 277.

5. *History of the Church*, 1:386.

6. Ibid., 1:386; 2:55.

7. Ibid., 4:473.

8. Ibid., 4:93; see also D&C 104:11–14.

9. Smith, *Teachings of the Prophet Joseph Smith*, p. 231.

10. *History of the Church*, 1:364; or Smith, *Teachings of the Prophet Joseph Smith*, pp. 22–23.

11. *History of the Church*, 1:365–66. While these forms are included in the *History of the Church*, there is no evidence that they were used, for they are not dated or notarized. In addition, they ignore some of the principles given in the revelations. For example, Billings agreed to relinquish all his property if he transgressed the laws of the Church. While it is true the transgressor did not have claim upon previously donated property, he did have claim on his inheritance

because the deed should have guaranteed him that right. Another instruction ignored in the documents pertained to the right of a wife to sign with her husband. (*History of the Church*, 1:364.)

12. Ibid., 1:298.

13. Smith, *Personal Writings of the Prophet Joseph Smith*, p. 258.

14. *History of the Church*, 1:365–66.

15. Ibid., 2:49.

16. Smith, *Teachings of the Prophet Joseph Smith*, p. 24; *History of the Church*, 2:56.

17. *History of the Church*, 2:193.

18. Parley P. Pratt, *Autobiography of Parley Parker Pratt*, ed. Parley P. Pratt, Jr. (Salt Lake City: Deseret Book Co., 1966), p. 50.

19. *History of the Church*, 1:146–47.

20. Milton V. Backman, Jr., *The Heavens Resound: A History of the Latter-day Saints in Ohio, 1830–1838* (Salt Lake City: Deseret Book Co., 1983), p. 66.

21. *History of the Church*, 1:180.

22. Backman, *Heavens Resound*, p. 66.

23. Max H. Parkin, *Conflict at Kirtland* (Salt Lake City: Department of Seminaries and Institutes, 1967).

24. Smith, *Teachings of the Prophet Joseph Smith*, pp. 24, 215.

25. Pratt, *Autobiography*, pp. 92, 95–96.

26. Smith, *Personal Writings of Joseph Smith*, p. 258.

27. Smith, *Teachings of the Prophet Joseph Smith*, pp. 23–25.

28. *History of the Church*, 6:85.

29. Ibid., 2:118.

30. *History of the Church*, 2:229 n.; *Messenger and Advocate*, vol. 1, no. 8, pp. 137–38.

31. *History of the Church*, 2:505.

32. Donald Q. Cannon and Lyndon W. Cook, eds., *Far West Record: Minutes of The Church of Jesus Christ of Latter-day Saints, 1830–44* (Salt Lake City: Deseret Book Co., 1983), pp. 145–49.

33. *History of the Church*, 4:93.

34. Smith, *Personal Writings of Joseph Smith*, p. 93.

35. In Conference Report, Apr. 1974, p. 184.

36. Thomas S. Monson, "Goal Beyond Victory," *Ensign*, Nov. 1988, pp. 44–47.

CHAPTER NINE

The Doctrines of Submission and Forgiveness

Daniel K. Judd

Instructor, East Lansing Michigan Institute of Religion
East Lansing, Michigan

Doctrine and Covenants 64 contains doctrines essential to personal peace in this world and exaltation in the world to come. The intent of this paper is to focus specifically on the life-giving doctrines of submission and forgiveness as expounded in the scriptural and historical contexts of Doctrine and Covenants 64:1–21 and to contrast the doctrines of submission and forgiveness with the impotent philosophies of men that permeate our culture.

SUBMISSION VS. SELFISHNESS

Each of the brethren to whom Doctrine and Covenants 64 was addressed—Joseph Smith, Jr., Ezra Booth, Isaac Morley, Edward Partridge, Sidney Gilbert, Frederick G. Williams, and Newel K. Whitney—was invited to overcome the world by making his will consistent with the Lord's will for him. Section 64 begins with the Lord inviting these elders of the Church to "hearken ye and hear, and receive *my will* concerning you. For verily I say unto you, I will that ye should overcome the world; wherefore I will have compassion upon you." (D&C 64:1–2; italics added.)

The scriptures teach repeatedly that submitting to the will of God rather than following our own wills is essential to exaltation: "For although a man may have many revelations, and have power to do many mighty works, yet if he boasts in his own strength, and sets at naught the counsels of God, and follows after the dictates of his own will and carnal desires, he must fall and incur the vengeance of a just God upon him." (D&C 3:4.) The Savior exemplified the doctrine of submission most poignantly in Gethsemane, saying, "Father, if thou be willing, remove this cup from me: nevertheless not my will, but thine, be done."

(Luke 22:42.) The Apostle Paul wrote of yielding his own desires to the needs of others: "For I am in a strait betwixt two, having a desire to depart, and to be with Christ; which is far better: nevertheless to abide in the flesh is more needful for you." (Philippians 1:23–24.) Shortly before Nephi, son of Helaman, was given the sealing power, the Lord said to him, "Blessed art thou, Nephi.... thou ... hast not sought thine own life, but hast sought my will, and to keep my commandments." (Helaman 10:4.)

We, as well, are asked to submit and sacrifice our lives in the service of God. Although we may not be asked to die, we are asked to live and serve God in ways that may not always be convenient or consistent with our own desires. Many times, those whom we are called to sacrifice for are those who give us the most reason not to. "Ye have heard that it hath been said, Thou shalt love thy neighbour, and hate thine enemy. But I say unto you, Love your enemies, bless them that curse you, do good to them that hate you, and pray for them which despitefully use you, and persecute you." (Matthew 5:43–44.) Being "saviours ... on mount Zion" (Obadiah 1:21) may require that we mercifully bear the sins and ignorance of others.

Yielding our own desires to the commands of God is the key to peace in this life and exaltation in the next. Elder Boyd K. Packer wrote, "Perhaps the greatest discovery of my life, without question the greatest commitment, came when finally I had the confidence in God that I would loan or yield my agency to Him."[1] Not only are we to do physically as the Lord would have us do, but we must learn to put off the natural man and learn to feel as He would feel and think as He would think. "Behold, the Lord requireth the heart and a willing mind; and the willing and obedient shall eat the good of the land of Zion in these last days. And the rebellious shall be cut off out of the land of Zion, and shall be sent away, and shall not inherit the land." (D&C 64:34–35.) A few years ago a friend of mine visited with a member of the Quorum of the Twelve Apostles. During their conversation on the importance of serving willingly, this apostle taught my friend an important lesson by saying, "The day that doing the right thing became a quest and not an irritation was the day I gained power."

SELF-IMAGE VS. THE IMAGE OF CHRIST

The emphasis on "overcoming the world" through submission to God's will stressed in Doctrine and Covenants 64 and throughout the scriptures contrasts sharply with false educational ideas of today such as self-actualization, self-esteem, self-image, and others that are so prevalent in our culture. These ideas have "a form of godliness, but they deny the power thereof." (Joseph Smith–History 1:19.) Doing "what's best for me" has generally replaced doing what God wills concerning us and our lives. Paradoxically, it is in doing the will of our Father in heaven and overcoming the world that we realize our own desires. "For whosoever will save his life shall lose it; but whosoever shall lose his life for my sake and the gospel's, the same shall save it.

"For what shall it profit a man, if he shall gain the whole world, and lose his own soul?

"Or what shall a man give in exchange for his soul?" (Mark 8:35–37.)

The adversary's philosophy is one of deception. Whatever gospel truth is being taught, he provides both its opposite and its counterfeit. Personally, I have come to believe "high self-image" is the adversary's counterfeit of what the scriptures describe as "confidence" and is the opposite of meekness. "Low self-image" is the adversary's counterfeit of meekness and is the opposite of confidence.

Having a "high self-image" or a "low self-image" is generally based upon the prideful presence or absence of things temporal, such as physical appearance (1 Samuel 16:7), wealth (Proverbs 13:7), and learning (2 Nephi 9:28). Godly confidence is a spiritual gift that develops from recognizing our own nothingness. (Mosiah 4:5; Moses 1:10.) If we do the will of our Father in heaven, our "confidence" shall "wax strong." (D&C 121:45.)

Ammon taught this same doctrinal comparison in his dialogue with his brother Aaron concerning their missionary success:

"For if we had not come up out of the land of Zarahemla, these our dearly beloved brethren, who have so dearly beloved us, would still have been racked with hatred against us, yea, and they would also have been strangers to God.

"And it came to pass that when Ammon had said these words, his brother Aaron rebuked him, saying: Ammon, I fear that thy joy doth carry thee away unto boasting.

"But Ammon said unto him: I do not boast in my own strength, nor in my own wisdom; but behold, my joy is full, yea, my heart is brim with joy, and I will rejoice in my God.

"Yea, I know that I am nothing; as to my strength I am weak;

therefore I will not boast of myself, but I will boast of my God, for in his strength I can do all things; yea, behold, many mighty miracles we have wrought in this land, for which we will praise his name forever." (Alma 26:9–12.)

President Ezra Taft Benson has stated: "In the scriptures there is no such thing as righteous pride. It is always considered as a sin. We are not speaking of a wholesome view of self-worth, which is best established by a close relationship with God. But we are speaking of pride as a universal sin."[2]

In place of being consumed with the selfish notion of enhancing self-image through personal, worldly pursuits, the Lord has invited the Saints, past and present, to be concerned with doing his will and thus taking upon ourselves his image. "And now behold, I ask of you, my brethren of the church, have ye spiritually been born of God? Have ye received his image in your countenances? Have ye experienced this mighty change in your hearts?" (Alma 5:14.)

A comprehensive search of all the revelations in the Doctrine and Covenants reveals that the "elders of [the] church" (D&C 64:1) to whom section 64 was addressed were struggling to follow the Lord's will as they sought to overcome an array of intellectual, spiritual, and temporal trials. Following are brief analyses of the challenges these brethren faced and how they fared in overcoming the world and submitting to the will of God as represented by the Lord through the scriptures and Church history.[3]

Ezra Booth. Ezra Booth, formerly a Baptist minister, had been baptized after witnessing the Prophet Joseph Smith heal a woman of a lame arm.[4] After witnessing this miracle, Booth desired the power to "convert" others in the same manner. He soon became embittered, however, when he was confronted with the doctrine that "faith cometh not by signs, but signs follow those that believe. Yea, signs come by faith, not by the will of men, nor as they please, but by the will of God." (D&C 63:9–10.) Booth later apostatized and published several articles against the Prophet Joseph and the Church in the *Ohio Star,* which provoked much opposition to the work of the Restoration.[5] Elder B. H. Roberts identified Booth as being the "first apostate . . . to publish anything against the Church."[6]

Booth's preoccupation with physical manifestations of spiritual truths serves as a warning to those with similar desires. Whenever we seek to base our own faith or encourage others to base their faith on physical "proofs," emotional sentiment, or intellectual argument, our faith and theirs lack the solid foundation of personal and prophetic revelation.

Isaac Morley. Both Isaac Morley and Ezra Booth were chastised for having "evil in their hearts" (D&C 64:16), but unlike Booth, Morley repented and was forgiven. While he was also reproved for faultfinding and not selling his farm as he had been commanded (D&C 64:15–16, 20), he proved himself a man of conviction when he later offered his life as a ransom for the safety of the Saints in Missouri.[7] Isaac Morley died in Sanpete County, Utah, after having been a great strength to the establishment of the Church in that area.[8]

Edward Partridge. The Lord described Edward Partridge as one whose "heart is pure before me, for he is like unto Nathanael of old, in whom there is no guile." (D&C 41:11.) A little over a month before section 64 was given, the Lord revealed to Edward Partridge that if he did not repent of his "unbelief and blindness of heart," he would "fall." (D&C 58:15.) The Lord told Edward Partridge in Doctrine and Covenants 64 that he had "sinned, and Satan [sought] to destroy his soul." (D&C 64:17.) Bishop Partridge was guilty of putting "forth his hand to steady the ark of God" and if he didn't repent he would "fall by the shaft of death." (D&C 85:8; see also 2 Samuel 6:1–11.) Edward Partridge did repent and was granted eternal life. (D&C 124:19.)

Sidney Gilbert. Algernon Sidney Gilbert was first called by the Lord to preach the gospel and be "an agent" for the Church in its business dealings. (D&C 53:3–4.) Over a year later, the Lord revealed to Joseph Smith that Brother Gilbert had "many things to repent of." (D&C 90:35.) Although Sidney Gilbert was faithful in many things (at one point he, along with Isaac Morley, offered his life as a ransom for his fellow Saints), he lacked confidence in his ability to preach the gospel and died soon after turning down a mission call. The Lord had previously counseled Brother Gilbert, "Ye should learn that he only is saved who endureth unto the end." (D&C 53:7.) The Prophet Joseph commented on Brother Gilbert's turning down his mission call and on his subsequent death by saying, "He had been called to preach the Gospel, but had been known to say that he 'would rather die than go forth to preach the Gospel to the Gentiles.'" Elder Heber C. Kimball remarked, "The Lord took him [Sidney Gilbert] at his word."[9]

Frederick G. Williams. Frederick G. Williams was obedient to the Lord's command to "not . . . sell his farm," which property assisted the Lord in establishing "a strong hold in the land of Kirtland." (D&C 64:21.) Some two and a half years later, the Lord revealed that Frederick G. Williams had not taught his children properly and was commanded to set his house in order:

"But verily I say unto you, my servant Frederick G. Williams, you have continued under this condemnation;

"You have not taught your children light and truth, according to the commandments; and that wicked one hath power, as yet, over you, and this is the cause of your affliction.

"And now a commandment I give unto you—if you will be delivered you shall set in order your own house, for there are many things that are not right in your house." (D&C 93:41–43.)

In addition to this warning to Frederick G. Williams and others of the brethren in Doctrine and Covenants 93:40–50, the scriptures contain many other warnings relative to the relationship of family and church responsibilities. The Savior chastised the ancient Pharisees for perverting the gospel when he indicted them for abdicating the care of their families on the grounds of "Corban." (Mark 7:11.) The Bible Dictionary (p. 650) teaches that the Pharisees "misused the opportunity of dedicating their material possessions to God, in order to avoid responsibility to care for their parents." Although this same indictment of "Corban" may or may not be true of the early brethren and their families, it is important that those facing similar challenges in the present be aware of the danger of not being as "diligent and concerned at home" (D&C 93:50) as they are in their professional or ecclesiastical assignments. Never should serving our neighbors become a rationalization for not serving those at home.

Frederick G. Williams continued to have difficulty and was excommunicated twice and re-baptized twice between 1837 and 1840; however, he "died as a faithful member of the Church, October 10, 1842 at Quincy, Illinois."[10]

Newel K. Whitney. Newel K. Whitney was obedient to the Lord's command not to sell his "store and . . . possessions." (D&C 64:26.) Three years later Brother Whitney was also admonished to "set in order his family, and see that they are more diligent and concerned at home." (D&C 93:50.) After being called to be the second bishop of the Church (Edward Partridge being the first), Bishop Whitney was admonished by the Lord to forsake his worldly ways and devote more time to his duties as a bishop: "Let my servant Newel K. Whitney be ashamed of the Nicolaitane band and of all their secret abominations, and of all his littleness of soul before me, saith the Lord, and come up to the land of Adam-ondi-Ahman, and be a bishop unto my people, saith the Lord, not [only] in name but [also] in deed, saith the Lord." (D&C 117:11.) There are no scriptural details available about why the Lord chastened Newel K. Whitney for his involvement in the "Nicolaitane band," but the scriptures do give us some clues. The designation "Nicolaitane" apparently was derived from "Nicolas," mentioned in Acts 6:5. Nicolas was one of seven men designated to administer the temporal affairs of the Church during New Testament times. Apparently, Nicolas used his position in the Church for personal gain; hence, the Lord stated in Revelation 2:6, he "[hated] the deeds of the Nicolaitans." Elder Bruce R. McConkie taught that those who involve themselves in Nicolaitane interests are "members of the Church who [are] trying to maintain their church standing while continuing to live after the manner of the world."[11]

Whether it be Nicolas of biblical times, Newel K. Whitney, or those of us in the present, there is much to be lost by those who use their membership in the Church for their own selfish interests. This self-interest is a form of priestcraft, which Nephi described: "For, behold, priestcrafts are that men preach and set themselves up for a light unto the world, that they may get gain and praise of the world; but they seek not the welfare of Zion." (2 Nephi 26:29.) Those of us involved in the Church Educational System or various other academic disciplines need to be ever aware of the danger of selling our spiritual birthrights for the sake of being true to academic traditions. It is possible we can become as the scribes and Pharisees of old who were rebuked by the Savior for such practices: "Full well ye reject the commandment of God, that ye may keep your own tradition." (Mark 7:9.)

The Prophet Joseph Smith. John Taylor wrote: "Joseph Smith, the Prophet and Seer of the Lord, has done more, save Jesus only, for the salvation of men in this world, than any other man that ever lived in it." (D&C 135:3.) Scriptural perspectives relative to the weaknesses of the Prophet Joseph are few, but the Prophet himself has offered some insight. He wrote of his adolescence:

"I was left to all kinds of temptations; and, mingling with all kinds of society, I frequently fell into many foolish errors, and displayed the weakness of youth, and the foibles of human nature; which, I am sorry to say, led me into divers temptations, offensive in the sight of God. In making this confession, no one need suppose me guilty of any great or malignant sins. A disposition to commit such was never in my nature. But I was guilty of levity, and sometimes associated with jovial company, etc., not consistent with that character which ought to be maintained by one who was called of God as I had been. But this will not seem very strange to any one who recollects my youth, and is acquainted with my native cheery temperament." (Joseph Smith–History 1:28.)

The Lord, in Doctrine and Covenants 3:6–11, chastened the Prophet Joseph for allowing himself to be influenced by the "persuasions of men" (v. 6) and fearing "man more than God" (v. 7). This rebuke came as a consequence of Joseph's yielding to Martin Harris's repeated request to show the Book of Mormon manuscript to others whom the Lord had not designated.

From Doctrine and Covenants 64:7 we learn that the Prophet Joseph had sinned but had repented and been forgiven: "Nevertheless, he [Joseph] has sinned; but verily I say unto you, I, the Lord, forgive sins unto those who confess their sins before me and ask forgiveness, who have not sinned unto death."

From Doctrine and Covenants 93:47–49 we learn that the Prophet Joseph and his family had sins and weaknesses to overcome:

"And now, verily I say unto Joseph Smith, Jun. – You have not kept the commandments, and must needs stand rebuked before the Lord;

"Your family must needs repent and forsake some things, and give more earnest heed unto your sayings, or be removed out of their place.

"What I say unto one I say unto all; pray always lest that wicked one have power in you, and remove you out of your place."

Joseph Smith "lived great, and he died great in the eyes of God and his people." (D&C 135:3.) While recognizing there are many greater than I who have testified of the prophetic call of the Prophet Joseph Smith, I add my personal witness of his call and ministry as a prophet of God.

FORGIVENESS

The brethren of the Restoration were counseled concerning the dangers of hardening their hearts toward one another: "My disciples, in days of old, sought occasion against one another and forgave not one another in their hearts; and for this evil they were afflicted and sorely chastened." (D&C 64:8; see also Acts 15:1–11, 36–40; Galatians 2:11–14.) These brethren were also taught that forgiveness of those who had offended them was a requisite for their own forgiveness and exaltation:

"Wherefore, I say unto you, that ye ought to forgive one another; for he that forgiveth not his brother his trespasses standeth condemned before the Lord; for there remaineth in him the greater sin.

"I, the Lord, will forgive whom I will forgive, but of you it is required to forgive all men." (D&C 64:9–10).

An account from the writings of President Heber J. Grant illustrates that the "disciples" in the recent past have also "sought occasion against one another" (D&C 64:8) but then went on to understand and live the divine command to forgive. At the time this incident took place, Heber J. Grant was a junior member of the Quorum of Twelve Apostles. He participated in a Church court in which a fellow member of the Quorum of the Twelve was excommunicated. In the ensuing years, this man came several times before the court to ask for rebaptism. His request was denied each time, but eventually every member of the Quorum of Twelve consented to rebaptism except Elder Grant. Elder Grant felt that because of the magnitude of the sin (adultery) and this man's former position in the Church, he should never be forgiven. At this time Elder Grant was brought to truly understand Doctrine and Covenants 64:10. Following is Elder Grant's own description of how this came about:

"I was reading the Doctrine and Covenants through for the third or fourth time systematically, and I had my bookmark in it, but as I picked it up, instead of opening where the bookmark was, it opened to D&C 64:10: 'I, the Lord, will forgive whom I will forgive, but of you it is required to forgive all men.' I closed the book and said: 'If the devil applies for baptism, and claims that he has repented, I will baptize him.'

"After lunch I returned to the office of President Taylor and said, 'President Taylor, I have had a change of heart. One hour ago I said, never while I live did I expect to ever consent that Brother So and So should be baptized, but I have come to tell you he can be baptized, so far as I am concerned.' President Taylor had a habit, when he was particularly pleased, of sitting up and laughing and shaking his whole body, and he laughed and said, 'My boy, the change is very sudden, very sudden. I want to ask you a question. How did you feel when you left here an hour ago? Did you feel like you wanted to hit that man squarely between the eyes and knock him down?'

"I said, 'That is just the way I felt.' He said, 'How do you feel now?' 'Well, to tell you the truth, President Taylor, I hope the Lord will forgive the sinner.' He said, 'You feel happy, don't you, in comparison? You had the spirit of anger, you had the spirit of bitterness in your heart toward that man, because of his sin and because of the disgrace he had brought upon the Church. And now you have the spirit of forgiveness and you really feel happy, don't you?' And I said, 'Yes, I do . . . now I feel happy.' "

President Taylor explained to Elder Grant: "Forgiveness is in advance of justice, where there is repentance, and that to have in your heart the spirit of forgiveness and to eliminate from your hearts the spirit of hatred and bitterness, brings peace and joy; that the gospel of Jesus Christ brings joy, peace and happiness to every soul that lives it and follows its teachings."[12]

JUSTICE AND MERCY

The doctrines of justice and mercy are to be understood and lived by each of us. These doctrines do, however, have their counterfeits. I have come to believe that a blaming and punishing attitude is the adversary's counterfeit of justice. Indulgence is the adversary's counterfeit of mercy. Punishment is laden with anger, resentment, and blame, whereas justice denotes charity—a heartfelt desire to help another repent. Indulgence is doing what comes easily, whereas mercy requires personal, loving sacrifice. Punishment and indulgence are both selfish. Justice and mercy are selfless. Negative, accusing feelings such as anger and resentment, although "natural" (Mosiah 3:19), are not of God, no matter the reasons we may have for harboring them. (Compare 3 Nephi 12:22 with Matthew 5:22 and JST Matthew 5:25.)

Although the scriptures speak of the Savior's anger, his anger is much different from ours. His only concern is that we attain "immortality and eternal life." (Moses 1:39.) As he dealt with the Pharisees, he "looked round about on them with anger, being grieved for the hardness of their hearts." (Mark 3:5.) His anger is selfless.

THE GREATER SIN

Doctrine and Covenants 64:9 teaches that we have the "greater sin" if we do not forgive another. How is this possible especially if others have sinned against us in a most loathsome and degrading way? How can such sins as adultery, incest, and rape be lesser sins than the sin of an offended person not forgiving the offender? Perhaps the following account can teach us the truth of the matter:

"As a child I was abused by my older brother. At the time I knew what my brother did was wrong, yet I still loved him. As I grew older, however, I learned to hate him. As I came face to face with the everyday problems of life, I didn't accept the responsibility for my own mistakes and faults. I looked for an excuse—a way out. I looked for someone or something else to blame. I began having problems with my physical health, but when I began to get well I refused to accept it. I didn't want to return to the everyday problems that would be waiting for me. That was when the hate for my brother really grew. In my mind, all of my problems were his fault. I realize now, it was then that it became my sin. My hate, my anger was what hurt me—it made me sick. The hate for my own brother had grown so strong and fierce that it left him behind. I hated myself, my family, my friends, this earth, and its creator. I think that when you hate everyone, the void is so powerful that if you don't find love, if you don't give love, you die. That's where the gospel came in. That was when I finally realized there was something more to life than my bitterness. Being part of the Church had never really been important to me. It became worthless, because I didn't do my part. So I began for the first time to work, to really live the gospel. I found that in return Heavenly Father began to give more to me than anything I could ever give him. My happiness and peace became his gift to me. With each day of my life as I give all that I can give, I can't even comprehend the blessings he gives me."[13]

This young woman came to understand that it was her sin and not her brother's that was consuming her life. Even though she had been receiving counsel from a host of professionals either to "vent" or to "control" her anger, she found peace only when she began to understand and live the gospel of Jesus Christ. She found that the peace she was seeking did not come either in expressing her anger or in controlling it, but peace came as she repented of the hate she harbored. If one were to take incest and hate without regard to context, incest would obviously be the greater sin. But within the context of our own lives, it is what we do, not what others do to us, that either blesses us or condemns us. Lehi taught that individuals are free "to act for themselves and not to be acted upon." (2 Nephi 2:26.) The Book of

Mormon prophet Samuel also taught this truth: "And now remember, remember, my brethren, that whosoever perisheth, perisheth unto himself; and whosoever doeth iniquity, doeth it unto himself; for behold, ye are free; ye are permitted to act for yourselves; for behold, God hath given unto you a knowledge and he hath made you free." (Helaman 14:30; see also Mark 7:15.)

President Spencer W. Kimball wrote: "If we have been wronged or injured, forgiveness means to blot it completely from our minds. To forgive and forget is an ageless counsel. 'To be wronged or robbed,' said the Chinese philosopher Confucius, 'is nothing unless you continue to remember it.' . . . Man can overcome. Man can forgive all who have trespassed against him and go on to receive peace in this life and eternal life in the world to come."[14]

Many of the brethren mentioned in Doctrine and Covenants 64 overcame the challenges they faced and died faithful to the covenants they had made to the Lord. Those who were faithful eventually yielded "to the enticings of the Holy Spirit, and [put] off the natural man and [became] a saint through the atonement of Christ the Lord, and [became] as a child, submissive, meek, humble, patient, full of love, willing to submit to all things which the Lord [saw] fit to inflict upon [them], even as a child doth submit to his father." (Mosiah 3:19.)

The gospel of Jesus Christ contains the answers to life's problems. The scriptures, the words of our living prophets, and individual revelation can teach us the doctrines that will enable us to overcome the sins and deceptions of this world and receive exaltation in the next. It is my prayer that we, as individuals and families, teachers and faculties, will overcome the world and do the will of him who sent us. Let us review the words of our Savior:

"Behold, I stand at the door, and knock: if any man hear my voice, and open the door, I will come in to him, and will sup with him, and he with me.

"To him that overcometh will I grant to sit with me in my throne, even as I also overcame, and am set down with my Father in his throne."(Revelation 3:20–21.)

NOTES

1. Boyd K. Packer, *That All May Be Edified* (Salt Lake City: Bookcraft, 1982), pp. 256–57.

2. Ezra Taft Benson, "Cleansing the Inner Vessel," *Ensign*, May 1986, p. 6.

3. These analyses reflect the Lord's perspective of these men's problems and not their own or another mortal's. (Ether 12:27.) Scriptural commentary outside the general time period of D&C 64 was based on the assumption that these men's strengths and weaknesses remained fairly consistent over time.

4. Joseph Smith, *History of The Church of Jesus Christ of Latter-day Saints*, 2d ed. rev., ed. B. H. Roberts (Salt Lake City: The Church of Jesus Christ of Latter-day Saints, 1932–51), 1:215.

5. Ibid., 1:241.

6. Ibid., 1:216.

7. Ibid., 1:394.

8. Andrew Jensen, *LDS Biographical Encyclopedia* (Salt Lake City: Western Epics, 1971) 1:235–36.

9. *History of the Church*, 2:118.

10. Jensen, *Biographical Encyclopedia*, 1:51–52.

11. Bruce R. McConkie, *Doctrinal New Testament Commentary* (Salt Lake City: Bookcraft, 1975), 3:446.

12. Heber J. Grant, in Conference Report, Oct. 1920, pp. 2–11.

13. Personal correspondence with the author.

14. Spencer W. Kimball, *The Miracle of Forgiveness* (Salt Lake City: Bookcraft, 1969), pp. 299–300.

CHAPTER TEN

Revelation on the Priesthood: The Dawning of a New Day in Africa

E. Dale LeBaron

Assistant Professor of Church History and Doctrine
Brigham Young University

When the revelation giving the priesthood to all worthy males was announced, I was presiding over the only mission in Africa. Because we had no black, male, Church members, the revelation did not have a noticeable immediate effect upon the Church there. It was obvious, however, that in the days ahead this revelation would have a much greater effect upon the continent of Africa than upon any other part of the world. The announcement of the revelation also brought understanding to many unusual happenings I had observed during the previous months. There had been numerous inquiries by black people of southern Africa who wanted information about the Church. These inquiries, although rarely occurring before this time, greatly increased following the revelation, and few of these inquirers knew anything about the revelation or the priesthood. There was abundant evidence that the Lord had poured out his Spirit upon the prophet in giving this revelation and also upon the blacks of Africa, who had long been deprived of the fulness of the gospel blessings and ordinances.

As an observer of many unusual evidences of the Lord's power upon the blacks of Africa, I felt a great concern that this marvelous chapter of Church history was not being adequately recorded because the blacks are an oral history people, unaccustomed to keeping a written history. I also felt a concern that any delay in record-keeping could rob us of valuable histories due to the death or illness of important participants. The opportunity of addressing these concerns came a decade later when the David M. Kennedy Center for International Studies approved my proposal to travel to Africa to collect oral histories from black converts to the Church. This project also received support from the General Authorities, who provided invaluable assistance in opening the way for support from mission presidents throughout Africa. In addition to this help, there were also frequent experiences that gave evidence that the Lord wanted this project accomplished. Divine intervention — from contacting interviewees to providing a replacement for a broken microphone — allowed the project to succeed as it did. One of my concerns about the urgency of this project was verified when Violet Dube, a pioneer among the black Saints of Soweto, South Africa, passed away two weeks after I interviewed her in the Johannesburg temple. This interview is the only recorded history of her life.

During the summer of 1988 I traveled in ten different African countries obtaining more than four hundred oral histories. The countries I visited were Ghana, Nigeria, Zaire, Zimbabwe, South Africa, Ciskei, Transkei, Swaziland, and the islands of Maritius and Reunion, located off the east coast of Africa.

THE RESTORATION FOR BLACK AFRICA

Prior to the revelation on the priesthood in 1978, no mission was organized among the blacks of Africa. In many respects, this divine directive brought the restoration of the gospel and all its blessings to these people. There are many parallels between the restoration of the gospel and the establishment of the Church in black Africa. This paper will compare some of these parallels, using examples from oral histories that reflect the divine origin of the revelation and the power of the Lord guiding and blessing people of Africa.

SPIRITUAL DARKNESS PENETRATED

One hundred and fifty-five years ago, the Lord promised, "Then cometh the day when the arm of the Lord shall be revealed in power in convincing the nations, the heathen nations, . . . of the gospel of their salvation." (D&C 90:10.) The restoration was accompanied by an immense thrust of spiritual power that penetrated the spiritual darkness and moved the kingdom forward. Like a rocket launching into space, this thrust of power overcame opposition and moved the Church upward on its divinely decreed course. After liftoff, continued energy was provided, but not as much as at first. Similarly, the revelation granting the priesthood and all its blessings to all worthy males was of such tremendous import and eternal significance that the Lord "poured out the Holy Ghost upon the First Presidency and the Twelve in a miraculous and marvelous manner, beyond anything that any then present had ever experienced."[1] Just as the Spirit was poured out upon many people about the time of the First Vision, preparing many for the message of the gospel, the Lord extended his Spirit with power upon people and parts of Africa near the time of the priesthood revelation.

Although the Church was established in South Africa in 1853, more than a century passed before work officially began among the blacks in Africa. In 1960 Glen G. Fisher returned to Canada from South Africa after serving as mission president there. The First Presidency asked President Fisher to stop in Nigeria and investigate groups who had organized themselves into church units, and had taken the name of The Church of Jesus Christ of Latter-day Saints. During the next six years, efforts were made to send missionaries to Nigeria. LaMar Williams was called and set apart by President McKay for this work. Others were also called, but the effort was abandoned in 1966 because visas could not be procured.

AFRICAN ELIASES

At the time of the restoration of the gospel, there were people who exerted leadership by breaking away from dominant churches and preparing themselves and others for the message of the restoration. Some of these were Sidney Rigdon and his Disciples group; John Taylor and his study group in Toronto, Canada, converted by Parley P. Pratt; and John Benbow and the United Brethren, taught by Wilford Woodruff in England. These courageous and inspired souls did much to prepare many to receive the gospel even before they had received it themselves.

For many years before 1978, unbaptized converts in Africa had received Church literature and divine direction. Their faith penetrated the spiritual darkness, and they sought more of the teachings of the Church. Often these devoted people made great efforts to communicate with Church headquarters and missions to obtain more information and to receive direction. They also pleaded for visits from Church representatives. Invariably, they shared their newfound knowledge and conviction generously. Though the Church and all of its blessings were not available to them, they found spiritual nourishment from "the crumbs which fall from their masters' table," and have testified of a spiritual confirmation that assured them, "Great is thy faith." (Matthew 15:27–28.)

One such pioneer in Ghana is Joseph W. B. Johnson. In 1964 he prayerfully read the Book of Mormon. He relates: "One early morning about 5:30 A.M., while about to prepare for my daily work, I saw the heavens open and angels with trumpets singing songs of praise unto God. . . . In the course of this I heard my name mentioned thrice, 'Johnson, Johnson, Johnson. If you will take up my work as I will command you, I will bless you and bless your land.' Trembling and in tears I replied, 'Lord, with thy help I will do whatever you will command me.' From that day onward, I was constrained by that spirit to go from street to street . . . to deliver the message which we had read from the Book of Mormon. . . . I did exactly as the Lord commanded me . . . and immediately . . . our persecution started."[2] Fourteen years later, when the missionaries arrived, there were already many congregations named The Church of Jesus Christ of Latter-day Saints. They had been organized by Brother Johnson. Hundreds were baptized into the Church.

In Nigeria, Anthony Obinna was a faithful and persistent pioneer. As a lifelong seeker after truth, he relates the following, which occurred in the late 1960s: "One night I was sleeping and a tall man came to me . . . and took me to one of the most beautiful buildings and showed me all the rooms. At the end he showed himself in the crucified form. Then in 1970 I found this book to read. It was the September, 1958, *Readers Digest*. There was an article entitled, 'The March of the Mormons' with a picture of the Salt Lake Temple. It was exactly the same building I had seen in my dream."[3]

Brother Obinna persistently wrote to Church headquarters and to missions, seeking Church literature and hoping for personal visits from Church representatives. After years of waiting, he wrote the following to the Quorum of the Twelve Apostles on 28 September 1978: "Your long silence about the establishment of the Church in Nigeria is very embarrassing. . . . What could hinder this church from having a foothold here? Did Christ not say, 'Go ye and teach all nations?' "[4] When the Obinna family learned of the revelation on the priesthood, they wrote to the First Presidency: "We are happy for the many hours in the upper room of the temple you spent supplicating the Lord to bring us into the fold. We thank our Heavenly Father for hearing your prayers and ours and [that he] by revelation has confirmed the long promised day. . . . We thank you for extending the priesthood which has been withheld [from] us and to prepare us to receive every blessing of the gospel."[5]

When the missionaries arrived in Nigeria, they found many prepared for the gospel through the teaching and leadership of Brother Obinna. He became the first person to be baptized by the missionaries sent to West Africa, and Sister Obinna became the first Relief Society president in black Africa. The first Latter-day Saint chapel built in Nigeria is in Aboh Mbaise, of the Imo State, near the home of the Obinna family.

I first met Moses Mahlangu in 1976 when I presided over the South Africa Mission. Living in the township of Soweto, Brother Mahlangu prayerfully read the Book of Mormon and patiently waited sixteen years for baptism. His dedication and persistence in living gospel principles deeply impressed me. Fluent in nine languages, he shared his testimony with many people during that time. While reflecting upon his long wait to join the Church, Brother Mahlangu compared himself to Cornelius, "who was very good in waiting to receive the word of God or to be a member of the church . . . till the angels came and told him what to do."[6] Today, at age sixty-three, Brother Mahlangu is a groundskeeper at the Johannesburg temple, which he regularly attends. He is the elders quorum president in the Soweto branch.

PREPARED FOR THE MESSAGE

The Lord assured us that at the time of the Restoration he would pour out his spirit upon all flesh and many would dream dreams and see visions. (Joel 2:28.) This is evidenced by the experiences of many early converts to the Church, including Solomon Chamberlain, who received a message about the Restoration from a vision before the organization of the Church, and Wilford Woodruff, who was promised in a vision to Robert Mason that he would participate in the Lord's restored church.[7]

In a similar way, many Africans have been guided to the Church and prepared for the gospel. Typical of them is Adjei Kwame, who grew up in a religious atmosphere in Ghana. Being an excellent student, he was given a seven-year scholarship to study engineering in the Soviet Union. He completed a master's degree in mechanical engineering but felt that his spiritual life suffered because he was not allowed to attend church meetings. Upon graduating, Brother Kwame took a teaching position in Gweru, Zimbabwe. There he began to experience spiritual yearnings, which he described: "I have always been searching for the truth and for the true church. . . . Then, February of this year (1988), I kept having dreams about a church building. When I went through

Que Que, I saw this church building and wanted to go in to find out what kept coming into my dreams all the time. . . . The building looked like a big temple. It had big spires like the temple that we see. The people were dressed in long white robes which ended at their feet, not in suits. . . . It was not in my thoughts that I should become a member of the church, but I wanted to find out why that church kept coming into my dreams. I felt like I was being pushed to that area. So I went into that church one Sunday. When I got there I felt that I had been released from some burden and I felt that this was the true church which I should join. . . . When I got to that church I felt that I was actually with some people that I knew a long time ago. I don't know how to express that feeling, but the only thing I can say is that I felt that I knew them a long time ago and that they have been good friends. And so I just felt that I was at home."[8]

Reflecting upon his first Latter-day Saint meeting, Brother Kwame related: "The first time I went to church in Que Que, I didn't know what was going on. It was a fast Sunday. . . . Now, people got up to give testimonies. The meeting was started when I got there. I sat at the back. The sacrament was served, and I participated without knowing what I was doing. After that, people were giving testimonies and I didn't know what they were doing. I got up and went straight to the pulpit and started talking. . . . I said that it is not easy for somebody to . . . talk to people that you don't know, but they should forgive me if I have made a mistake but I believe in the Supreme Being, whom I call God, and I want to be a member of that church. . . . After that I met Sister Hamstead and what actually descended upon the two of us I can not explain. Before I became aware I was weeping. . . . I can't explain the feeling. I was released of all burdens. . . . I felt that I had gone to a place where I visited often. And now I was at home."[9]

A FOUNDATION OF FAITHFUL AND ABLE LEADERS BRINGS GROWTH

The quality of leadership brought into the Church between 1830 and 1840 made possible its survival and growth. The four presidents of the Church who succeeded the Prophet Joseph, as well as many other great leaders, all joined the Church in that decade. The strength of that leadership is reflected by the Church's unusual growth in spite of the persecutions and hardships that the members endured.

In the first decade after the revelation on the priesthood, the Church in Africa was blessed with an unusual quality of converts. A surprisingly large number of African converts are educated. Take, for example, the educational achievements of the Church leadership in Ghana and Nigeria. Because of widespread poverty and unemployment, it is unusual for a person to complete high school in these countries. In 1987, the literacy level was reported at 30 percent for Ghana and 25 percent for Nigeria.[10] Yet, of the Church leaders I interviewed in Ghana and Nigeria, 82 percent of the district and stake presidents are college or university graduates. In Ghana 76 percent of the Relief Society presidents interviewed are college or university graduates; in Nigeria, 58 percent. Of 104 persons interviewed in Ghana and 100 interviewed in Nigeria, 74 percent in Ghana and 55 percent in Nigeria have received some college or university training. This foundation of leadership, in only ten years, is impressive. The Philippines, which is considered one of the most rapidly growing areas of the Church, organized its first stake twelve years after the missionaries arrived; a new stake was organized in Nigeria in less than ten years' time after the missionaries arrived. Church leaders are confident that there will be accelerated growth throughout Africa because of the quality of the converts who are responding to the gospel.[11]

The Church in Africa has grown rapidly as converts have shared the gospel with their families and friends. In 1840, ten years after the Church was organized, there were 16,865 members. (*Church Almanac,* 1985, p. 248.) Today, ten years after the revelation on the priesthood, there are approximately 17,000 black Saints in Africa. (As reported by mission presidents.)

One example of why Church growth is spectacular in Africa is the experience of Rueben Okuchukwu Onuoha, the newly ordained patriarch of the Aba Nigeria Stake, which was organized three weeks before our interview. When he received his call from Elder Neal A. Maxwell, Brother Onuoha had been a member less than three years and had never met a patriarch. Reflecting upon that interview, he said: "I don't know anything about it. The only thing I've got to do is to be prayerful about it. . . . I know that by the grace of God I will succeed when the time comes for me to be at peace in the job." All his life Brother Onuoha has felt spiritual yearnings and restlessness. Disillusioned and disappointed about religion, he stopped attending Christian meetings. "But then, as soon as this church came to me," he reflected, "I picked up interest, and I have not missed attending sacrament meeting even one day since the 25th of August, 1985, . . . regardless of whether I am sick or not." The same week he was baptized, Brother Onuoha introduced the gospel to eighteen people, who later joined the Church. Because he lived about twenty miles from the nearest chapel, meetings were held in the parlor of Brother Onuoha's home. Four months after his baptism, there was no longer space in his parlor for the eighty people whom he had introduced to the gospel.[12]

Besides the two hundred members in his branch, Brother Onuoha has shared the gospel with many others, including Dr. Clement Nwafor. Dr. Nwafor is the chief medical officer for about two million Nigerians, a prominent and popular citizen in the Aba area. Brother Onuoha visited Dr. Nwafor when Brother Onuoha's wife was ill. To the chain-smoking doctor, Brother Onuoha said, "Look, doctor, you have achieved almost everything. I know you to be a very hard-working man. You are very popular in your area. You have been given the chieftainship title and several other positions from the government and from the community which you come from. But you still lack one thing, and that is serving the Lord who has brought you into this universe." From this bold declaration followed pamphlets, the Book of Mormon, and the missionaries. Dr. Nwafor accepted the gospel: "My whole system was like it was a break from prison right from that time. . . . I felt like a new person. I felt like somebody that was born again. I felt anew." Less than six months after Dr. Nwafor's baptism, he was set apart as a high councilor in the new stake in Nigeria.[13]

THE LORD USES "THE WEAK" TO DO HIS WORK

One of the great testimonies of the restoration of the gospel is the work that was accomplished by the Prophet Joseph and those who were faithful to him and the gospel teachings. From the beginning of this dispensation the Lord promised that he would use the weak things of the world to accomplish his great purposes. (D&C 1:19, 23–24.) There are many examples of the application of this principle in the Church in Africa, from preaching to prophesying, from teaching to translating.

Missionaries in Africa are awed by the childlike faith of those they teach. One pair of missionaries in South Africa, after telling and testifying of the First Vision, asked the family if they understood what they had heard and whether they had any questions. The father replied, pointing to the flip-chart drawing of the First Vision, "Yes, I have a question. Who took that photograph?"[14]

Unusual blessings have come to the Saints in Africa because of the faith and sacrifice of some of the members there. The accomplishments of Sister Priscilla Sampson-Davis, who joined the Church in 1979, provide one example. Through her faith and encouragement, her oldest son gave up a lifelong dream and forfeited a four-year scholarship to an Anglican seminary theological school, to be baptized. Twenty months later, he was one of the first full-time missionaries from West Africa. One day after sacrament meeting, Sister Sampson-Davis had an experience that changed her life and ultimately affected many others.

"I had a vision. I wasn't asleep. I saw things as if I was at the sacrament meeting and someone in white apparel came and stood in front of the stand, and beckoned me and called me. I came and stood by him, and then he asked me to turn around and look at the congregation — to look at the faces of the people to see if they were all enjoying the service. I looked around. I couldn't see any differences, so I told him that I couldn't see any differences in their faces. Then he asked me . . . to look again carefully, and I saw that some of them had bent down their heads.

"He asked me why some of those people were not joining in the singing. Then I said, 'Because they didn't go to school and they couldn't read English. They couldn't sing, and that is the reason why they bent down their heads.' Then he said, 'Wouldn't you like to help your sisters and brothers who couldn't read and who couldn't join you in singing praises to our Heavenly Father?' Though I wasn't very good in the language, I could speak. It is my mother tongue, but I couldn't write well. I didn't say, 'No.' I said, 'I will try. I will do my best.' And then the vision passed away. So I immediately got up. I took paper and pencil and started translating 'Redeemer of Israel' right away into Fante."

As Fante is the language of 85 percent of the Ghanaian people, the hymns were eagerly received by the Ghanaian Saints. After translating the hymnbook, Sister Sampson-Davis translated missionary pamphlets and film strips, *Gospel Principles, Stories of the Book of Mormon,* and the Book of Mormon. She is now translating the Doctrine and Covenants and the Pearl of Great Price. She bears powerful testimony that the Holy Ghost has been her teacher and guide in this great and important project.[15]

Another example of perseverance and faith is the life of Celestine Onuka. While conducting interviews in Aba, Nigeria, I observed Brother Onuka as he studied the scriptures each day in the chapel. I was told that he was one of the first Nigerians to serve a mission, and now unemployed, he studies the scriptures daily to stay mentally and spiritually alert. Brother Onuka told me of his father, who died when he was seven. His father had taught him that he should get an education and become an engineer. Education became an obsession for him, though there was little to hope for because of his family's poverty. "I had faith. I had hope that I would finish secondary school, too. But how I was going to do that I did not know."

By working and saving in every way, Brother Onuka completed elementary school. But secondary school was a greater challenge — to attend he had to pay tuition approximately equivalent to a laborer's monthly salary. He would also have to walk six miles to school every day. As impossible as this seemed to him at age fifteen, Brother Onuka was determined to do it. He worked many jobs to buy a few books and a pen. Most books he borrowed from friends. Many days he didn't attend school so he could work. A family friend counseled him to get a steady job, but he said he must go to school. So his friend agreed to help him with his expenses. Brother Onuka was active in school: speech, debate, and choir. He rose to the top of his class. Then, his generous friend died and again Brother Onuka was discouraged and in despair. When he couldn't pay tuition, he was asked to leave the school. Some teachers pitied him and allowed him to stay in class, but others asked him to leave. When required to leave a class, Brother Onuka sat under the classroom window and listened, taking notes on the lectures. "I would not give up!" he declared. Through help from sympathetic administrators, teachers, and friends, he finished his final year of high school. His goal for his last year was to receive top grades on his final exams and thereby get a scholarship to a university — his only hope of attending. After writing the national exams, he felt he had done well, but the examining committee determined that a student from his school had cheated, and they disqualified all exams from his school. His hopes were dashed again.

Brother Onuka's interests changed from education to religion. Usually unemployed, he studied religions and the scriptures. He was disturbed by many teachings of churches that he felt did not agree with the Bible. Upon receiving a Book of Mormon, he read, felt its truthfulness, and asked to be baptized. At about this time, he found a copy of the Book of Mormon that had been read and marked by his father many years before. Along with it was correspondence from Church headquarters that revealed that his father had planned to join the Church and go to school in Utah.

Immediately after Brother Onuka's baptism he obtained a job, and about one year later, he was the second Nigerian to serve a full-time mission. As a missionary, he participated in more than seven hundred baptisms and helped to create entire branches. He spoke of his mission with deep emotion and love for the people and the work.

Although he had several jobs after his mission, he chose to quit those that took him away from Church activity. Now the ward clerk and music director of the Aba Ward, this valiant young man spends most days studying the scriptures alone in the chapel.

I asked Brother Onuka of his goal to become an engineer and of the future. He solemnly replied: "I do not know. No, I do not know. I really do not know. Education is one thing that I had hoped to have in my life, but I have tried. With all the money I have received, I have tried to get a good education. But I do not know. I want to have a good job and to get married but when I think about all I have tried, I become depressed. I don't want people seeing me depressed and thinking I am in the wrong church and that God is punishing me. I want them to see me as an example of God's church." Then, with tearful eyes he observed, "I want to be able to serve the Lord and do something for the dead — baptisms for the dead. I know my father loves me." After weeping for some time, he continued, "He loves me! I would like to be with him always." He sobbed uncontrollably, and concluded, "I would like to be with him anytime." I embraced Brother Onuka as we both wept. I felt to bless and assure him as well as encourage him.[16]

Upon my return home from Africa, a letter from Brother Onuka was waiting for me. He happily shared the news that, the week following our interview, he was offered employment by a new convert to the Church who also agreed to train him as a surveyor, free of charge. Brother Onuka wrote, "I have started training and will graduate in about two and a half year's time."

CONCLUSION

A year before the establishment of the Lord's church in this dispensation, he assured the Saints, "Be faithful and diligent in keeping the commandments of God, and I will encircle thee in the arms of my love." (D&C 6:20.) Through his Book of Mormon prophet, the Lord also declared that "he inviteth them all to come unto him and partake of his goodness; and he denieth none that come unto him, black and white, bond and free, male and female; and he remembereth the heathen; and all are alike unto God." (2 Nephi 26:33.)

Indeed, there is abundant evidence of the Lord's love for the people of Africa and of his desire to bless these patient people. It is thrilling to see that they are beginning to have a vision of the important role that they must take in the Lord's kingdom, so recently established among them. This was illustrated through a dream related by Jude Inmpey of the Aba area of Nigeria. He dreamed that he observed a person playing an organ, which emitted a terrible sound. Upon investigating, he found the person was playing only the white keys. Some time later, in a Church gathering, he saw the interpretation of this dream as he related, "The Church has for many years played only the white keys on the keyboard, and now they're playing both the white and the black, and the music is much sweeter."[17]

NOTES

1. Bruce R. McConkie, "All Are Alike unto God," *A Symposium on the Book of Mormon* (Salt Lake City: The Church of Jesus Christ of Latter-day Saints, 1978), p. 4.

2. Document on file with author.

3. Document on file with author.

4. Copy of letter on file with author.

5. Copy of letter on file with author.

6. Oral history on file with author.

7. See David F. Boone, "Prepared for the Restoration," *Ensign,* Dec. 1984, pp. 17–21.

8. Oral history on file with author.

9. Oral history on file with author.

10. *World Fact Book 1987* (Washington, D.C.: Central Intelligence Agency, 1987).

11. Oral history on file with author.

12. Oral history on file with author.

13. Oral history on file with author.

14. Oral history on file with author.

15. Oral history on file with author.

16. Oral history on file with author.

17. Oral history on file with author.

CHAPTER ELEVEN

The Doctrine and Covenants Leads Us to Christ

Robert England Lee

Curriculum Writer, Church Educational System
Salt Lake City, Utah

Sometime during the summer of 1828, the Lord taught the Prophet Joseph a doctrine, which He called "my doctrine." Even though this doctrine was taught before the Church was formally organized, it states, "Whosoever repenteth and cometh unto me, the same is my church." (D&C 10:67.)

The Savior clarified this doctrine somewhat in 1831 when he told us how we can know if a person has repented. "By this ye may know," said he, "if a man repenteth of his sins — behold, he will confess them and forsake them." (D&C 58:43.) Yet, in all the Doctrine and Covenants, there is no succinct definition of the expression "come unto Christ." The Lord has not said, "By this you may know if a man cometh to Christit. . . . " It is my feeling that he has offered a definition of "come unto Christ" within the holy scriptures. I believe that there are elements of the definition of "come unto Christ" lying before us as we read the scriptures, but we must seek for them before we find them.

The Lord declared, "Come unto me, all ye that labour and are heavy laden, and I will give you rest." (Matthew 11:28.)

The Prophet Joseph Smith said that, "this rest is of such perfection and glory, that man has need of a preparation before he can . . . enter it and enjoy its blessings. This being the fact, God has given certain laws to the human family, which, if observed, are sufficient to prepare them to inherit this rest." (*Teachings of the Prophet Joseph Smith,* sel. Joseph Fielding Smith [Salt Lake City: Deseret Book Co., 1938], p. 54.)

The rest offered by the Lord comes to us when we obey his counsel and keep his commandments, or, in other words, when we come unto him. We can therefore assume that the counsel and commandments of the Lord, as found in the revelations of the Doctrine and Covenants, constitute a definition of the expression "come unto Christ." We may

read the Doctrine and Covenants and translate the counsel and commandments of the Lord into a "come unto Christ statement"; then, we
may evaluate our lives in the light of our findings. Our evaluation of
our lives will be based upon what the Lord expects and not upon what
the world expects. Once we have evaluated our lives, we will be inclined
to repent and come unto Christ and be his church. We will therefore
examine the revelations of the Doctrine and Covenants with the specific
purpose in mind of learning principles relative to our coming to Christ.

Before we begin our search, however, we will briefly explore the
Doctrine and Covenants to learn who Christ is. On several occasions
the Lord has used titles to describe himself and his relationship to God,
to us, and to the world. Insofar as his relationship with God is concerned,
he is "the Son of the living God" (D&C 14:9), "the Firstborn" (D&C
93:21), "the Son of Man" (D&C 61:38), and "Son Ahman" (D&C 78:20).

To us as individuals, he is "the Lord thy God" (D&C 10:15), "your
Lord, your God, and your Redeemer" (D&C 27:1), "thy Savior" (D&C
19:41), "your Maker" (D&C 30:2), and "your advocate" (D&C 62:1).

Relative to the world, he is "the Redeemer of the world" (D&C
19:1) and "the Savior of the world" (D&C 43:34). He is "Alpha and
Omega, . . . the beginning and the end" (D&C 19:1), "the Lord of Sa-
baoth, . . . the creator of the first day" (D&C 95:7), "the Lord" (D&C
44:1), "the Lord Almighty" (D&C 84:118), "the Most High God" (D&C
39:19), "the Holy One of Zion" (D&C 78:15), "the Mighty One of Israel"
(D&C 36:1), "the Lord God of hosts" (D&C 56:10), "the Spirit of truth"
(D&C 93:26). He is "the Bridegroom" (D&C 33:17; 65:3; 88:92), "the
good shepherd" (D&C 50:44), "the stone of Israel" (D&C 50:44), "the
Great I Am" (D&C 39:1), "Endless" (D&C 19:10), "he who hath established the foundations of Adam-ondi-Ahman" (D&C 78:15), "he who
led the children of Israel out of the land of Egypt" (D&C 136:22), "the
light which shineth in darkness" (D&C 10:58), and "the life and the
light of the world" (D&C 11:28).

With this clearer picture of the Savior in mind, we turn to the
revelations of the Doctrine and Covenants to learn what it means to
come to Christ. We will not examine all the counsel and commandments
given by the Lord in this book of scripture. Rather, we will examine
the directives given to a portion of a group of people known as the
members of the Church.

Just as the Lord refers to himself by different titles, even so, in the Doctrine and Covenants, the Lord calls his people, the members of the Church, by different titles. We shall look at some of these titles and examine what the Lord says to and about these people. We will assume that what he asks them to do is calculated to bring them to Christ. We will therefore examine what the Lord asks these people to do and translate those instructions into actions performed by one who is striving to come to Christ. Then, we will search the scriptures to verify that living these instructions will bring us to Christ.

The titles of the Lord's people that we will examine are "the church," "the elect," "the people of the Lord," "the sons of God," and "saints."

THE CHURCH

"The church," as we shall use the term, is a title sometimes used by the Lord when referring to the members of the Church as a whole. Each use of the term "the church" as it appears in the revelations of the Doctrine and Covenants will be examined to determine what "the church" does to demonstrate that it is coming to Christ. Those of "the church" who are striving to come to Christ "take heed and pray always, lest they fall into temptation." (D&C 20:33.) They meet together often to partake of the sacrament in remembrance of the Lord Jesus. (D&C 20:75.) They give heed to all the words of the prophet and walk in holiness before God. (D&C 21:4.) They sustain those among them who have been appointed to care for the poor and the needy. (D&C 38:34–35.) They repent of their sins. (D&C 63:63.) They assist and support the families of those who have been called to preach the gospel to the world. (D&C 75:24.) They have respect or reverence for the name of the Supreme Being. (D&C 107:4.) They uphold the First Presidency with their confidence, faith, and prayers. (D&C 107:22.)

In connection with the title "the church," there is an emphasis on prayer and brotherhood that is not associated with other titles. Do the scriptures validate the assumption that prayer and brotherhood will lead us to Christ?

In 4 Nephi we learn that after the appearance of Christ among the Nephites, "the disciples of Jesus had formed a church of Christ in all the lands round about." (4 Nephi 1:1.) Those who belonged to the church of Christ came to these disciples, repented, were baptized, and received the Holy Ghost. (4 Nephi 1:1.) They had no contentions or other forms of wickedness among them. (4 Nephi 1:15–17.) Mighty miracles were performed among them. (4 Nephi 1:5.) Mormon indicates why this condition existed when he says, "They did walk after the commandments which they had received from their Lord and their God, continuing in fasting and prayer, and in meeting together oft both to pray and to hear the word of the Lord." (4 Nephi 1:12.)

Of them Mormon said, "Surely there could not be a happier people among all the people who had been created by the hand of God. . . . they were in one, the children of Christ, and heirs to the kingdom of God." (4 Nephi 1:16–17.) They demonstrated for us how "the church" comes to Christ. By contrast, when they became lifted up in pride and divided into social classes, they denied the true church of Christ and "the more parts of his gospel," and Satan "did get hold upon their hearts." (4 Nephi 1:27–28.)

The Lord declared to "the church" in this dispensation, "Whosoever is of my church, and endureth of my church to the end, him will I establish upon my rock, and the gates of hell shall not prevail against them." (D&C 10:69.)

THE ELECT

Our examination reveals that the "elect," and therefore those who are striving to come to Christ, hear the voice of the Lord and do not harden their hearts. (D&C 29:7.) They believe in Christ and hearken to his voice. (D&C 33:6.) They magnify their callings. (D&C 84:33.) They are on guard concerning their own lives and give diligent heed to the words of eternal life. (D&C 84:43.) They live by every word that comes forth from the mouth of God. (D&C 84:44.) The "elect" of God are sensitive to the word of the Lord which comes from his voice. They hear, and hearken, and heed, and live by the words which come from his mouth.

Again we look to the scriptures to seek confirmation that such behavior will lead us to Christ. We look at Nephi, in the Book of Mormon. When he returned to the land of Jerusalem to obtain the brass plates, he was "led by the Spirit, not knowing beforehand the things which [he] must do." (1 Nephi 4:6.) He was "constrained by the Spirit" (1 Nephi 4:10), and he "did obey the voice of the Spirit" (1 Nephi 4:18). This is the pattern he followed in his relationship with the Lord throughout his life. In his parting testimony he revealed the motto by which he lived: "Thus hath the Lord commanded me, and I must obey." (2 Nephi 33:15.) Nephi saw the Lord, and received great revelations concerning the future, and he obtained the land of promise the Lord had reserved for him. Furthermore, he promised us that we will see him as we stand before the judgment bar of God. (2 Nephi 33:11.) He followed the pattern of those called the "elect" and came unto Christ.

Of the "elect" in the last days the Lord declared, "They will hear my voice, and shall see me, and shall not be asleep, and shall abide the day of my coming; for they shall be purified, even as I am pure." (D&C 35:21.)

THE PEOPLE OF THE LORD

The title "people of the Lord" appears only once, as such, in the Doctrine and Covenants. It is used in the first verse of the revelation recorded in section 63. In this revelation the Lord addresses those who *call themselves* the people of the Lord. From this revelation we learn that there is a difference between people calling themselves the people of the Lord and actually being his people. The Lord indicates that among those who call themselves "the people of the Lord" there are those who have turned away from the commandments and have not kept them. Of those people, the Lord says, "Let such beware and repent speedily, lest judgment shall come upon them as a snare, and their folly shall be made manifest, and their works shall follow them in the eyes of the people." (D&C 63:15.)

The revelations of the Doctrine and Covenants declare that to be the people of the Lord, we must be striving to come to Christ and refrain from seeking after signs and wonders to sustain our faith. Rather, we must seek for the glory of God to be made manifest to mankind through signs and wonders. (D&C 63:12.) We will keep the commandments. (D&C 63:13.) We will not commit adultery, even in our hearts; therefore, we will not lose the Spirit, but we will keep the faith, and will not fear. (D&C 63:14, 16.) We will believe. We will be honest. We will not love and make a lie. We will not be whoremongers or sorcerers. (D&C 63:17.) We will endure in faith and do the will of the Lord. (D&C 63:20.) As the people of the Lord we will be virtuous and honest in our dealings with each other and with God. To be worthy of this title today we must be out of step with the commonly accepted practices of the world. Will such behavior lead us to Christ?

In the Book of Mormon we read of Ammon, a missionary to the Lamanites. I believe he was one who possessed great virtue and honesty. His motivation to preach the gospel sprang from a sincere desire to serve the Lord. He faithfully defended the king's flocks, when lesser men would have made excuses and run away. He took no glory to himself when great miracles were performed in his behalf. King Lamoni was astonished by the great physical and spiritual power Ammon possessed, but "he was more astonished, because of the faithfulness of Ammon," because "he doth remember all my commandments to execute them." (Alma 18:10.) Ammon revealed the mystery of the Great Spirit to King Lamoni. Furthermore, "he began at the creation of the world, and also the creation of Adam, and told him all things concerning the fall of man, and rehearsed and laid before him the records and the holy scriptures of the people." (Alma 18:36.) Ammon's efforts resulted in many souls' being brought to Christ, and the Church was established among Lamoni's people.

Of Ammon and his brothers Mormon declares: "They had waxed strong in the knowledge of the truth; for they were men of a sound understanding and they had searched the scriptures diligently, that they might know the word of God. . . . They had given themselves to much prayer, and fasting; therefore they had the spirit of prophecy, and the spirit of revelation, and when they taught, they taught with power and authority of God." (Alma 17:2–3.) Such were the power and the example of Ammon that those who were converted by his preaching "never did fall away." (Alma 23:6.) Mormon declares Ammon to be a man of God. (Alma 48:18.) Ammon followed the pattern of all those who are called the "people of the Lord" and came unto Christ.

To the people of the Lord, the promise is given that they "shall receive an inheritance upon the earth when the day of transfiguration shall come." (D&C 63:20.) Unto them shall the mysteries of the kingdom of God be revealed, which mysteries shall become for them "a well of living water, springing up unto everlasting life." (D&C 63:23.)

THE SONS OF GOD

The title "sons of God" is frequently associated with the future. It is generally a title *yet to be bestowed*. In the revelations of the Doctrine and Covenants the Lord gives men power *to become* the sons of God when certain conditions are met. The only time that the term is used in the present tense is in the vision of the three degrees of glory, found in section 76: "Wherefore, . . . they *are* gods, even the sons of God" (D&C 76:58; italics added.) Those who are familiar with the context of this statement recognize that we are reading of those "who *shall come forth* in the resurrection of the just" (D&C 76:50; italics added.) There-fore, it too has a strong orientation toward the future.

Those who are striving to come to Christ, and therefore those who will receive the power to become the sons of God, must receive a testimony of Christ and believe on his name. (D&C 11:30; 34:3; 35:2; 45:8; 76:51.) In the Doctrine and Covenants, the Lord never mentions this title without also listing these qualifications. In section 76 the Lord indicates how one manifests that he has received the testimony of Christ and that he believes on Christ's name. He is baptized after the manner of the burial of Christ. He is "buried" in the water in the name of Christ. (D&C 76:51.) He keeps the commandments and receives the Holy Spirit by the laying on of hands by one who has authority. (D&C 76:52.) And he overcomes the world by faith. (D&C 76:53.)

The title "sons of God" is more closely linked to receiving a tes-timony of Jesus and manifesting it through faithfulness and the recep-tion of ordinances than any other title used by the Lord when referring to his people. We will look to the scriptures once again to verify our assumption that this behavior will lead us to Christ.

The people of Alma, who gathered at the waters of Mormon, pos-sessed the qualities we have described. They received a testimony of Jesus and the saving ordinances. They kept the commandment given to them by Alma that they should "look forward with one eye, having one faith and one baptism, having their hearts knit together in unity and in love one towards another. . . . And thus," Mormon declares, "they became the children of God." (Mosiah 18:21–22.)

The Lord revealed to Moses that Adam was baptized and that the Spirit of God descended upon him and he was born of the Spirit. After-ward, "he heard a voice out of heaven, saying: Thou art baptized with fire, and with the Holy Ghost. This is the record of the Father, and the Son, from henceforth and forever;

"And thou art after the order of him who was without beginning of days or end of years, from all eternity to all eternity.

"Behold, thou art one in me, a son of God; and thus may all become my sons. Amen.

" . . . Behold, our father Adam taught these things, and many have believed and become the sons of God, and many have believed not, and have perished in their sins, and are looking forth with fear, in torment, for the fiery indignation of the wrath of God to be poured out upon them." (Moses 6:66–68; 7:1.)

Speaking of the sons of God, the Prophet Joseph Smith declared, "These shall dwell in the presence of God and his Christ forever and ever." (D&C 76:62.)

Relative to those who could have become the sons of God but do not, the Prophet Joseph revealed that they are people "who received not the testimony of Jesus in the flesh, but afterwards received it. These are they who are the honorable men of the earth, who were blinded by the craftiness of men. . . . These are they who are not valiant in the testimony of Jesus; wherefore, they obtain not the crown over the kingdom of our God." (D&C 76:74–75, 79.)

SAINT

Jacob, the brother of Nephi, provides us with a poignant definition of a saint. He declares saints to be "they who have believed in the Holy One of Israel, they who have endured the crosses of the world, and despised the shame of it." (2 Nephi 9:18.)

How do saints demonstrate that they are striving to come to Christ?

During an earlier time in the Church, they assembled themselves to the land of Zion (D&C 63:24, 36); now, they assemble themselves to those places appointed by the Lord through his prophet (D&C 125:2). They keep the commandments and hearken to observe all the words which the Lord speaks to them. (D&C 103:7–8.) They are a light to the world and the saviors of men. (D&C 103:9.) They impart of their substance to the poor and the needy among them. (D&C 105:3.) They build temples and are baptized for the dead and participate in all the ordinances associated with the temple. (D&C 124:29–40.)

The title "saint" is used by the Lord when he addresses the members of the Church in the revelation called the Word of Wisdom. (D&C 89.) This revelation shows the "order and will of God in the temporal salvation of *all* saints in the last days." (D&C 89:2; italics added.) The Lord also indicates that it is within the capacity of all those who can be called saints to obey this law. (D&C 89:3.) Therefore, those who are called saints, and those who are striving to come to Christ, will not drink wine or strong drinks. (D&C 89:5.) They will use tobacco only for the healing of cattle, and they will not take hot drinks into their bodies. (D&C 89:8–9.) They will use wholesome herbs with prudence and thanksgiving. (D&C 89:11.) They will eat the flesh of beasts and fowl sparingly, and with thanksgiving, in times of winter, cold, famine, or excess of hunger. (D&C 89:12–15.) They will eat grain, fruits, and vegetables. (D&C 89:14–16.) They will remember to keep and do these sayings, and they will walk in obedience to the commandments. (D&C 89:18.)

Those whom the Lord calls "saints" manifest that they are striving to come to Christ by the spiritual nature of the actions which flow from them and by the physical nourishment which they take in. We will search the scriptures to see if such behavior will lead us to Christ.

Daniel, the Old Testament prophet, and his friends Hananiah, Mishael, and Azariah elected not to defile themselves with the meat and wine of the king. Therefore their "countenances appeared fairer and fatter in flesh than all the children which did eat the portion of the king's meat." (Daniel 1:15.) The Lord gave them "knowledge and skill in all learning and wisdom." (Daniel 1:17.) King Nebuchadnezzar found them to be "in all matters of wisdom and understanding . . . ten times better than all the magicians and astrologers that were in all his realm." (Daniel 1:20.)

Later, Daniel's friends were asked to defile themselves spiritually by bowing down to a false god. This they also refused to do. As a result they were cast into a fiery furnace. Yet, when the king who had condemned them looked into the furnace, he exclaimed, "Lo, I see four men loose, walking in the midst of the fire, and they have no hurt; and the form of the fourth is like the Son of God." (Daniel 3:25.) They lived as saints, striving to come to Christ; he came to them and delivered them from destruction.

Those who are worthy of the title "saint" in this dispensation "shall receive health in their navel and marrow to their bones; and shall find wisdom and great treasures of knowledge, even hidden treasures; and shall run and not be weary, and shall walk and not faint." Furthermore, the Lord promises the saints "that the destroying angel shall pass by them, as the children of Israel, and not slay them." (D&C 89:18–21.)

Traditionally, we have associated this deliverance from destruction as a promise of good health. While that is a significant part of the promise associated with the Word of Wisdom, there may be a larger meaning to the promise as it applies to saints. That larger meaning is understood when we examine the prophecy in section 45.

Concerning the destruction of the wicked prior to his second coming, the Lord declared, "But before the arm of the Lord shall fall, an angel shall sound his trump, and the saints that have slept shall come forth to meet me in the cloud.

"Wherefore, if ye have slept in peace blessed are you; for as you now behold me and know that I am, even so shall ye come unto me and your souls shall live, and your redemption shall be perfected; and the saints shall come forth from the four quarters of the earth.

"Then shall the arm of the Lord fall upon the nations." (D&C 45:45–47.)

Relative to the blessings that await the saints, Jacob, the brother of Nephi, declared, "They shall inherit the kingdom of God, which was prepared for them from the foundation of the world, and their joy shall be full forever." (2 Nephi 9:18.)

SUMMARY

We have read the revelations of the Doctrine and Covenants to learn what it means to come to Christ, and we have verified from the scriptures that we can come to Christ by following the counsel and commandments found in these revelations. Our answer is not complete because we did not examine every commandment given to every person or group mentioned in the document. But we have explored a way to study the Doctrine and Covenants, which will bless our lives as we apply that which we learn.

It is my belief that the Lord has given us these sacred writings for the purpose of teaching us how we come to him. Consider the statement made by the Savior to the Jews, relative to the scriptures available to them in their day: "Search the scriptures; for in them ye think ye have eternal life: and they are they which testify of me. *And ye will not come to me, that ye might have life.*" (John 5:39–40; italics added.)

The Lord taught the Jews of his day that, despite what they thought, they were not saved by the scriptures. They were saved as they used what they learned from the scriptures to come to Christ. It cannot be any different today. We are not saved according to our knowledge of the scriptures. Only insofar as we use that knowledge to come unto Christ will we have eternal life.

There are no references in the Old or the New Testament that contain the admonition from the Lord, or anyone else, to "repent and come unto Christ." That coming to Christ is inextricably tied to true repentance is clearly taught only in the Book of Mormon, in the revelations of the Doctrine and Covenants, and in the words of the living prophets. I believe that it is one of the "plain and most precious parts of the gospel of the Lamb which have been kept back." (1 Nephi 13:32.)

As we review the words of the Lord on this matter, notice the tandem nature of these principles. The resurrected Savior taught the Nephites:

"Whoso *repenteth and cometh unto me* as a little child, him will I receive, for of such is the kingdom of God. Behold, for such I have laid down my life, and have taken it up again; therefore *repent, and come unto me* ye ends of the earth, and be saved." (3 Nephi 9:22; italics added.)

"I have given you the law and the commandments of my Father, . . . that ye shall *repent of your sins, and come unto me* with a broken heart and a contrite spirit." (3 Nephi 12:19; italics added.)

"Ye shall not cast [a man who is unworthy] out of your synagogues, or your places of worship, for unto such shall ye continue to minister; for ye know not but what they will return and *repent, and come unto me* with full purpose of heart, and I shall heal them; and ye shall be the means of bringing salvation unto them." (3 Nephi 18:32; italics added.)

To those of our generation who are the church, the elect, the people of the Lord, the sons of God, and saints, the Savior says:

"Remember the worth of souls is great in the sight of God;

"For, behold, the Lord your Redeemer suffered death in the flesh; wherefore he suffered the pain of all men, that all men might *repent and come unto him.*

"And he hath risen again from the dead, *that he might bring all men unto him, on conditions of repentance.*

"And how great is his joy in the soul that repenteth!

"Wherefore, you are called to cry repentance unto this people.

"And if it so be that you should labor all your days in *crying repentance unto this people, and bring, save it be one soul unto me,* how great shall be your joy with him in the kingdom of my Father!" (D&C 18:10–15; italics added.)

Therefore, search the scriptures, for they truly testify of Christ. And they will tell us how to come to him and show us how to bring others to him. And if we apply what the scriptures teach, we shall have eternal life.

CHAPTER TWELVE

What Is the Dispensation of the Fulness of Times?

Robert J. Matthews

Dean of Religious Education
Brigham Young University

I am happy to be associated with this great effort that takes place each year to honor Dr. Sidney B. Sperry and to teach the gospel of Jesus Christ. I want to present a doctrinal dimension to the story of the restoration of the gospel, which began with the personal appearance of the Father and the Son to Joseph Smith in the sacred grove near Palmyra, New York, in 1820. We will discuss the ministry of angels in the literal establishment of the kingdom of God on the earth. That is what the Prophet Joseph Smith has called "the established order of the kingdom of God."

For this presentation I alone am responsible. I do not speak for the Church or for the university. I will quote numerous authorities and passages of scripture and endeavor to quote them correctly and in the proper context. I fully believe the doctrine to be true and correct, yet the arrangement and presentation are my own.

"AS A BABE UPON ITS MOTHER'S LAP"

We will begin with the words of President Wilford Woodruff, speaking in the sixty-eighth general conference of the Church, 8 April 1898. He was telling of a meeting that had been held in Kirtland, Ohio, sixty-four years earlier, on Sunday, 27 April 1834:

"I arrived in Kirtland on Saturday and there met with Joseph and Hyrum Smith in the street. I was introduced to Joseph Smith. It was the first time that I had ever seen him in my life. He invited me home to spend the Sabbath with him, and I did so. They had meeting on Sunday.

"On Sunday night the Prophet called on all who held the Priesthood to gather into the little log school house they had there. It was a small

150

house, perhaps 14 feet square. But it held the whole of the Priesthood of the Church of Jesus Christ of Latter-day Saints who were then in the town of Kirtland, and who had gathered together to go off in Zion's camp. That was the first time I ever saw Oliver Cowdery, or heard him speak; the first time I ever saw Brigham Young and Heber C. Kimball, and the two Pratts, and Orson Hyde and many others. There were no Apostles in the Church then except Joseph Smith and Oliver Cowdery. When we got together the Prophet called upon the Elders of Israel with him to bear testimony of this work. Those that I have named spoke, and a good many that I have not named, bore their testimonies. When they got through the Prophet said, 'Brethren I have been very much edified and instructed in your testimonies here tonight, but I want to say to you before the Lord, that you know no more concerning the destinies of this Church and kingdom than a babe upon its mother's lap. You don't comprehend it.' I was rather surprised. He said, 'it is only a little handfull of Priesthood you see here tonight, but this Church will fill North and South America — it will fill the world.' "[1]

We are witnessing today the worldwide expansion of the Church. It has covered a great area in North and South America and is reaching throughout the world. Wherever a temple is built, that is a reliable indicator that the gospel has taken root and that the Church is stable in that particular area. Today, besides the many temples in North and South America, there are Latter-day Saint temples in England, Germany, Switzerland, Sweden, South Africa, the Philippines, Japan, Korea, Taiwan, New Zealand, Australia, Tahiti, Tonga, Samoa, and Hawaii. And we are just getting started with a worldwide dispensation of the gospel. It is 169 years since Joseph Smith received his first vision, yet in many parts of the world, expansion of the Church has come in just the last few decades. This is the dispensation of the fulness of times — the last of many dispensations that first began with father Adam. *This* time the gospel and the kingdom are going to stay upon the earth, and *this* time the eternal purposes of the Lord pertaining to the salvation of the human family on this earth are going to be fulfilled.

While there are many things we do not know, we do not need to remain in the same condition as those of whom the Prophet Joseph spoke, as knowing little more than "babes upon their mother's lap." That was in 1834. The Lord has revealed much since then, and we have seen a number of things unfold pertaining to the dispensation of the fulness of times.

THE ESTABLISHED ORDER OF THE KINGDOM OF GOD

One of the fundamental concepts of The Church of Jesus Christ of Latter-day Saints is that there is an established, revealed order, or system, for doing gospel things. We have it as a basic principle that all blessings are governed by law. Both the earth and the heavens are governed by law — divine law, instituted by the Lord himself.

I will read an excerpt from a sermon delivered by the Prophet Joseph Smith at the funeral of James Adams, 9 October 1843:

"The organization of the spiritual and heavenly worlds, and of spiritual and heavenly beings, was agreeable to the most perfect order and harmony: their limits and bounds were fixed irrevocably, and voluntarily subscribed to in their heavenly estate by themselves, and were by our first parents subscribed to upon the earth. . . .

"I assure the Saints that truth, in reference to these matters, can and may be known through the revelations of God in the way of His ordinances, and in answer to prayer. The Hebrew Church 'came unto the spirits of just men made perfect and unto an innumerable company of angels, unto God the Father of all, and to Jesus Christ the Mediator of the new covenant.' . . . What object was gained by this communication with the spirits of the just? It was the established order of the kingdom of God: The keys of power and knowledge were with them to communicate to the Saints."[2]

The Prophet spoke several times about "fixed principles." You noted that term in the quotation just given. In the same address he uses the term at least two more times, and he also uses it in other discourses.[3]

These words from the Prophet Joseph extend our understanding of some earlier statements found in the Doctrine and Covenants.

"There is a law, irrevocably decreed in heaven before the foundations of this world, upon which all blessings are predicated —

"And when we obtain any blessing from God, it is by obedience to that law upon which it is predicated." (D&C 130:20–21.)

And also:

"For all who will have a blessing at my hands shall abide the law which was appointed for that blessing, and the conditions thereof, as were instituted from before the foundation of the world. . . .

"Behold, mine house is a house of order, saith the Lord God, and not a house of confusion.

"Will I accept of an offering, saith the Lord, that is not made in my name?

"Or will I receive at your hands that which I have not appointed?

"And will I appoint unto you, saith the Lord, except it be by law, even as I and my Father ordained unto you, before the world was?

"I am the Lord thy God; and I give unto you this commandment — that no man shall come unto the Father but by me or by my word, which is my law, saith the Lord. . . .

"I am the Lord thy God, and will give unto thee the law of my Holy Priesthood, as was ordained by me and my Father before the world was." (D&C 132:5, 8–12, 28.)

Even a casual look at these passages is sufficient to inform us that the Lord works by the law that he and his Father ordained and established before the creation of this earth. The angels obey and are governed by such laws, and man also is obligated to obey these divine laws that are older than the world is old, if he wants the blessing. That is the plain meaning of these declarations. The Lord is not adding to or changing the plan of salvation. There are no bargain days, no special sales, no days for double coupons. The plan of redemption through the gospel and its ordinances has always been the same.

The Lord has a plan, an order, a system for the salvation of the human family. It is an old plan, an ancient plan, an eternal plan. It was explained to us and implemented in the premortal life, and it has been introduced several times to mankind on the earth through chosen prophets beginning with father Adam. When the Lord Jesus Christ reveals his plan anew and confers his holy priesthood upon his prophets, that is called a dispensation of the gospel. Since the plan is older than the earth, there is no difficulty or problem in the Lord revealing the entire plan to the ancient prophets, beginning with Adam. The Lord has established and re-established gospel dispensations several times among people on the earth. Each dispensation endured for a while, and then each ceased to function on earth because of wickedness and unbelief. The last and final gospel dispensation has now been established, and it is destined to fill the whole earth. It is appropriately called the dispensation of the fulness of times, because it is a dispensation consisting of all previous dispensations plus some unique and particular things never accomplished before on the earth.

My presentation deals with these two questions: What is the dispensation of the fulness of times? and a related question, How was it established? The first question has been at least partially answered, and so I will turn to the second: How was the dispensation of the fulness of times established? We can almost answer that in one sentence: It was done by the prophets of former dispensations extending the gospel and priesthood they have to the prophets of the last dispensation. But we need to examine and discuss the details.

FORMING A COLONY

I have ofttimes thought of the establishment of a dispensation of the gospel on the earth as something like establishing a colony in a new land. When the European settlers came to America in the sixteenth century, they found a people already here (the American Indians, or Lamanites), but the settlers brought a different culture, a different mode of life, and new laws and authority. These settlers named their colonies after the places from whence they came, hence we had New England, New Holland, New France, and New Spain, etc. We still have New York, New Amsterdam, and New Orleans. A new culture became established among the previous occupants. It was really an *old* culture transplanted from Europe, but it was new to America in that generation.

In something of the same way, a new dispensation is brought about by angels from an older world coming to visit this world and calling upon new prophets, introducing what to the new prophets is a new culture, a new authority or priesthood, and new laws. These heavenly visitors have brought to earth a celestial priesthood, a celestial order of marriage and family, a celestial economic system, and a celestial social system. The parallel to a colony can be carried too far, but there are some similarities.

The dispensation of the fulness of times was established on this earth by heavenly messengers coming from another world, conferring their laws and doctrines and authority upon Joseph Smith and Oliver Cowdery, thus initiating a new colony on the earth that represented and bore traces of the world from whence these angels came.

The ancient prophets who had been the leaders of their dispensations during earlier ages of the earth are angels now, and they minister to the current prophets on the earth. Although all are engaged in the same holy work of the Lord, these heavenly angels are not all alike and do not all come for the same precise and detailed purpose—some bring information, others bring keys and priesthood. But they are all engaged in the gospel of Jesus Christ. It makes a difference who is sent to do what. Our clue to understanding that is in becoming acquainted with the established order of the kingdom of God.

Who were the divine messengers who came to the Prophet Joseph Smith? We know of at least the following:

The Father and the Son. They initiated this dispensation and brought a correct knowledge of the Godhead. They removed all doubt that there is a God, that he hears and answers prayers, and that the Father and Son are two different, distinct persons.

The Angel Moroni. He brought forth the Book of Mormon — the stick of Ephraim.

John the Baptist. He restored the Aaronic Priesthood.

Peter, James, and John. They restored the Melchizedek Priesthood.

Moses. He brought the keys of the gathering of Israel.

Elias. He brought the dispensation of the gospel of Abraham, thus establishing the patriarchal order of marriage and family.

Elijah. He brought the keys of sealing and turning the hearts of the children to the fathers and to the promises that had been made to the fathers.

No doubt Adam also came, and Enoch, Noah (Gabriel), and many others. We do not have the exact record, date, place, or occasion for some of these coming to Joseph Smith to extend to him their particular keys, but because we know the rules that govern the system, we know it has to be so.

What qualified each of these prophets to come to Joseph Smith and be the one to restore those particular keys and priesthood for this dispensation? First, they were chosen and ordained in the premortal life. Second, they were righteous and diligent in mortal life and held the keys in their day on earth. Third, they went into eternity still holding those keys and thus were appointed as angels, on an errand, to return and bestow their authority.

There seems to be another essential consideration also. When keys and priesthood are bestowed, two persons are always the recipients. In every documented case Oliver Cowdery was present with the Prophet Joseph Smith when priesthood and keys were restored. This is no doubt a demonstration of the law of witnesses. When the revelation is personal, or consists of information only, no such witness seems to be necessarily present.

In addition to the visits of those angels whom we have already mentioned, we are given a wider view by President John Taylor:

"If you were to ask Joseph what sort of a looking man Adam was, he would tell you at once; he would tell you his size and appearance and all about him. He would do the same about Peter, James, and John, because he had seen them."[4]

"I know of what I speak for I was very well acquainted with him [Joseph Smith]. The principles which he had, placed him in communication with the Lord, and not only with the Lord, but with the ancient apostles and prophets; such men, for instance, as Abraham, Isaac, Jacob, Noah, Adam, Seth, Enoch, and Jesus and the Father, and the apostles that lived on this continent as well as those who lived on the Asiatic continent. He seemed to be as familiar with these people as we are with one another."[5]

THE DISPENSATION OF THE FULNESS OF TIMES

The dispensation of the fulness of times is a period of restoration and of gathering. It is the plan of Jesus Christ for completing the redemption of mankind and the earth. There are some very interesting statements in the scriptures on this subject:

First, from Peter, as recorded in Acts 3:20–21:

"And he shall send Jesus Christ, which before was preached unto you:

"Whom the heaven must receive until the times of restitution of all things, which God hath spoken by the mouth of all his holy prophets since the world began."

And from Paul to the Ephesians, 1:9–10:

"Having made known unto us the mystery of his will, according to his good pleasure which he hath purposed in himself:

"That in the dispensation of the fulness of times he might gather together in one all things in Christ, both which are in heaven, and which are on earth; even in him."

At the conclusion of the visits of Jesus Christ, Moses, Elias, and Elijah in the Kirtland Temple, Elijah said to Joseph Smith and Oliver Cowdery: "Therefore, the keys of this dispensation are committed into your hands." (D&C 110:16.) And a few months later the Lord said to Thomas B. Marsh, president of the Quorum of the Twelve Apostles:

"For unto you, the Twelve, and those, the First Presidency, who are appointed with you to be your counselors and your leaders, is the power of this priesthood given, for the last days and for the last time, in the which is the dispensation of the fulness of times.

"Which power you hold, in connection with all those who have received a dispensation at any time from the beginning of the creation;

"For verily I say unto you, the keys of the dispensation, which ye have received, have come down from the fathers, and last of all, being sent down from heaven unto you." (D&C 112:30–32.)

The Prophet Joseph Smith wrote: "It is necessary in the ushering in of the dispensation of the fulness of times, which dispensation is now beginning to usher in, that a whole and complete and perfect union, and welding together of dispensations, and keys, and powers, and glories should take place, and be revealed from the days of Adam even to the present time. And not only this, but those things which never have been revealed from the foundation of the world, but have been kept hid from the wise and prudent, shall be revealed unto babes and sucklings in this, the dispensation of the fulness of times." (D&C 128:18.)

Elder David W. Patten, a member of the Quorum of the Twelve Apostles, wrote in July 1838:

"Now the thing to be known is, what the fullness of times means, or the extent or authority thereof. It means this, that the dispensation of the fullness of times is made up of all the dispensations that ever have been given since the world began, until this time. Unto Adam first was given a dispensation. . . . And unto Noah also was a dispensation given. . . . And from Noah to Abraham, and from Abraham to Moses, and from Moses to Elias, and from Elias to John the Baptist, and from then to Jesus Christ, and from Jesus Christ to Peter, James, and John, the Apostles—all received in their time a dispensation by revelation from God, to accomplish the great scheme of restitution, spoken of by all the holy prophets since the world began; the end of which is the dispensation of the fullness of times, in the which all things shall be fulfilled that have been spoken of since the earth was made.

" . . . this deliverer [Joseph Smith] must be clothed with the power of all the other dispensations, or his dispensation could not be called the dispensation of the fullness of times."[6]

This dispensation therefore represents all other dispensations, and Elder Patten continues by saying if we treat lightly the calling of Joseph Smith we likewise "sin not against him only, but against Moroni, who

holds the keys of the stick of Ephraim [Book of Mormon], and also
Elias, who holds the keys of bringing to pass the restitution of all things,
and also John . . . ; and also Elijah . . . ; and also Joseph and Jacob and
Isaac and Abraham, your fathers, by whom the promises remain; and
also Michael, or Adam, the Father of all, the Prince of all, the Ancient
of Days; and also Peter and James and John. . . .

"Therefore, brethren, beware concerning yourselves, that you sin
not against the authority of this dispensation, nor think lightly of those
whom God has counted worthy for so great a calling."[7]

Elder Patten's words bring us an awareness of the high calling of
the Prophet Joseph Smith, and also of each of his successors, right
down to President Ezra Taft Benson. It is not a matter of personality,
or of popularity; it is not a charismatic thing, it is a matter of a man
holding the keys of the priesthood and of being the Lord's anointed.

The saving principles and ordinances of the gospel are the same
in every dispensation. We do not have any doctrines or ordinances in
the Church today that have not been had at some time or other in the
world in earlier dispensations. There are, however, some things to be
accomplished in this dispensation that have not been done before, such
as the building of the New Jerusalem, the second coming of the Savior,
the Millennium, and the earth receiving its paradisiacal glory.

How many dispensations have there been? We often hear that there
have been seven — Adam, Enoch, Noah, Abraham, Moses, Jesus, and
Joseph Smith. This list is far too shallow. The seven are only a few of
the dispensations mentioned in the Bible (what about Melchizedek,
Elijah, John the Baptist?), and this list completely ignores what we
know about the gospel being among the Nephites, the Jaredites, and
the ten lost tribes. There have been many, many dispensations, and
the dispensation of the fulness of times is a combination of them all.

THE HEAVENLY ORDER OF PRIESTHOOD

Since the ancient prophets are angels now, let us read some things
about the order and the organization that exists among these celestial
beings as they relate to the Church upon the earth.

First, from Elder Orson Pratt about the priesthood: "There are
authorities in heaven as well as upon the earth, and the authorities in
heaven are far greater in number than the few who are upon the earth.
This [church] is only a little branch of the great tree of the priesthood —
merely a branch receiving authority from heaven, so that the inhabitants

of the earth may be benefited as well as the inhabitants of the eternal world; but the great trunk of the tree of the Priesthood is in heaven."[8]

Now from the Prophet Joseph Smith: "[The Melchizedek priesthood] is the channel through which all knowledge, doctrine, the plan of salvation and every important matter is revealed from heaven.

"Its institution was prior to 'the foundation of this earth.' . . . It is the channel through which the Almighty commenced revealing His glory at the beginning of the creation of this earth, and through which He has continued to reveal Himself to the children of men to the present time, and through which He will make known His purposes to the end of time."[9]

As to the special functions and powers of the priesthood, we read the following: "For him to whom these keys [of the Holy Priesthood] are given there is no difficulty in obtaining a knowledge of facts in relation to the salvation of the children of men, both as well for the dead as for the living." (D&C 128:11.)

THE SPECIAL STATUS OF ADAM

The Prophet Joseph taught that Adam was not only the first man on the earth but also the first in a lot of other things. He was the first prophet for Jesus Christ. These are the words of Joseph Smith: "Commencing with Adam, who was the first man, who is spoken of in Daniel as being the 'Ancient of Days,' or in other words, the first and oldest of all, the great, grand progenitor of whom it is said in another place he is Michael, because he was the first and father of all, not only by progeny, but the first to hold the spiritual blessings, to whom was made known the plan of ordinances for the salvation of his posterity unto the end, and to whom Christ was first revealed, and through whom Christ has been revealed from heaven, and will continue to be revealed from henceforth."[10]

Adam presides over all of the dispensations: "Adam holds the keys of the dispensation of the fullness of times; i.e., the dispensation of all the times have been and will be revealed through him from the beginning to Christ, and from Christ to the end of the dispensations that are to be revealed. . . .

"Now the purpose in [God] in the winding up scene of the last dispensation is that all things pertaining to that dispensation should be conducted precisely in accordance with the preceding dispensations.

"And again, God purposed in Himself that there should not be an eternal fullness until every dispensation should be fulfilled and gathered together in one, and that all things whatsoever, that should be gathered together in one in those dispensations unto the same fullness and eternal glory, should be in Christ Jesus; therefore He set the ordinances to be the same forever and ever, and set Adam to watch over them, to reveal them from heaven to man, or to send angels to reveal them. . . .

"These angels are under the direction of Michael or Adam, who acts under the direction of the Lord."[11]

"Moses sought to bring the children of Israel into the presence of God, through the power of the Priesthood, but he could not. In the first ages of the world they tried to establish the same thing; and there were Eliases raised up who tried to restore these very glories, but did not obtain them; but they prophesied of a day when this glory would be revealed. Paul spoke of the dispensation of the fullness of times, when God would gather together all things in one, etc.; and those men to whom these keys have been given, will have to be there; and they without us cannot be made perfect.

"These men are in heaven, but their children are on the earth. Their bowels yearn over us. God sends down men for this reason. . . . All these authoritative characters will come down and join hand in hand in bringing about this work."[12]

"There has been a chain of authority and power from Adam down to the present time."[13]

In view of what we have just read, we ask ourselves these questions: Who sent John the Baptist to Joseph Smith? Answer: Adam. Who sent Peter, James, John, Moroni, Elijah, Moses, and all the others to Joseph Smith? The answer is the same: Adam. Who sent angels to minister in any age of the world? Who sent Moses and Elijah to the Mount of Transfiguration? It has to have been Adam, or someone acting under his direction. Adam holds all of the keys, and keys are the directing power. In every dispensation Adam reveals the gospel of Jesus Christ, or he sends someone to do it. He is the father of the human family and wants as many of his children saved as possible. Since there is no salvation outside of Jesus Christ, every dispensation is a gospel dispensation. All of the prophets and all of the angels are servants of Jesus Christ.

When we see the relationship between the dispensations as explained by the Prophet Joseph and that all are conducted on the same plan, we come to the conclusion that all of the former dispensations were open-ended. That is, they had a starting point but have not had a closing date as such. They ceased to function on earth because of apostasy, but the work of the earlier dispensations is not yet ended. The leaders of each dispensation, still holding the keys, have come back again to continue their work, until "the Great Jehovah says the work is done." In the words of Elder Bruce R. McConkie, "As rivers flow into an ocean, all the dispensations of the past flow into this final great dispensation."[14] In the meantime, those who held the keys and were once mortal prophets are continuing their work on the other side of the veil, in the spirit world, or elsewhere as translated beings or as resurrected beings.

Continuing with the words of the Prophet Joseph, we learn that Adam holds the keys of the First Presidency: "The Priesthood was first given to Adam; he obtained the First Presidency, and held the keys of it from generation to generation. He obtained it in the Creation, before the world was formed, as in Genesis 1:26, 27, 28. He had dominion given him over every living creature. . . .

"The Priesthood is an everlasting principle, and existed with God from eternity, and will to eternity, without beginning of days or end of years. The keys have to be brought from heaven whenever the Gospel is sent. When they are revealed from heaven, it is by Adam's authority.

" . . . He (Adam) is the father of the human family, and presides over the spirits of all men, and all that have had the keys must stand before him in this grand council.

" . . . He (Adam) is the head, and was told to multiply. The keys were first given to him, and by him to others. He will have to give an account of his stewardship, and they to him."[15]

That Adam held the keys of the First Presidency was the subject of remarks by Elder Mark E. Petersen at the Mexico City Conference, 26 August 1972:

"Now tonight we had the prophet of the Church visit us. Do you know how much authority the President of the Church holds? Let us think for a moment about the Prophet Joseph Smith. The Prophet Joseph Smith was ordained to the Aaronic Priesthood by whom?

"*Answer:* John the Baptist.

"The Prophet Joseph Smith an apostle was ordained by whom?

"*Answer:* Peter, James, and John.

"Joseph Smith then was ordained an apostle by Peter, James, and John. This was part of his ordination to the Melchizedek Priesthood, but other men also came and ordained Joseph to other powers. Can you tell us, any one, what other angels came and ordained Joseph Smith to certain powers?

"*Answer:* Moses and Elijah, the prophet.

"Who else? What angels came? We have Moses and Elijah, and Elias, and who else?

"*Answer:* Adam.

"What power did Adam bring back to Joseph Smith.

"*(No answer)* Then I will tell you. Adam brought the keys of the First Presidency. Joseph Smith received the keys of the First Presidency from Adam, who came back and visited him. Joseph Smith received the power of the gathering of Israel through Moses, who came back to see him. Elijah brought back the powers that we use in connection with our temple work."[16]

The Prophet Joseph Smith wrote:

"The Priesthood is everlasting. The Savior, Moses, and Elias, gave the keys to Peter, James and John, on the mount, when they were transfigured before him. . . .

"How have we come at the Priesthood in the last days? It came down, down, in regular succession. Peter, James, and John had it given to them and they gave it to others. Christ is the Great High Priest; Adam next."[17]

"This, then, is the nature of the Priesthood; every man holding the Presidency of his dispensation, and one man holding the Presidency of them all, even Adam; and Adam receiving his Presidency and authority from the Lord."[18]

These clear and direct statements about Adam's special status are in complete harmony with yet another declaration found in D&C 78:16 that Adam holds the keys of salvation:

"[The Lord] hath appointed Michael your prince, and established his feet, and set him upon high, and given unto him the keys of salvation under the counsel and direction of the Holy One, who is without beginning of days or end of life."

THE SPECIAL STATUS OF NOAH (GABRIEL)

The Prophet Joseph had some special things to say about the great prophet Noah: "Noah, who is Gabriel . . . stands next in authority to Adam in the Priesthood; he was called of God to this office, and was the father of all living in this day, and to him was given the dominion."[19]

Noah was like a second Adam, the father of all living in his day after the Flood. Doctrine and Covenants 27:6–7 states that a prophet named Elias holds the keys of "bringing to pass the restoration of all things" in the last days. This Elias is further identified as the angel who visited Zacharias, the father of John the Baptist, and gave him promise of a son (as recorded in Luke 1). Since Luke identifies this angel as Gabriel, and Gabriel is Noah, we conclude that the Elias of Doctrine and Covenants 27 is Noah. It therefore appears that Noah has a major role, under Adam, in bringing about the restoration of the gospel in the fulness of times. That is, Noah, as well as Adam, is closely linked with The Church of Jesus Christ of Latter-day Saints.

Again from the Prophet Joseph: "[Jehovah talked with Noah] in a familiar and friendly manner, that He continued to him the keys, the covenants, the power and the glory, with which He blessed Adam at the beginning; . . . for all the ordinances and duties that ever have been required by the Priesthood, under the directions and commandments of the Almighty in any of the dispensations, shall all be had in the last dispensation, therefore all things had under the authority of the Priesthood at any former period, shall be had again, bringing to pass the restoration spoken of by the mouth of all the Holy Prophets."[20]

These teachings from the Prophet show us an order, a priesthood organization in the heavens, and they explain to us the doctrinal background of the Church and the dispensation in which we live. These things give us a perspective on the work of the Lord in our own day.

DIFFERENCES BETWEEN ANGELS AND SPIRITS

We have said quite a lot about angels and the priesthood order that exists among them, but we have not dealt with the different levels among the angels. The word *angel* means a messenger and is often used to refer to any heavenly messenger, but in the strict sense, an angel is a resurrected or translated being with a body.

There are also ministering spirits, who are not tabernacled with a body of flesh and bones — for example, those who have passed through mortality and are awaiting the resurrection. It appears from what has been revealed that if priesthood or keys are to be conferred, a resurrected or translated being is employed because of the laying on of hands, whereas spirits can convey knowledge but cannot lay on hands. Such is the fundamental principle of Doctrine and Covenants 129, which first defines an angel as having a tangible body as contrasted to a spirit, and then indicates that mortals could not feel the physical touch of a spirit, therefore righteous spirits will not attempt to touch a mortal. Hence a mortal could not be ordained by a spirit, but either an angel or a spirit could deliver a message. Because of the necessity for the laying on of hands, we can thus discern that John the Baptist, Peter, James, John, Moses, Elias, Elijah, and any others who conferred priesthood and keys on Joseph Smith and Oliver Cowdery were tabernacled beings and not merely spirits.

We return again to the Prophet Joseph, who spoke of the distinction of missions, or assignments, between angels and spirits:

"Spirits can only be revealed in flaming fire and glory. Angels have advanced further, their light and glory being tabernacled; and hence they appear in bodily shape. . . .

" . . . Angels have advanced higher in knowledge and power than spirits."[21]

Joseph Smith "explained the difference between an angel and a ministering spirit; the one a resurrected or translated body, with its spirit ministering to embodied spirits — the other a disembodied spirit, visiting and ministering to disembodied spirits. Jesus Christ became a ministering spirit (while His body was lying in the sepulchre) to the spirits in prison, to fulfill an important part of His mission, without which He could not have perfected His work, or entered into His rest. After His resurrection He appeared as an angel to His disciples.

" . . . Jesus Christ went in body after His resurrection, to minister to resurrected bodies."[22]

The Prophet Joseph thus taught that there is an order that must be observed in the teaching of the gospel. That is, the general pattern is for mortals to teach mortals, spirits to teach spirits, and resurrected beings to minister among other resurrected beings. Only when there is no available mortal with the priesthood does an angel come from heaven to confer it or to teach the gospel. There is a law that governs who is assigned to preach to whom.

This law does not imply that angels or spirits do not minister to mortals, but only that such ministering would be the exception, when there is no mortal who can do what is needed. These basic principles seem to pertain to the preaching of the *first* principles to mankind, and not to pertaining to the prophets of God receiving guidance and direction from the Lord, from angels, and so on.

The Prophet Joseph Smith indicated still further that the order of heaven is that mortals will receive the gospel from mortals: "No wonder the angel told good old Cornelius that he must send for Peter to learn how to be saved: Peter could baptise, and angels could not, so long as there were legal officers in the flesh holding the keys of the kingdom, or the authority of the priesthood. There is one evidence still further on this point, and that is that Jesus himself when he appeared to Paul on his way to Damascus, did not inform him how he could be saved. He had set in the church first Apostles, and secondly prophets, for the . . . grand rule of heaven was that nothing should ever be done on earth without revealing the secret to his servants the prophets, agreeably to Amos 3:7, so Paul could not learn so much from the Lord relative to his duty in the common salvation of man, as he could from one of Christ's ambassadors called with the same heavenly calling of the Lord, and endowed with the same power from on high."[23]

This concept is in harmony with the parable in Luke 16 in which the rich man died and went to hell and asked for someone to come back from the dead and warn his five brothers before they died, lest they too come to that place. Father Abraham said they would be taught on earth by "Moses and the prophets." But Lazarus insisted it would be better if someone rose from the dead to teach them. Whereupon, in the parable, Abraham said: "If they hear not Moses and the prophets, neither will they be persuaded, though one rose from the dead." (Luke 16:26–30.)

SOME MISSIONARIES IN THE SPIRIT WORLD

We generally have supposed that soon after Jesus' resurrection, all of the righteous spirits in the spirit world were also resurrected; however, we may need to look at this supposition a little closer. Since there is a principle that spirits preach to spirits, I take it that not every one of the righteous spirits was resurrected immediately after Jesus was resurrected. Most of them, yes, but apparently not all. We have learned from Doctrine and Covenants 138 that between the time of his death and the time of his resurrection, Jesus went in spirit to the world of spirits. He did not go personally among the wicked in the spirit world but instead spent the time ministering among the righteous spirits, organizing a mission in the spirit world for them to preach to those in the spirit prison. Jesus' spirit thereafter returned to his dead body, and he became the first resurrected being on this earth. If *all* of the righteous were resurrected immediately after Jesus, the spirit world mission would essentially have been disorganized. It is my opinion that a few stalwart, righteous men and women spirits were asked to postpone their resurrection for a short time in order to conduct their missions in the spirit world among those in prison. It would not be very long before recruits would come from the earth, from among the Jewish, Nephite, and Ten Tribe churches which Jesus had established on earth. Stephen, James, and many others would soon be available to take up their labors in the spirit world. I don't know of any revelation that says that this is not so, and I believe this conclusion is entirely consistent with the known laws that govern the preaching of the gospel.

THE ANGELS AT THE TOMB

One more application of these principles. Who were the two angels who came to the tomb at Jesus' resurrection? Although they are nowhere named in scripture, we are not without information on the matter. Things are done according to law and order in the priesthood. The resurrection of Jesus from the dead is the greatest event that occurred on this earth since the creation and fall of man. In the King James Version of the Bible, Matthew and Mark say there was one angel at the tomb. Luke and John say "two angels." The Joseph Smith Translation uniformly reads two angels in all four of the Gospels. (See JST Matthew 28:2–5; Mark 16:3–6.) This is a strong suggestion that these two angels came as witnesses of Christ's resurrection. Who among all the hosts of heaven deserved such a privilege? Surely not just anyone would be so selected and chosen. There is an ancient tradition in early Christianity that the two angels were Michael and Gabriel. That to us means Adam and Noah. When we consider that Adam is the chief angel, the Archangel, and that Noah stands next to Adam, it is easy for me to be comfortable with this identification of the two angels.

Of what form would they be? Jesus was already resurrected at the time. The stone needed to be rolled away, not to let Jesus out, but to let mortals in to observe that Jesus was not there. Who would deserve to be among the first to rise from the dead, after Jesus? No doubt Adam and Noah. They could be freshly resurrected, just after the Savior, and could come to the tomb to roll the stone away and announce to the women, to Peter, John, and others that Jesus was risen from the dead.

CONCLUSION: LIGHT AND DARKNESS

All that we have read today teaches us that there is "an established order in the kingdom of God," whether that kingdom is on earth or in heaven. I will cite again for emphasis a statement from the Prophet quoted earlier:

"The organization of the spiritual and heavenly worlds, and of spiritual and heavenly beings, was agreeable to the most perfect order and harmony: their limits and bounds were fixed irrevocably, and voluntarily subscribed to in their heavenly estate by themselves, and were by our first parents subscribed to upon the earth."[24]

When we contemplate the heavenly order of things with its intelligence, purpose, and light, as it has been given to us in the dispensation of the fulness of times, and contrast that with the confusion, disorder, contention, and lack of vision found among man-made organizations on the earth, we can appreciate the need for the gospel of Jesus Christ to be taught carefully to all men and women everywhere.

The world is in spiritual darkness. We can plainly see that as yet the dispensation of the fulness of times, with its celestial laws and promises and celestial authority, is still but a system of colonies in a strange earth among people with different laws and customs who have not yet learned of the established order of heaven. Who cannot see that those mortals who are limited to the secular and religious beliefs of the world, great as they may be, are "as babes upon their mothers' laps" with respect to the scope, the plan, the order, and the purposes of Jesus Christ manifested in the dispensation of the fulness of times. The Church of Jesus Christ of Latter-day Saints is the kingdom of God on the earth in the dispensation of the fulness of times.

NOTES

1. In Conference Report, 8 Apr. 1898, p. 57.

2. Joseph Smith, *Teachings of the Prophet Joseph Smith*, sel. Joseph Fielding Smith (Salt Lake City: Deseret Book Co., 1938), p. 325.

3. See Smith, *Teachings of the Prophet Joseph Smith*, pp. 197–98.

4. John Taylor, in *Journal of Discourses* (London: Latter-day Saints' Book Depot, 1854–86), 18:326.

5. Ibid., 21:94.

6. Joseph Smith, *History of The Church of Jesus Christ of Latter-day Saints*, 2d ed. rev., ed. B. H. Roberts (Salt Lake City: The Church of Jesus Christ of Latter-day Saints, 1932–51), 3:49, 52; or *Elders' Journal*, July 1838.

7. *History of the Church*, 3:53; or *Elders' Journal*, July 1838.

8. Orson Pratt, in *Journal of Discourses*, 7:84.

9. Smith, *Teachings of the Prophet Joseph Smith*, pp. 166–67.

10. Ibid., p. 167.

11. Ibid., pp. 167–68.

12. Ibid., p. 159.

13. Ibid., p. 191.

14. Bruce R. McConkie, *Mormon Doctrine*, 2d ed. (Salt Lake City: Bookcraft, 1958), p. 186.

15. Smith, *Teachings of the Prophet Joseph Smith*, pp. 157–58.

16. Mark E. Petersen, in Mexico Area Conference Report, Aug. 1972, p. 61.

17. Smith, *Teachings of the Prophet Joseph Smith*, p. 158.

18. Ibid., p. 169.

19. Ibid., p. 157.

20. Ibid., pp. 171–72.

21. Ibid., p. 325.

22. Ibid., p. 191.

23. Ibid., p. 265.

24. Ibid., p. 325.

CHAPTER THIRTEEN

Quest for the City of God: The Doctrine of Zion in Modern Revelation

Robert L. Millet

Chairman, Department of Ancient Scripture
Brigham Young University

"We ought to have the building up of Zion as our greatest object,"[1] Joseph Smith taught in 1839. Indeed, the vision of Zion was a strong motivating force for the Saints in the 1830s and 1840s, it was central to the establishment of a holy commonwealth among a beleaguered band of Mormons who crossed the plains and settled a hostile basin, and it has been the ensign, or banner, under which the Saints in the twentieth century have rallied and gathered. Further, the prophetic vision of Zion does now and will yet provide what might be called the eschatological ideal — the scriptural pattern for the pure society in the last days — the holy community, "a city which hath foundations, whose builder and maker is God." (Hebrews 11:10.) This paper deals with the concept of Zion as made known through Joseph Smith and his successors, focusing primarily upon the philosophy and ideal of Zion as set forth in modern revelation.

ZION: FROM THE BOOK OF MORMON

The word *Zion* first appears in the biblical record in conjunction with David's conquest of Jerusalem, in which it is written that David has taken "the strong hold of Zion: the same is the city of David." (2 Samuel 5:7.) With the movement of the Ark of the Covenant to the Temple Mount, *Zion* came to be used interchangeably with the idea of the holy mountain of Jehovah and thus with the city of Jerusalem. "Great is the Lord," wrote the Psalmist, "and greatly to be praised in the city of our God, in the mountain of his holiness. Beautiful for situation, *the joy of the whole earth, is mount Zion*." (Psalm 48:1–2; italics added.) "Sons of Zion" (Psalm 149:2; Joel 2:23) or "daughters of Zion" (Isaiah 3:16; Zechariah 9:9) came to refer to the men and women of Jerusalem who were recipients of either God's wrath or his blessing.

Joseph Smith's first serious encounter with the concept of *Zion* probably came in his translation of the Book of Mormon. Other than on those occasions where Isaiah is quoted (and thus where Zion has reference to the city of Jerusalem), the word Zion takes on a different meaning and is used in an expanded way. Consider the following:

"And blessed are they who shall seek to bring forth my Zion at that day, for they shall have the gift and power of the Holy Ghost." (1 Nephi 13:37.)

"And this land [America] shall be a land of liberty unto the Gentiles, and there shall be no kings upon the land, who shall raise up unto the Gentiles.

"And I will fortify this land against all other nations.

"And he that fighteth against Zion shall perish, saith God." (2 Nephi 10:11–13.)

"He [God] commandeth that there shall be no priestcrafts; for, behold, priestcrafts are that men preach and set themselves up for a light unto the world, that they may get gain and praise of the world; but they seek not the welfare of Zion.

"Behold, the Lord hath forbidden this thing; wherefore, the Lord God hath given a commandment that all men should have charity, which charity is love. And except they should have charity they were nothing. Wherefore, if they should have charity they would not suffer the laborer in Zion to perish.

"But the laborer in Zion shall labor for Zion; for if they labor for money they shall perish." (2 Nephi 26:29–31.)

"For behold, at that day shall he [Satan] rage in the hearts of the children of men, and stir them up to anger against that which is good.

"And others will he pacify, and lull them away into carnal security, that they will say: All is well in Zion; yea, Zion prospereth, all is well— and thus the devil cheateth their souls, and leadeth them away carefully down to hell. . . .

"Therefore, wo be unto him that is at ease in Zion." (2 Nephi 28:20–21, 24.)

"Verily, verily, I say unto you [the resurrected Christ speaking to the Nephites], thus hath the Father commanded me—that I should give unto this people this land for their inheritance.

"And then the words of the prophet Isaiah shall be fulfilled, which say:

"Thy watchmen shall lift up the voice; with the voice together shall they sing; for they shall see eye to eye when the Lord shall bring again Zion." (3 Nephi 16:16–18.)

The word *Zion* in the Book of Mormon is thus seen to be much broader than a reference to the Old Testament city of Jerusalem. Zion is to be established or "brought forth" under God's direction, and those who fight against it incur the displeasure of the Almighty. From the passages in 2 Nephi 26 and 2 Nephi 28 we are introduced to the word *Zion* in a context of what seems to be a community, or society, of the Saints. This society is one in which the citizens are to labor for "the welfare of Zion" and not for personal aggrandizement; further, the members of the community are to avoid the attitude that "all is well in Zion." The words of Jesus in 3 Nephi 16 are instructive in that a prophecy from Isaiah (52:8) is given a unique interpretation: the inheritance of the land of America by the descendants of the tribe of Joseph is seen to be a fulfillment of the prophecy that "the Lord shall bring again Zion." Thus two usages of *Zion* emerge in the Book of Mormon, each of which would play a key role in the development of the concept of Zion among the Latter-day Saints: (1) Zion as community of the Saints, and (2) Zion as place, the land of America.

ZION: FROM THE PROPHET'S TRANSLATION OF THE BIBLE

In June 1830 Joseph Smith began a careful study of the King James Version of the Bible. With Oliver Cowdery as scribe, he began to prepare what he called a "new translation" of the scriptures, what was called for years the Inspired Version and what we now know as the Joseph Smith Translation of the Bible (JST). John Whitmer, Emma Smith, Frederick G. Williams, Newel K. Whitney, and Sidney Rigdon served, at one time or another, as scribes. Rigdon joined the Church in November 1830, traveled from Ohio to meet the Prophet, and began to labor with Joseph in early December. A journal entry of Joseph Smith in December 1830 regarding his work with the King James Bible is instructive:

"It may be well to observe here, that the Lord greatly encouraged and strengthened the faith of his little flock . . . which had embraced the fulness of the everlasting Gospel, as revealed to them in the Book of Mormon, by giving some more extended information upon the Scriptures, a translation of which had already commenced. Much conjecture and conversation frequently occurred among the Saints, concerning the books mentioned, and referred to, in various places in the Old and New Testaments, which were now nowhere to be found. The common remark was, 'They are lost books'; but it seems the Apostolic Church had some of these writings, as Jude mentions or quotes the prophecy of Enoch, the seventh from Adam. To the joy of the little flock . . . did the Lord reveal the following doings of olden times, from the prophecy of Enoch."[2]

Whereas the biblical record in Genesis 5 contains only three verses descriptive of the ministry of Enoch, Genesis in the Joseph Smith Translation consists of more than one hundred verses. A careful reading of the text reveals the following about Enoch:

1. At the age of sixty-five Enoch was called of God to cry repentance to a wicked people.

2. Though shy, hesitant, and slow of speech, Enoch was given divine assurance and promised great power: "Behold my spirit is upon you, wherefore all thy words will I justify; and the mountains shall flee before you, and the rivers shall turn from their course; and thou shalt abide in me, and I in you; therefore walk with me." (JST Genesis 6:36.)

3. Enoch became a seer and was given a knowledge of "things which were not visible to the natural eye." (JST Genesis 6:38.)

4. Enoch's preaching led many people to repent. The city became so righteous that "the Lord came and dwelt with his people, and they dwelt in righteousness." Further, "the fear of the Lord was upon all nations, so great was the glory of the Lord, which was upon his people." (JST Genesis 7:20–21.)

5. Enoch established an economic order for the poor and needy. "And the Lord called his people Zion, because they were of one heart and one mind, and dwelt in righteousness; and there was no poor among them." The city of Enoch came to be known as "the City of Holiness, even Zion." (JST Genesis 7:23, 25.)

6. Enoch saw in vision a future day when the "elect" would be gathered to a "Holy City," a latter-day community that "shall be called Zion, a New Jerusalem." (JST Genesis 7:70.)

7. Enoch and his people were eventually translated, taken into heaven without experiencing death. "And Enoch and all his people walked with God, and he dwelt in the midst of Zion; and it came to pass that Zion was not, for God received it up into his own bosom; and

from thence went forth the saying, Zion is fled." (JST Genesis 7:77–78.) Later in Genesis, by the way, we learn (through the Prophet's inspired translation) of the people of Melchizedek, a people who "wrought righteousness, and obtained heaven, and sought for the city of Enoch which God had before taken, separating it from the earth, having reserved it unto the latter days, or the end of the world." (JST Genesis 14:34.)

Joseph Smith's discovery of the Zion of Enoch through his work of Bible translation became pivotal in the quest for a society of Zion among the Mormons. Enoch became the pattern, the scriptural prototype by which all social, economic, or spiritual programs were to be judged. "The vision of Enoch," one anthropologist has written, "helped define Zion's social order, which was called on occasion the 'city' or 'order of Enoch.' " In addition, Enoch's city "came to be the divine model for the Mormons' earthly undertakings, the platonic essence, if you will, of [the Prophet's] subsequent commandments and revelations on the subject. According to this vision, Zion's ideal urban order would be permeated by religion. Religion, not politics, would ensure domestic tranquility. Religion, not the military, would provide for the common defense. Religion, not economics, would promote the general welfare." In short, the Prophet's revelation of Enoch "gave theological, cosmological, eschatological, social, and personal sanction to the quest for Zion."[3]

ZION: A SPECIFIC LOCATION

As we have seen, Joseph Smith would have encountered the notion of Zion as a community of the believers from the Book of Mormon and from his translation of the Bible. Among the earliest revelations given in this dispensation was the repeated command: "Now, as you have asked, behold, I say unto you, keep my commandments, and seek to bring forth and establish the cause of Zion." (D&C 6:6; see also 11:6; 12:6; 14:6.) Zion thus came to be associated with the restored Church and the grander work of the Restoration, and the faithful could take heart in the midst of their troubles, for Zion was the city of God (D&C 97:19); indeed, in speaking of the sacred spot where the people of God congregated, the Lord said, "Behold, the land of Zion—I, the Lord, hold it in mine own hands." (D&C 63:25.)

Isaiah the prophet had spoken some seven hundred years before Christ of the "mountain of the Lord's house" being established in the

tops of the mountains. (Isaiah 2:2.) In harmony with what was made
known to him through his translation of the Book of Mormon, Joseph
the Prophet declared in July 1840 that "the land of Zion consists of all
North and South America, but that any place where the Saints gather
is Zion."[4] That Isaiah's phrase "mountain of the Lord's house" referred
to a place of gathering is attested by a statement of Joseph Smith made
just two months before his death: "The whole of North and South
America," he taught, "is Zion; the mountain of the Lord's house is in
the center of North and South America."[5]

The idea that there was a more specific location for the city of Zion
within the whole of North and South America began to be made known
very early. To Oliver Cowdery — in his call to a preaching mission among
the Lamanites — the Lord explained as early as September 1830 that
"it is not revealed, and no man knoweth where the city Zion shall be
built, but it shall be given hereafter." The Lord then added that the
location "shall be on the borders by the Lamanites." (D&C 28:9.) It
was on 20 July 1831, just as the leaders of the Saints had begun to
arrive in Missouri, that the word of the Lord came concerning the
specific location of Zion in that early day of restoration: "Hearken, O
ye elders of my church," the revelation began, "who have assembled
yourselves together, according to my commandments, in this land,
which is the land of Missouri, which is the land which I have appointed
and consecrated for the gathering of the saints. Wherefore, *this is the
land of promise, and the place for the city of Zion. . . . the place which is
now called Independence is the center place;* and a spot for the temple is
lying westward." (D&C 57:1–3; italics added.)

That the Master intended that Independence, Jackson County, Missouri, be recognized as Zion in the early nineteenth century — and
further, that this was to be the eventual site of the New Jerusalem and
a vital location in the winding up scenes prior to the coming of Christ
in glory — is attested by the Lord's explanation that he will "contend
with Zion, and plead with her strong ones, and chasten her until she
overcomes and is clean before me." And then, significantly, the Savior
adds, "For she shall not be removed out of her place. I, the Lord, have
spoken it. Amen." (D&C 90:36–37; compare 101:17.) Even years later
the leaders of the Church continued to preach that a return to Missouri
was a necessary part of the establishment of Zion. For example, Orson
Pratt stated emphatically in 1870 that "there is one thing sure — as
sure as the sun shines forth in yonder heavens, so sure will the Lord

fulfil one thing with regard to this people. What is that? He will return them to Jackson county, and in the western part of the State of Missouri they will build up a city which shall be called Zion, which will be the head-quarters of this Latter-day Saint Church; and that will be the place where the prophets, apostles and inspired men of God will have their head-quarters. It will be the place where the Lord God will manifest Himself to His people, as He has promised in the Scriptures, as well as in modern revelation.

" 'Do you believe that?' says one. Just as much as we believed, long before it came to pass, what has taken place. The world can believe what has taken place, because it has been fulfilled. The Latter-day Saints believe in prophecies before they take place. We have just as much confidence in returning to Jackson county and the building of a great central city that will remain there a thousand years before the earth passes away, as the Jews have in returning to Jerusalem and re-building the waste places of Palestine."[6]

ZION: A STATE OF BEING

In time the concept of Zion began to expand in the minds of the Saints, so that *Zion* came to refer not only to a specific location — be it Jackson County or even Kirtland, Ohio (see D&C 94:1; 96:1) — but also to a state of being, a state of righteousness. "Let Zion rejoice," the prophetic word acclaimed, "for this is Zion — THE PURE IN HEART; therefore, let Zion rejoice, while all the wicked shall mourn." (D&C 97:21.) Zion was to be the abode of the faithful, the gathering place of the pure in heart, no matter its location. The rebellious had no place in Zion (D&C 64:35), for Zion was to become a holy commonwealth wherein the law of the celestial kingdom was to be in effect (D&C 105:5, 32). President Brigham Young thus spoke of the Saints having Zion in their heart. "Unless the people live before the Lord in the obedience of His commandments, they cannot have Zion within them. They must carry it with them, if they expect to live in it, to enjoy it, and increase in it. . . .

" . . . As to the spirit of Zion, it is in the hearts of the Saints, of those who love and serve the Lord with all their might, mind, and strength."[7]

On another occasion he affirmed: "Zion will be redeemed and built up, and the Saints will rejoice. This is the land of Zion; and who are Zion? *The pure in heart are Zion; they have Zion within them.* Purify yourselves, sanctify the Lord God in your hearts, and have the Zion of God within you, and then you will rejoice more and more."[8]

Finally, President Young alluded to the scriptural warning found in Doctrine and Covenants 45:68. "The time is nigh," he taught, "when every man that will not take up his sword against his neighbour must needs flee to Zion. *Where is Zion? Where the organization of the Church of God is. And may it dwell spiritually in every heart;* and may we so live as to always enjoy the Spirit of Zion!"[9]

ZION AND THE ECONOMY

From the very beginning the Saints were encouraged to put their trust "in that Spirit which leadeth to do good—yea, to do justly, to walk humbly, to judge righteously; and this is my Spirit." (D&C 11:12.) This spirit of unselfishness, of brotherhood and equity, was what had characterized the Nephites during their golden era. Of that supernal season Mormon wrote: "And they taught, and did minister one to another; and they had all things common among them, every man dealing justly, one with another." (3 Nephi 26:19.) People who trust in the Spirit of the Lord, who give themselves over to the mind of the Almighty, come to love as he loves, to seek out and succor the needy, to see to the wants of those who hunger and thirst. It follows naturally, therefore, that the Lord should reveal those principles by which individuals and societies can be made one. Joseph the Prophet had learned of Enoch's day that "the Lord called his people Zion, because they were of one heart and one mind, and dwelt in righteousness; and there was no poor among them." (Moses 7:18.) Less than a month after teaching his latter-day Saints about the ancient City of Holiness enjoyed by his former-day Saints, the Lord counseled his people by parable: "Let every man esteem his brother as himself, and practise virtue and holiness before me.

"And again I say unto you, let every man esteem his brother as himself.

"For what man among you having twelve sons, and is no respecter of them, and they serve him obediently, and he saith unto the one: Be thou clothed in robes and sit thou here; and to the other: Be thou clothed in rags and sit thou there—and looketh upon his sons and saith I am just?

"Behold, this I have given unto you as a parable, and it is even as

I am. I say unto you, be one; and if ye are not one ye are not mine."
(D&C 38:24–27.)

God soon made known to the Latter-day Saints those ideals and
principles by which a modern Zion could be set up. Indeed, fundamental
laws and principles of consecration and stewardship occupy a substantial
portion of the Doctrine and Covenants; further, the economic implementation of the law of consecration in Ohio and Missouri, as well as
the dissemination of the higher covenants of consecration in Nauvoo,
proved to be a righteous obsession of Joseph Smith and the early leaders
of the Church.[10] Formal instructions began with the revelation known
as the law of the Church, section 42 of the Doctrine and Covenants,
and pressing particulars concerning the role of the bishop in the care
of the poor (D&C 41; 72), the deeding of properties (D&C 51), and the
care of widows and the fatherless (D&C 83) soon followed. When the
Saints proved unable, because of circumstances and selfishness, to live
fully the economic principles set forth in the revelations and which
characterize the society of Zion, the Lord explained that "were it
for the transgressions of my people, speaking concerning the ch
and not individuals, they might have been redeemed even now.

"But behold, they have not learned to be obedient to the th   s
which I required at their hands, but are full of all manner of evil,   d
do not impart of their substance, as becometh saints, to the poor   d
afflicted among them;

"And are not united according to the union required by the la v of
the celestial kingdom;

"And Zion cannot be built up unless it is by the principles of the
law of the celestial kingdom; otherwise I cannot receive her unto myself." (D&C 105:2–5.)

ZION: THE PLACE OF GATHERING

Zion is a place of gathering. Those who accept the true Messiah
and unite with the true church are gathered into the fold of the true
Shepherd. The Latter-day Saints in the days of Joseph Smith anticipated
the complete realization of the prophesied day when "the Lord thy God
will turn thy captivity, and have compassion upon thee, and will return
and gather thee from all the nations." (Deuteronomy 30:3.) The society
of Zion was the ensign, and the converts to the faith were those who
would gather to the city of holiness. In the words of the modern seer,
the gathering "is a principle I esteem to be of the greatest importance

to those who are looking for salvation in this generation. . . . All that the prophets that have written, . . . in speaking of the salvation of Israel in the last days, goes directly to show that it consists in the work of the gathering."[11]

There were a number of reasons for a gathering, or clustering, of modern Israel. First, the gathering served to establish a sense of identity and focus for a people who were often shunned or persecuted for their peculiar beliefs. The one thing that all Saints from all parts of the world could share was an identity as a people, a "nation," a remnant drawn to a central site.

Second, the gathering provided the Latter-day Saints with a broader base from which to conduct missionary activities. Israel was to be gathered to her rightful locale through an acceptance and worship of the true God as taught by the true Church. "We are gathering the people as fast as we can," President Brigham Young stated. "We are gathering them to make Saints of them and of ourselves."[12] "Ye are called to bring to pass the gathering of mine elect," six elders were told in 1830, "for mine elect hear my voice and harden not their hearts." (D&C 29:7.)

Third, modern Israel gathered to a central location to escape the perils and the pull of Babylon and the coming destruction upon the wicked. A revelation received in November 1831 thus announced: "Yea, verily I say unto you again, the time has come when the voice of the Lord is unto you: Go ye out of Babylon; gather ye out from among the nations." Those in the world who were among the Gentiles were to "flee unto Zion." (D&C 133:7, 12.) "The time is near," Joseph Smith warned, "when the sun will be darkened, and the moon turn to blood, and the stars fall from heaven, and the earth reel to and fro. Then, if this is the case, and if we are not sanctified and gathered to the places God has appointed, with all our former professions and our great love for the Bible, we must fall; we cannot stand; we cannot be saved; for God will gather out his Saints from the Gentiles, and then comes desolation and destruction, and none can escape except the pure in heart who are gathered."[13]

Fourth, the Saints gathered to a central location in order to build temples, holy houses wherein the heavens were tied to the earth and the infinite powers of heaven extended to finite man. Joseph Smith asked: "What was the object of gathering the Jews, or the people of God in any age of the world? . . .

"The main object was to build unto the Lord a house whereby He could reveal unto His people the ordinances of His house and the glories of His kingdom, and teach the people the way of salvation; for there are certain ordinances and principles that, when they are taught and practiced, must be done in a place or house built for that purpose."[14]

In summary, people were to gather to Zion to prepare a city of holiness on earth similar to the one enjoyed by our scriptural prototype, Enoch. "In speaking of the gathering," the Prophet explained, "we mean to be understood as speaking of it according to scripture, the gathering of the elect of the Lord out of every nation on earth, and bringing them to the place of the Lord of Hosts, when the city of righteousness shall be built, and where the people shall be of one heart and one mind, when the Savior comes: yea, when the people shall walk with God like Enoch, and be free from sin. The word of the Lord is precious; and when we read that the veil spread over all nations will be destroyed, and the pure in heart see God, and reign with Him a thousand years on earth, we want all honest men to have a chance to gather and build up a city of righteousness, where even upon the bells of the horses shall be written *'Holiness to the Lord.'* "[15]

With the powers to gather Israel restored to Joseph Smith and Oliver Cowdery through the theophanies of the Kirtland Temple in 1836 (D&C 110), the Latter-day Saints became serious about the obligations resting upon them in the matter of gathering. During the first ten years of the British Mission's operation, 17,849 persons were baptized.[16] Such persons were not only counseled in matters of doctrine and theology, but were also encouraged to gather to Zion in the United States; more than 4,700 of these converts uprooted themselves and traveled to Nauvoo, Illinois.[17] Immigration to Utah totaled more than 85,000.[18] The directive to gather became a duty and a commandment. "You can serve Him just as well anywhere else [as in the Salt Lake valley]," President Brigham Young taught in 1855, *"when it is your duty to be there. If it is not your duty to be anywhere else, if you would serve him acceptably, it must be where He calls you."*[19]

By the end of the nineteenth century the leaders of the Church began to sense the need for strength in remote areas, to envision the necessity of establishing the central tent of Zion with numerous stakes being driven solidly into the soil of distant lands. That the Lord himself had anticipated such development is seen in a revelation received in

December 1833. In the midst of the Missouri persecutions, the word of the Lord came to modern Israel:

"Zion shall not be moved out of her place, notwithstanding her children are scattered.

"They that remain, and are pure in heart, shall return, and come to their inheritances, they and their children, with songs of everlasting joy, to build up the waste places of Zion—

"And all these things that the prophets might be fulfilled.

"And, behold, there is none other place appointed than that which I have appointed; neither shall there be any other place appointed than that which I have appointed, for the work of the gathering of my saints—

"*Until the day cometh when there is found no more room for them; and then I have other places which I will appoint unto them, and they shall be called stakes,* for the curtains or the strength of Zion." (D&C 101:17–21; italics added.)

By 1911 the First Presidency of the Church had issued the following statement regarding the gathering to a central location: "The establishment of the latter-day Zion on the American continent occasions the gathering of the Saints from all nations. This is not compulsory, and particularly under present conditions, is not urged, because it is desirable that our people shall remain in their native lands and form congregations of a permanent character to aid in the work of proselyting."[20] Some six decades later Elder Bruce R. McConkie delivered an address to the Saints in Mexico and Central America that serves as a doctrinal benchmark in the matter of gathering to Zion: "This gathering has commenced and shall continue until the righteous are assembled into the congregations of the Saints in all the nations of the earth." And then, becoming more specific, Elder McConkie pointed out that "the place of gathering for the Mexican Saints is in Mexico; the place of gathering for the Guatemalan Saints is in Guatemala; the place of gathering for the Brazilian Saints is in Brazil; and so it goes throughout the length and breadth of the whole earth. Japan is for the Japanese; Korea is for the Koreans; Australia is for the Australians; *every nation is the gathering place for its own people.*"[21]

ZION: THE IDEAL SOCIETY

The establishment of a Zion society entailed more to Joseph Smith than simply the explication of religious doctrine on Sunday mornings. Although religion was the foundation for such a community, yet the ultimate challenge was to so structure the activities of the citizens as to engender the principles of Zion within all phases of life — social, economic, political, and, of course, spiritual. "I intend to lay a foundation," Joseph Smith boldly declared, "that will revolutionize the whole world." And then, emphasizing the source of this revolutionary movement, he added, "It will not be by sword or gun that this kingdom will roll on: the power of truth is such that all nations will be under the necessity of obeying the Gospel."[22] Zion was to stand as a banner, an ensign, to the people of the earth.

"Zion as the heart of the kingdom of God was to be an ensign and a standard to the world, that all men might look to her and pattern their lives and their social arrangements after her example of truth and righteousness. An ensign is a distinguished flag or banner, used in ancient times to direct the actions of men such as in a military campaign. As an ensign to the world in the last days, Zion was to be a rallying point of truth — to attract the attention of all men and direct them into the paths of peace and progression.

"As a messenger before the Lord, the society of Zion was to be a nucleus of the millennial kingdom — an opening wedge — containing the basic principles and powers through which, eventually, peace and good will could be established universally among men. The divine system was to be developed among the Saints first, and then expanded throughout the earth as the millennial kingdom of Christ was ushered in."[23]

Zion was and is to be the focus of all that is good, all that is ennobling, all that is instructive and inspirational. In Zion all things were to be gathered together in one in Christ. (Ephesians 1:10.) In addition, the Saints were to judge by a set of standards derived and obtained from a source beyond that of unenlightened man. "Behold, I, the Lord, have made my church in these last days like unto a judge sitting on a hill, or in a high place, to judge the nations. For it shall come to pass that the inhabitants of Zion shall judge all things pertaining to Zion." (D&C 64:37–38.) In short, "every accomplishment, every polished grace, every useful attainment in mathematics, music, in all science and art belong to the Saints."[24] The Saints "rapidly collect the intelligence that is bestowed upon the nations, for all this intelligence belongs to Zion."[25] The following ideas, attributed to Joseph Smith, illustrate the spirit of Zion that was meant to be a part of every facet of life among the Saints:

"He [the Prophet] recommended the Saints to cultivate as high a state of perfection in their musical harmonies as the standard of the faith which he had brought was superior to sectarian religion. To obtain this, he gave them to understand that the refinement of singing would depend upon the attainment of the Holy Spirit. . . . When these graces and refinements and all the kindred attractions are obtained that characterized the ancient Zion of Enoch, then the Zion of the last days will become beautiful, she will be hailed by the Saints from the four winds, who will gather to Zion with songs of everlasting joy."[26]

In seeking to expand the Latter-day Saints' vision of what could be accomplished through the elevated perspective provided by the gospel, President Spencer W. Kimball observed that "our own talent, obsessed with dynamism from a CAUSE" could produce masterpieces in literature and art that will yet surpass what has been rendered by the world's greatest. "Take a da Vinci or a Michelangelo or a Shakespeare and give him a total knowledge of the plan of salvation of God and personal revelation and cleanse him, and then take a look at the statues he will carve and the murals he will paint and the masterpieces he will produce. Take a Handel with his purposeful effort, his superb talent, his earnest desire to properly depict the story, and give him inward vision of the whole true story and revelation, and what a master you have!"[27]

Perhaps one of the most glorious and expansive visions of Zion and the people of God was shared by President John Taylor. He explained that the Saints shall yet "rear splendid edifices, magnificent temples and beautiful cities that shall become the pride, praise and glory of the whole earth. We believe that this people will excel in literature, in science and the arts and in manufactures. In fact, there will be a concentration of wisdom, not only of the combined wisdom of the world as it now exists, but men will be inspired in regard to all these matters in a manner and to an extent that they never have been before, and we shall have eventually, when the Lord's purposes are carried out, the most magnificent buildings, the most pleasant and beautiful gardens, the richest and most costly clothing, and be the most healthy and the most intellectual people that will reside upon the earth. This is part and parcel of our faith. . . . the people, from the President down, will all be under the guidance and direction of the Lord in all the pursuits of human life, until eventually they will be enabled to erect cities that will be fit to be caught up—that when Zion descends from above, Zion will also ascend from beneath, and be prepared to associate with those from above. . . . This is the idea, in brief, that we have entertained in relation to many of these things."[28]

Truly, "Zion must increase in beauty, and in holiness; her borders must be enlarged; her stakes must be strengthened; yea, verily I say unto you, Zion must arise and put on her beautiful garments." (D&C 82:14.)

CONCLUSION

The quest for the city of God among the Latter-day Saints – the quest for Zion – has been and continues to be a noble cause among our people, providing both direction and motivation toward that eschatological ideal we have come to know as a society of the pure in heart. Zion, "the highest order of priesthood society,"[29] is a concept that has grown and expanded since the time Joseph Smith encountered it in the Book of Mormon in the early part of the last century. It, like many other aspects of the restored gospel, has been unfolded to the people of modern Israel by the God of Israel in "line upon line, precept upon precept" fashion. "New circumstances," Elder Orson Pratt noted, "require new power, new knowledge, new additions, new strength."[30]

Elder Erastus Snow pointed out in 1884 that when the early Saints "first heard the fullness of the Gospel preached by the first Elders, and read the revelations given through the Prophet Joseph Smith, *our ideas of Zion were very limited.* But as our minds began to grow and expand, why we began to look upon Zion as a great people, and the Stakes of Zion as numerous. . . . *We ceased to set bounds to Zion and her Stakes.*"[31] As Zion has grown, so has our understanding of Zion. And a part of that understanding is an appreciation for the patient maturity required for the regeneration of a people and the renovation of a society, an awareness that Zion is established "in process of time." (Moses 7:21.) Neither spiritual marathons nor excessive zeal are required; rather, the peaceful plodding that characterizes those who have a "steadfastness in Christ" (2 Nephi 31:20) will result in purity of heart and achievement of the prophetic ideal. "Let our anxiety be centred upon this one thing," President Brigham Young counseled, "the sanctification of our own hearts, the purifying of our own affections, the preparing of ourselves for the approach of the events that are hastening upon us." And then in a manner that has particular relevance to those of us who grow impatient with the Lord's timetable, President Young added: "Be satisfied to let the Lord have his own time and way, and

be patient. Seek to have the Spirit of Christ, that we may . . . prepare
ourselves for the times that are coming. This is our duty."[32]

NOTES

1. Joseph Smith, *Teachings of the Prophet Joseph Smith*, sel. Joseph Fielding
Smith (Salt Lake City: Deseret Book Co., 1976), p. 160.

2. Joseph Smith, *History of The Church of Jesus Christ of Latter-day Saints*,
ed. B. H. Roberts, 2d ed. rev. (Salt Lake City: Deseret Book Co., 1957), 1:131–
33.

3. Steven L. Olsen, "Zion: The Structure of a Theological Revolution," *Sunstone*, vol. 6, no. 6 (November-December 1981), pp. 24–25.

4. Andrew F. Ehat and Lyndon W. Cook, eds., *The Words of Joseph Smith*
(Provo, Utah: Religious Studies Center, Brigham Young University, 1980), p. 415;
spelling and punctuation standardized.

5. Ibid., p. 363; spelling and punctuation standardized. See also Smith, *Teachings of the Prophet Joseph Smith*, p. 362.

6. Orson Pratt, in *Journal of Discourses* (London: Latter-day Saints' Book
Depot, F. D. Richards & Sons, 1855–86), 13:138; see also 2:57, 60; 11:324; 17:291–
306. Note the following from Brigham Young: "Where is the centre stake of Zion?
In Jackson County, Missouri. Were I to try to prevent you from going there, I
could not do it. Can the wicked? No. Can the devils in hell? No, they cannot."
(Ibid., 8:198.)

7. Brigham Young, in *Journal of Discourses*, 2:253.

8. Ibid., 8:198; italics added.

9. Ibid., 8:205.

10. For a detailed treatment of the various phases and periods of consecration
in the Church during the administration of Joseph Smith, see Lyndon W. Cook,
Joseph Smith and the Law of Consecration (Provo, Utah: Grandin Books, 1985).

11. Smith, *Teachings of the Prophet Joseph Smith*, p. 83.

12. Brigham Young, in *Journal of Discourses*, 9:137–38.

13. Smith, *Teachings of the Prophet Joseph Smith*, p. 71; see also p. 101.

14. Ibid., pp. 307–8; see also Brigham Young, in *Journal of Discourses*, 12:161.

15. Smith, *Teachings of the Prophet Joseph Smith*, p. 93.

16. *Latter-day Saints' Millennial Star*, 8:90 (15 October 1846).

17. Leonard J. Arrington and Davis Bitton, *The Mormon Experience* (New York:
Alfred A. Knopf, 1979), p. 129.

18. Ibid., p. 136.

19. Brigham Young, in *Journal of Discourses*, 2:253; italics added.

20. *Messages of the First Presidency*, comp. James R. Clark, 6 vols. (Salt Lake
City: Bookcraft, 1965–75), 4:222.

21. Mexico and Central America Area Conference Report, Aug. 1972, pp. 43,
45.

22. Smith, *History of the Church*, 6:365.

23. Hyrum L. Andrus, *Doctrines of the Kingdom* (Salt Lake City: Bookcraft, 1973), pp. 28, 29.

24. Brigham Young, in *Journal of Discourses*, 10:224.

25. Ibid., 8:279.

26. Cited in Joseph Young, "Vocal Music," in *History of the Organization of the Seventies* (Salt Lake City: Deseret Steam Printing Establishment, 1878), pp. 14–15.

27. Spencer W. Kimball, "The Gospel Vision of the Arts," *Ensign*, July 1977, p. 5.

28. John Taylor, in *Journal of Discourses*, 10:147.

29. Spencer W. Kimball, in Conference Report, Oct. 1977, p. 125.

30. Orson Pratt, in *Journal of Discourses*, 22:36.

31. Erastus Snow, in *Journal of Discourses*, 25:30–31; italics added.

32. Brigham Young, in *Journal of Discourses*, 9:3.

CHAPTER FOURTEEN

The Second Gathering of the Literal Seed

Monte S. Nyman

Associate Dean of Religious Education
Brigham Young University

The tenth article of faith of The Church of Jesus Christ of Latter-day Saints (hereafter referred to as the Church) declares, "We believe in the literal gathering of Israel." The second gathering of Israel was foreseen by Moses, Isaiah, Jeremiah, Ezekiel, and other Old Testament prophets.[1] The Book of Mormon prophets also foretold this great latter-day event.[2] The evidence given through scripture, both ancient and modern, is that the house of Israel has been, is being, and will be literally gathered in these latter days and that this gathering is being consummated in The Church of Jesus Christ of Latter-day Saints.

Twenty-six sections in the Doctrine and Covenants confirm that the literal blood of Israel is in most members of the Church today. Twenty-three of these sections are quite definite in this declaration, whereas three other sections are not quite as definite. This literal gathering is further supported by statements in the Book of Mormon and the Pearl of Great Price and by statements made by presidents of the Church and members of the Quorum of the Twelve Apostles.[3] All of these sources confirm that many biblical statements are being fulfilled. This work will not attempt to include all of these supporting evidences, however, but will focus on the testimony of the Doctrine and Covenants.

THE COVENANT OF ABRAHAM

Father Abraham was promised that "in [his] seed shall all the kindreds of the earth be blessed."[4] The Pearl of Great Price establishes that this blessing to Abraham would be fulfilled through "the literal seed, or the seed of the body."[5] That the early brethren of the Church were of that

186

seed and were fulfilling that covenant is repeatedly stated in the Doctrine and Covenants.

In reiterating those who would again "drink of the fruit of the vine" with him on the earth at a future great meeting,[6] the Lord named "Joseph and Jacob and Isaac, and Abraham, your fathers, by whom the promises remain."[7] The designation of these great patriarchs as "your fathers, by whom the promises remain" confirms that the early brethren were literal descendants and also that the covenants, or promises, made to them were still in effect and not yet fulfilled. The Saints' identification with the ancient patriarchs as their "fathers" is made repeatedly in the revelations in the Doctrine and Covenants.

Following the Latter-day Saints' being driven out of Missouri, in 1834 the Lord revealed to them that the redemption of Zion would come and that he would raise up a man to lead them as Moses had led the children of Israel, "For ye are the children of Israel, and of the seed of Abraham." He further verified that they would be led as their "fathers" had been led, and he gave promise to them of angelic forerunners as he had to their "fathers."[8] Upon the completion of the Kirtland Temple two years later, the Lord appeared and accepted that temple, and Elias also appeared. Elias "committed the dispensation of the gospel of Abraham, saying that in us and our seed all generations after us should be blessed."[9] Thus were restored the keys, or directing power, for the fulfillment of the promise made to Abraham that through his seed all nations would be blessed. The covenant made to Abraham to bless all nations was under way.

In an earlier revelation, the Lord had instructed the Saints to "renounce war and proclaim peace, and seek diligently to turn the hearts of the children to their *fathers*, and the hearts of the *fathers* to the children."[10] Although this revelation is not as pronounced regarding Abraham as the previous one cited, the use of "fathers" when compared to other contexts and the fact that Abraham had seen the future days[11] make it seem obvious that the fathers spoken of in this revelation in the Doctrine and Covenants are Abraham and the succeeding patriarchs to whom the restoration promises were made.

One other revelation in the Doctrine and Covenants has some relevance to Abraham's literal seed. In Section 84 the Lord traced for latter-day Israel the Melchizedek Priesthood authority from Moses back to Abraham and from Abraham back to Adam. He spoke of the responsibilities of this priesthood and of the priesthood of Aaron in making "an acceptable offering and sacrifice in the house of the Lord" in the New Jerusalem. Although it does so indirectly, this passage shows that Moses' and Aaron's literal seed, who are also literal seed of Abraham, are to be involved in the latter-day temple in the new Jerusalem. Furthermore, through these priesthoods, the faithful recipients "become the sons of Moses and of Aaron and the seed of Abraham, and the church and kingdom, and the elect of God."[12] This passage means not only that those who are faithful in their rightful heirship will finally be the covenant people of Abraham but also that those who are not of the literal seed are adopted into the covenant line. The literal seed and those adopted into that lineage are today fulfilling the covenant of Abraham. The Church and kingdom and the elect of God (the covenant people) are once more upon the earth. Because Abraham's literal seed are promised to be the heirs of that covenant, it has to involve them.

JOSEPH SMITH FULFILLS ABRAHAM'S COVENANT

In March 1838 Joseph Smith answered certain questions on the writings of Isaiah. The Prophet's answers were all prefaced by "thus saith the Lord," showing that they were given to him by revelation from the Lord. He identified the rod spoken of in Isaiah 11:1 as "a servant in the hands of Christ, who is partly a descendant of Jesse as well as of Ephraim, or of the house of Joseph, on whom there is laid much power."[13] Jesse is the father of King David and of the lineage of Judah. This descendant of Jesse (Judah) and Joseph is undoubtedly Joseph Smith himself, although in his modesty the Prophet did not identify himself in that role. He was given power to translate the Book of Mormon, which gift would fulfill the last part of the prophecy.[14] Joseph Smith further interpreted the root of Jesse spoken of in Isaiah 10:11 as "a descendant of Jesse, as well as of Joseph, unto whom rightly belongs the priesthood, and the keys of the kingdom, for an ensign, and for the gathering of my people in the last days."[15] The life of Joseph Smith also sustains himself as the root of Jesse spoken of by Isaiah. That the priesthood rightly belonged to him is evidenced by the angel Moroni's declaration to him in September 1823 that "God had a work for [him] to do."[16] He was foreordained to his very work in the premortal council.[17] The keys of the kingdom were delivered to him and were "never [to] be taken from [him], while [he was] in the world, neither in the world to come."[18] Thus, he holds the keys of this dispensation.

The keys committed to the foreordained prophet Joseph Smith

included those of "the dispensation of the gospel of Abraham," and the Prophet was told that "in us [the priesthood holders of this last dispensation] and our seed all generations after us should be blessed."[19] The covenant to Abraham was that through him and his seed all the kindreds of the earth were to be blessed,[20] and this blessing was to be accomplished through the literal seed of Abraham who would bear the priesthood and the ministry.[21] Earlier Joseph Smith had been told that he was from the loins of Abraham and that the promise of Abraham was Joseph Smith's also because of this lineage.[22] Therefore, he was to do the work of Abraham.[23] Six months after the question-and-answer revelation wherein were identified the rod and the root of Jesse, the Lord again revealed that Joseph Smith was the person through whom the covenant of Abraham would be fulfilled:

"And as I said unto Abraham concerning the kindreds of the earth, even so I say unto my servant Joseph: In thee and in thy seed shall the kindred of the earth be blessed."[24]

Further evidence of Joseph Smith's lineage being of Abraham is given later on in the same revelation. Hyrum Smith, Joseph's older brother, was called to "the office of Priesthood and Patriarch, which was appointed unto him by his father, by blessing and also by right; that from henceforth he shall hold the keys of the patriarchal blessings upon the heads of all my people."[25] Joseph Smith, Sr., the father of Hyrum and Joseph Smith, Jr., had been the first Patriarch to the Church. This office was now to be held by Hyrum, not only because of Hyrum's having been designated by his father but also because it was his right as the oldest, faithful, living descendant of Abraham. The Prophet Joseph explained:

"An Evangelist is a Patriarch, even the oldest man of the blood of Joseph or of the seed of Abraham. Wherever the Church of Christ is established in the earth, there should be a Patriarch for the benefit of the posterity of the Saints, as it was with Jacob in giving his patriarchal blessing unto his sons, etc."[26]

President Brigham Young said further that the Lord "has watched that family and that blood as it has circulated from its fountain to the birth of that man [Joseph Smith]."[27]

DESCENDANTS OF JOSEPH AND EPHRAIM

The covenant made to Abraham was passed on to Abraham's seed by birthright and went to Isaac, then to Jacob, and then to Joseph who was sold into Egypt.[28] Many great covenants and blessings were likewise promised to Joseph and his seed.[29] These promises were, of course, an extension of Abraham's covenant. Likewise, the fulfillment of Abraham's and Joseph's blessings was not limited to the family of Joseph Smith, Sr. Others of the lineage of Joseph of Egypt were recipients of the same fulfillment. At a conference of high priests on 4 June 1833, John Johnson was given "a promise of eternal life inasmuch as he keepeth my commandments from henceforth — for he is a descendant of Joseph and a partaker of the blessings of the promise made unto his fathers."[30] Again, the blessings of the fathers are the blessings of Abraham, Isaac, Jacob, and Joseph. Other members of the Church collectively had the same blessings extended to them but in the context of their being descendants of Ephraim, the son of Joseph of Egypt, to whom the birthright was granted.[31]

On 1 August 1831, the "residue of the elders" of the Church were told that it would be "many years" before they received their "inheritance" in the land of Zion (Jackson County, Missouri) because they were to "push the people together from the ends of the earth. Wherefore, . . . let them preach the gospel in the regions round about."[32] The pushing of the people together from the ends of the earth was the blessing given by Moses to the seed of Joseph. Those pushed together were to be the ten thousands of Ephraim and the thousands of Manasseh.[33] Therefore the elders of the Church are the descendants of Joseph who are sent out to gather Ephraim and Manasseh from among the Gentiles. Nearly three months later, on 25 October 1831, the Lord reiterated this mission at a conference of the Church in a revelation to William E. McLellin.[34]

The Lord establishes his word in the mouths of two or three witnesses.[35] At the same October conference, the Lord gave a third witness that those being pushed together were of Ephraim. At this conference it was determined to compile and publish the revelations given to Joseph Smith as the Book of Commandments, and what is now known as Doctrine and Covenants 133 was revealed as an appendix to the compilation. In this appendix, the Lord outlined future events in the gathering of Israel to the promised lands of Jerusalem and Zion. Those gathered, or returning from the north countries, are to "bring forth their rich treasures unto the children of Ephraim, my servants."[36] These servants are the members of the Church who have already been gathered, or "pushed together," in fulfillment of Joseph's blessing.

Those coming from the north countries to the everlasting hills shall "be crowned with glory, even in Zion [the Americas], by the hands of the servants of the Lord, even the children of Ephraim."[37] The Lord then confirmed that this will be "the blessing of the everlasting God upon the tribes of Israel, and the richer blessing upon the head of Ephraim and his fellows [others of Israel who have been gathered to Zion already or Gentiles who have been adopted into Israel]."[38] The literal gathering of Ephraim and their role as the birthright holder is thus firmly established.

Hosea, the Old Testament prophet, foreknew the role of Ephraim in the latter-day gathering.[39] The concept of Ephraim as the servant also opens up the interpretation of several other Old Testament prophecies. Israel, whom the Lord has taken, or gathered, from the ends of the earth, is repeatedly identified as the Lord's servant by the prophet Isaiah.[40]

The Prophet Joseph Smith further confirmed this concept of the servant in interpreting Isaiah's meaning of the phrase "Put on thy strength, O Zion" in Isaiah 52:1.

"He had reference to those whom God should call in the last days, who should hold the power of priesthood to bring again Zion, and the redemption of Israel; and to put on her strength is to put on the authority of the priesthood, *which she, Zion, has a right to by lineage;* also to return to that power which she had lost." The Prophet also identified those in Zion as "the scattered remnants" and "the remnants of Israel in their scattered condition among the Gentiles."[41] Ephraim was to fulfill the covenant of Abraham in gathering together Joseph's seed and others of the house of Israel in the latter days.

THE KEYS OF THE GATHERING

The role of the elders of the Church as legitimate gatherers of the remnants of Israel was established by Moses, the ancient leader of Israel's exodus from Egypt. He appeared to Joseph Smith and Oliver Cowdery on 3 April 1836 in the newly built Kirtland Temple "and committed unto [them] the keys of the gathering of Israel from the four parts of the earth, and the leading of the ten tribes from the land of the north."[42] That the gathering from the four parts of the earth and the leading of the ten tribes from the north are two separate movements that will be accomplished in that chronological order is supported by the servants (Ephraim) first being gathered and then blessing the ten tribes upon their return, as outlined in Doctrine and Covenants 133. The tenth article of faith also separates the two events: "We believe in the literal gathering of Israel and in the restoration of the Ten Tribes." The literal gathering of Israel would logically be accomplished through the birthright tribe, Ephraim, as Doctrine and Covenants 133 confirms. Further, Joseph F. Smith, then President of the Church, observed in November 1902: "A striking peculiarity of the Saints gathered from all parts of the earth is that they are almost universally of the blood of Ephraim."[43] The gathering of Ephraim is well under way. The prophecy of the ten tribes returning from the north is yet to be fulfilled.

The prayer dedicating the Kirtland Temple, given by revelation to Joseph Smith, further illustrates the servants' role in the gathering in the last days. The prayer asks that "thy [the Lord's] servants, the sons of Jacob, may gather out the righteous to build a holy city to thy [the Lord's] name"[44] from all the nations of the earth. The prophet Amos had prophesied that Israel would be sifted among all the nations of the earth.[45] Although the dedicatory prayer calls Church members the sons of Jacob, it acknowledges that they were "identified with the Gentiles."[46] The prayer also asked that the children of Judah, the Lamanites, and "all the scattered remnants of Israel, who have been driven to the ends of the earth, come to a knowledge of the truth, believe in the Messiah, and be redeemed from oppression, and rejoice."[47] The sequence of the gathering is reaffirmed: first, those among the Gentiles, and then those scattered upon the face of the earth.

The Old Testament prophets foretold of the gathering of these scattered remnants. It was a particular theme of the prophet Isaiah, whose writings we were commanded to search.[48] Many of his prophecies are confirmed in latter-day revelation.

THE PROPHECIES OF ISAIAH

The Savior declared to the Nephites that when the words of Isaiah "shall be fulfilled then is the fulfilling of the covenant which the Father hath made unto his people, O house of Israel."[49] The Savior further commanded that the prophecies of Isaiah be searched because "he spake as touching all things concerning my people which are of the house of Israel; therefore it must needs be that he must speak also to the Gentiles."[50] "Note that the Savior did not say that Isaiah spoke *about* the Gentiles, but that he was to speak '*to* the Gentiles.' The reason Isaiah (through his writings) was to speak to the Gentiles is that the house of Israel was scattered among them. If Isaiah were to speak *all things* concerning the house of Israel to them, he could not do so unless he spoke to the Gentiles among whom they were scattered. This is further confirmed by a subsequent verse in which the Savior declares that the words he was speaking to the Nephites should be written; then, 'according to the time and the will of the Father,' they would 'go forth unto the Gentiles.' (3 Nephi 23:4.)"[51] Jacob, son of Lehi, also said that "Isaiah spake concerning all the house of Israel."[52]

The Lord revealed anew the parable of the wheat and the tares and said that its fulfillment would come in the latter days. As a lesson to be drawn from this parable, the Lord told the brethren that their priesthood had "continued through the lineage of [their] fathers—for [they were] lawful heirs, according to the flesh, and have been hid from the world with Christ in God."[53] Because these brethren were first-generation members of the Church, the fathers through whom this priesthood continued would not have been their immediate fathers but, as previously shown, would logically be Abraham, Isaac, and Jacob, the covenant holders of past ages. This is further evidenced by the promise to Abraham that the priesthood would continue through the literal seed of his body.[54] The Lord declared that this priesthood would continue through the lineage of these first-generation Church members "until the restoration of all things spoken by the mouths of all the holy prophets since the world began."[55] He promised further that if they continued in his goodness, they would be "a light unto the Gentiles, and through this priesthood, a savior unto [his] people Israel."[56] These promises also relate to the covenant of Abraham.[57]

From these truths it can be discerned that the parable of the wheat and the tares teaches that the wheat is Israelites who are to be gathered from the tares who are the Gentiles. This interpretation is sustained by a later revelation:

"That the work of the gathering together of my saints may continue, that I may build them up unto my name upon holy places; for the time of harvest is come, and my word must needs be fulfilled.

"Therefore, I must gather together my people, according to the parable of the wheat and the tares, that the wheat may be secured in the garners to possess eternal life, and be crowned with celestial glory, when I shall come in the kingdom of my Father to reward every man according as his work shall be;

"While the tares shall be bound in bundles, and their bands made strong, that they may be burned with unquenchable fire."[58]

The basic concept of Israel's being gathered from among the Gentiles is taught in several other sections and is connected to other prophecies of Isaiah.

Joseph Smith understood that he was engaged in the second gathering of Israel prophesied by Isaiah.[59] He marveled when he saw that Alvin would be in the celestial kingdom when "he had departed this life before the Lord had set his hand to gather Israel the second time, and had not been baptized for the remission of sins."[60]

In a revelation the Lord commanded Sidney Rigdon to write for the Prophet Joseph, that he might receive the scriptures "to the salvation of [the Lord's] elect; for they will hear my voice, and shall see me, and shall not be asleep, and shall abide the day of my coming; for they shall be purified, even as I am pure."[61] The Lord then promised that Israel would be saved in his own due time, verifying that his elect is Israel. This promise in Doctrine and Covenants 35:25 is the same promise and in the same context as that in Isaiah 45:17. It is reminiscent of Jesus' declaration: "My sheep hear my voice, and I know them, and they follow me."[62] Those with the blood of Israel respond to the gospel message because they were numbered with the house of Israel in the premortal life, and they recognize the truths of the gospel.[63] Isaiah also speaks of the coming forth of the Book of Mormon and of things to come concerning the Lord's sons.[64]

A short time later the Lord revealed that the Church was to move to the Ohio and there be endowed with power from on high. From the Ohio the Lord would send his representatives among all nations, "for Israel shall be saved."[65] This is a second witness to Isaiah 45. Three days after this revelation, the Lord promised James Covill that if he would be baptized, he could participate in the covenant "to recover my people, which are of the house of Israel."[66] This promise is the same promise given in Isaiah 11:11 concerning the scattering of Israel in about 721 B.C.

In speaking of a conference to be held in Missouri in June 1831, the Lord referred to the Saints as "my people, which are a remnant of Jacob, and those who are heirs according to the covenant."[67] Isaiah had prophesied the gathering of the remnant of Jacob and the covenant of which they were heirs is, of course, the covenant of Abraham that Isaiah later referred to as the anointing.[68]

Two other concepts from Isaiah concerning Israel are verified in the Doctrine and Covenants.

First, Isaiah prophesied that the latter-day servants would seek after the Gentiles but would not find them.[69] The Lord revealed that the fulness of the gospel would come forth in the times of the Gentiles, "but they [the Gentiles] receive it not; for they perceive not the light."[70] Only those of the blood of Israel respond to the gospel message. Joseph Smith also declared, "But few of them will be gathered with the chosen family."[71]

Second, in speaking of the latter-day gathering to Zion, Isaiah said that the willing and the obedient would eat the good of that land.[72] That the Lord, through Isaiah, was speaking of latter-day Israel is confirmed by Oliver Cowdery's account of the angel Moroni's visit to Joseph Smith in September 1823. Oliver said, "Isaiah, who was on the earth at the time the ten tribes of Israel were led away captive from the land of Canaan, was shown not only their calamity and affliction, but the time when they were to be delivered."[73] In the same context, the Lord then warned that the rebellious would be cut off out of the land of Zion, for "the rebellious are not of the blood of Ephraim."[74] The New Testament also teaches that though these people who had been gathered were of the blood of Israel, they would not be entitled to the blessings if they were rebellious.[75]

OTHER REFERENCES TO ISRAEL

The Lord continually refers to the members of the Church as the children of Israel in one sense or another. The new song to be sung in Zion when it is established will declare that "the Lord hath redeemed his people, Israel."[76] He declared that he had much people in the area of New York and the regions round about.[77] He likewise spoke of Salem, Massachusetts.[78] "Much people" can refer only to Israel, because he was not speaking of total population. In speaking of the future establishment of the city of Zion (the New Jerusalem), he referred to the time when the army of Israel would become very great.[79] He spoke of his bishops as judges in Israel.[80]

In crossing the plains, President Brigham Young received a revelation regarding the organization of the people into companies. The Lord referred to the "Camp of Israel" and compared them to the children of Israel coming out of Egypt.[81] President Wilford Woodruff, in speaking of a vision that he saw before issuing the Manifesto, referred to the confusion that would reign throughout Israel if the practice of plural marriage had not ceased.[82]

In summary, then, the prophet Isaiah is quoted or paraphrased in twenty-six sections of the Doctrine and Covenants on the Latter-day Saints' being literal Israelites:

The promises to Abraham, Isaac, and Jacob remain. (D&C 27:10.)

The elect (covenant people) will hear his voice and be saved. (D&C 35:20–21, 25.)

Israel will be saved from all nations. (D&C 38:33.)

The covenant to recover the house of Israel is described. (D&C 39:11.)

The restoration of scattered Israel will take place among the Gentiles — few Gentiles will join the Church. (D&C 45:17, 28–29.)

The Church is a remnant of Jacob — heirs to the covenant. (D&C 52:2.)

The people are to be pushed together from the ends of the earth. (D&C 58:44–46; 65:11.)

The rebellious are not of Israel. (D&C 64:36.)

The priesthood line of authority from Moses to Abraham to Adam is outlined; the Lord redeems Israel. (D&C 84:6–34, 99–100.)

The parable of the wheat and the tares is explained: Israel is hidden among the Gentiles. (D&C 86:1–11, especially 8–11.)

The blessings belonging to the descendants of Joseph are spoken of. (D&C 96:6–7.)

The hearts of Abraham's children will be turned to their fathers. (D&C 98:16.)

Many people of Israel are in this place. (This indication is not as definite as others.) (D&C 100:3.)

The parable of the wheat and the tares: Israel is among the Gentiles. (This indication is not as definite as others.) (D&C 101:64–65.)

The Saints are of Israel and of Abraham. (D&C 103:15–19.)

The army of Israel will become great. (D&C 105:26–27, 30–31.)

The duties of judges in Israel are outlined. (D&C 107:72.)

The sons of Jacob will gather out the righteous from among the Gentiles. (D&C 109:58, 60, 67.)

The keys of the gathering and dispensation of the gospel of Abraham are committed to the Prophet. (D&C 110:11–12.)

Many people of Israel are in this city. (This indication is not as definite as others.) (D&C 111:2.)

Joseph Smith is a descendant of Judah and Joseph. (D&C 113:2–10.)

Joseph Smith fulfills the covenant of Abraham, being of the patriarchal lineage. (D&C 124:11, 58, 91–92.)

Joseph Smith is the seed of Abraham. (D&C 132:30–31.)

The servants of the Lord are of Ephraim. (D&C 133:12, 30, 32, 34.)

The camps of Israel will be led as were the children of Israel. (D&C 136:1, 22.)

The Restoration was the beginning of the Lord's gathering Israel the second time. (D&C 137:6.)

CONCLUSION

The literal gathering of Israel in the latter days has commenced. It began with the First Vision when the Prophet Joseph Smith was visited by the Father and the Son in the spring of 1820. As a literal descendant of Abraham and of Joseph and of Ephraim and of Judah, he was chosen in the premortal council of heaven to initiate and preside over the last dispensation of the gospel, the dispensation of the fulness of times, when all things from heaven and earth would be gathered together in Christ.[83]

After the First Vision, the Prophet was visited by various angels to restore their keys, power, and authority to gather Israel from among the Gentiles and from their being scattered upon all the face of the earth. The members of The Church of Jesus Christ of Latter-day Saints are those Israelites who have already been gathered and who now number over six million people. Nevertheless, there yet remain millions more to be gathered. When completed, this gathering will far exceed the previous gatherings of Israel in other dispensations. Not only will it include the thousands of Manasseh and the tens of thousands of Ephraim but it will also include millions of Lamanites, Jews, and descendants of the ten lost tribes of Israel. The members of the restored church of Jesus Christ are the literal seed of Abraham and of Israel who will be the Lord's servants to establish Israel as the kingdom of God and Zion as the New Jerusalem and to usher in the millennial reign of the Lord Jesus Christ. To these great truths the Doctrine and Covenants, as revelation to the apostles and prophets of the latter days, bears repeated witness.

NOTES

1. Deuteronomy 4:27–31; Isaiah 11:11–12; Jeremiah 16:14–16; Ezekiel 37:1–14; Joel 2:28–32; Amos 9:14–15.

2. 2 Nephi 29:1; Jacob 6:2.

3. The declaration that Latter-day Saints are the literal seed of Israel has been made by modern-day prophets and apostles periodically throughout the history of the Church. Some of these declarations have been cited in this paper. Recent verifications may be seen in Ezra Taft Benson, *A Witness and a Warning* (Salt Lake City: Deseret Book, 1988); Bruce R. McConkie, *A New Witness for the Articles of Faith* (Salt Lake City: Deseret Book, 1985); and Russell M. Nelson, Brigham Young University devotional address, 22 Nov. 1988.

4. 3 Nephi 20:27; Genesis 12:1–3.

5. Abraham 2:11.

6. D&C 27:5; see also Matthew 26:29; Mark 14:25; Luke 22:18.

7. D&C 27:10.

8. D&C 103:17, 19.

9. D&C 110:12.

10. D&C 98:16; italics added.

11. John 8:56; see also Helaman 8:16–18.

12. D&C 84:31, 34.

13. D&C 113:4.

14. See D&C 20:8.

15. D&C 113:6.

16. Joseph Smith–History 1:33.

17. Joseph Smith, *Teachings of the Prophet Joseph Smith,* sel. Joseph Fielding Smith (Salt Lake City: Deseret Book Co., 1938), p. 365.

18. D&C 90:3–4; see D&C 110:11–16; 128:20–21.

19. D&C 110:12.

20. Genesis 12:3; 1 Nephi 22:9; 3 Nephi 20:25.

21. Abraham 2:11.

22. Although the reference cited is D&C 132, recorded 12 July 1843, it was revealed to Joseph Smith much earlier than this date, as noted in the section heading.

23. See D&C 132:30–32.

24. D&C 124:58.

25. D&C 124:91–92.

26. Smith, *Teachings of the Prophet Joseph Smith,* p. 151.

27. In *Journal of Discourses* (London: Latter-day Saints' Book Depot, 1854–86), 7:289–90.

28. See Genesis 17:21; 25:23; 1 Chronicles 5:1–2.

29. See 2 Nephi 3:4; 4:1–2.

30. D&C 96:6–7.

31. See Genesis 48:15–20; Jeremiah 31:9.

32. D&C 58:44–46.

33. See Deuteronomy 33:13–17.

34. See D&C 66:11.

35. See Deuteronomy 19:15; Matthew 18:16; 2 Corinthians 13:1.

36. D&C 133:30.

37. D&C 133:32.

38. D&C 133:34.

39. See Hosea 14:1–9.

40. See Isaiah 41:9; Joseph Smith Translation, Isaiah 42:19; 43:10; 44:2, 21; 45:4; 49:3, 5–6.

41. D&C 113:8, 10; italics added.

42. D&C 110:11.

43. Joseph F. Smith, *Gospel Doctrine*, 5th ed. (Salt Lake City: Deseret Book Co., 1939), p. 115. Other presidents of the Church who have spoken on the unique role of Ephraim as the birthright holder and the gatherer of Israel include Brigham Young (in *Journal of Discourses*, 2:268–69) and Joseph Fielding Smith (*Doctrines of Salvation*, 3:250–54).

44. D&C 109:57–58.

45. See Amos 9:8–9.

46. D&C 109:60. President Wilford Woodruff referred to the Saints as Israelites but as Gentiles in a national capacity: "The Gospel is now restored to us Gentiles, for we are all Gentiles in a national capacity." (In *Journal of Discourses*, 18:220.)

47. D&C 109:67.

48. See 3 Nephi 20:11; 23:1.

49. 3 Nephi 20:12.

50. 3 Nephi 23:2.

51. Monte S. Nyman, *An Ensign to All People: The Sacred Message and Mission of the Book of Mormon* (Salt Lake City: Deseret Book Co., 1987), p. 39.

52. 2 Nephi 6:5.

53. D&C 86:8–9; compare Isaiah 49:2.

54. See Abraham 2:11.

55. D&C 86:10.

56. D&C 86:11.

57. See Abraham 2:9–11; Genesis 12:1–3.

58. D&C 101:64–66.

59. See Isaiah 11:11.

60. D&C 137:6.

61. D&C 35:20–21.

62. John 10:27.

63. See Deuteronomy 32:8–9; Acts 17:26; Abraham 3:22–23; Alma 13:1–5.

64. Isaiah 45:8, 11.

65. D&C 38:33.

66. D&C 39:11.

67. D&C 52:2.

68. Isaiah 10:20–22, 27.

69. Isaiah 41:12.
70. D&C 45:29.
71. Smith, *Teachings of the Prophet Joseph Smith,* p. 15.
72. See Isaiah 1:19.
73. *Messenger and Advocate,* Apr. 1835, pp. 109–10.
74. D&C 64:36.
75. Compare Matthew 3:9; Luke 13:28–30; Romans 9:6.
76. D&C 84:99.
77. See D&C 100:3.
78. D&C 111:2.
79. D&C 105:26–27, 30–31.
80. D&C 107:72.
81. D&C 136:1, 22.
82. See Official Declaration–1, p. 293.
83. See Ephesians 1:10.

CHAPTER FIFTEEN

Doctrine and Covenants 76 and the Visions of Resurrected Life in the Teachings of Elder John A. Widtsoe

Alan K. Parrish

Associate Professor of Ancient Scripture
Brigham Young University

Elder Bruce R. McConkie taught that many truths known by the ancient Saints but lost through the dark millennium have been restored to us in this age of restoration, things largely "Christ-centered, gospel-centered, priesthood-centered, church-centered." He declared that the doctrinal restoration, begun in 1820 with the Prophet Joseph Smith, is in our day still in its beginning stages and will continue through the Millennium.[1] As fundamental doctrine shaping the views of Church members on matters of life here and hereafter, few, if any, scriptural passages have had more influence than Doctrine and Covenants 76. From it we derive much information about our relationship to God and eternity and about the purpose of religion, the Church, and our individual lives. Viewing the great doctrines of eternal life through the eyes of our best teachers is profitable for our learning and edification. So, in addition to studying the doctrine in section 76 itself, many Church members have studied related teachings of early Church leaders, including the Prophet Joseph Smith, President Brigham Young, Elder Orson Pratt, and others. They have also studied the related teachings of recent Church leaders, including President Joseph Fielding Smith, President Spencer W. Kimball, Elder Bruce R. McConkie, and President Ezra Taft Benson. But many Church members are far less aware of the teachings on this subject by prominent Church leaders in the middle decades of the Church. Elder John A. Widtsoe was one of these leaders. This paper will look at some important teachings of section 76 through the eyes of this special witness, who had a particular devotion to the Doctrine and Covenants. Elder Widtsoe was one of the great teachers of this dispensation. His influential Church service covered the first half of the twentieth century. He was a stalwart witness of Christ and the Restoration and a gifted Church leader noted for his keen and inspired mind. A review of his background, especially as it relates to the Doctrine and Covenants and his Church service, is a necessary foundation for this analysis.

John Andreas Widtsoe, or Dr. Widtsoe, as he was popularly called throughout the Church, was born in Norway, 31 January 1872. In the fall of 1883, with his convert mother and six-year-old brother, Osborne, he emigrated to Utah to live among the Saints. His is a classic story of penniless beginnings, a single-parent family, and an arduous struggle to establish life in a new community with another language and unique religious customs. From that beginning John A. Widtsoe rose to extraordinary prominence. Between 1889 and 1891 he became a distinguished student at Brigham Young College in Logan, for which he, along with seven others, was invited to attend Harvard College by Dr. Joseph M. Tanner, president of Brigham Young College.

In 1894, after only three years, he graduated from Harvard, summa cum laude (with highest honors). Between 1894 and 1898 he was professor of chemistry at the Agricultural College of Utah in Logan, now Utah State University. For two years beginning in 1898, he studied chemistry and agriculture in Europe and received his doctorate from the distinguished Georg-August-Universität in Göttingen, Germany. In 1900 he returned to the Agricultural College of Utah as the director of the Agricultural Experiment Station, which was established as a result of land-grant college legislation. For the next five years he achieved academic distinction while juggling the demands of teaching, research, and administration. At the Agricultural Experiment Station, his duties encompassed the practical application of academic research to increased efficiency of farming and agriculture throughout the state of Utah.

Between 1905 and 1907 he established the agriculture program at Brigham Young University. Then for the nine years between 1907 and 1916, he was president of Utah State Agricultural College in Logan, Utah. His term there ended when he was appointed president of the University of Utah in Salt Lake City. Because of his devotion to the Church and his personal association with many of the early leaders of Brigham Young University he was prominent in the development of that university, and efforts were made by some to have him appointed its president. He never was appointed president of BYU, but in later years, as the LDS Church's commissioner of education, he had responsibilities for overseeing its administration. Following a remarkable career in Utah higher education, John A. Widtsoe was called to be a member of the Quorum of the Twelve Apostles, in which he served for more than thirty years, from 1921 to 1952.

Elder Widtsoe's devotion to the scriptures and the teachings of the Church permeated his home life, his academic training, his professional life, and his Church service. In his autobiography, written in the final years of his life, he looked back on his early education at Brigham Young College:

"Theology became our best loved subject. It formed our outlook upon life; and made us more sensitive to right and wrong. It shaped our characters and conduct in life. From my own experience and from the observation of the lives of those who have had parallel training in secular and sacred subjects, I have been throughout life an unchanging, firm believer in religious education for youth."[2]

Through the difficult and lonely years at Harvard his faith was tested, and, like so many others, he had to search for the truth. Of that search he wrote: "At that time I was having my religious battles. Was Mormonism what it pretended to be? Did Joseph Smith tell the truth? I read, listened, compared, thought, prayed. It was a real search for truth. Out of it in time came the certain knowledge that the restored gospel is true and that Joseph Smith was indeed a Prophet, and restorer of the simple true gospel of Jesus Christ. There has never been any doubt about it since that time of deep study and prayer."[3]

Upon graduation in 1894 he returned to Logan and began his teaching career at the Agricultural College. His passion for learning, especially religious learning, continued. Though he had studied widely the philosophies and religions of man at Harvard, he wrote, "the gospel impressed me as the foremost, all-encompassing system of truth. I liked to discuss its many implications."[4] Accordingly, he organized a small group of friends into weekly study sessions. Shortly thereafter, Orson Smith, president of the Cache Stake, learned of John's enthusiasm for the gospel, which, combined with the unusual advantage of his Harvard education, presented a rare opportunity for the stake. Anxious to fulfill the president's wishes, John agreed to bring his friends and meet President Smith in the regular meeting of the first quorum of elders of Cache Stake in the First Ward on the following Monday evening. In that meeting, President Smith reorganized the elders' quorum, and John was sustained as the first counselor and quorum instructor. That Church calling became an important landmark in Elder Widtsoe's life and was quite significant to the study of the Doctrine and Covenants throughout the Church. He wrote:

"We undertook to read and study the Doctrine and Covenants. However, we found it difficult to remember the places in the Book where certain thoughts were expressed. We needed to have an index to which we could refer. So I made a concordance of the ideas in the Book, which was used effectively in card index form. Some years later this concordance was presented to the Church and published. In all my priesthood work, none has been more enjoyable than in this elders quorum. The happy associations came to an end after four years, when I went abroad for more learning. But the love of the Doctrine and Covenants has been kept alive. It remains one of my favorite scriptures; and I have written and published much about it."[5]

Upon his return from Germany, Dr. Widtsoe resumed work on the concordance. He completed the project on his thirty-third birthday, 31 January 1905. The work was published in 1906 as a volume of 205 pages under the copyright of Joseph F. Smith, trustee-in-trust for the Church.[6] In 1908, an edition of the Doctrine and Covenants was published with this index and concordance in its entirety, including the title page. In its preface Dr. Widtsoe shared some personal impressions about the Doctrine and Covenants:

"Concordance making is not a work for vacation times. Yet the wearisome routine, which can not be avoided in such labors, has been more than compensated for, by the glorious visions of revealed truth that have sprung from every page of the Book. Thus, whatever reward is due for the work represented by this concordance I have already received. . . . The Book of Doctrine and Covenants is a mighty evidence of the divine inspiration of the Prophet Joseph Smith. The study of this holy Book has greatly strengthened my love for the Gospel."[7]

Among Church auxiliaries, interest in a regular course of study from the Doctrine and Covenants burgeoned with this new aid. Between 1902 and 1904 Dr. Widtsoe wrote a series of twenty-eight lessons for the Young Ladies Mutual Improvement Association under the title *The Book of Doctrine and Covenants*. In 1903 he wrote a series of lessons for the fourth-year theological department of the Deseret Sunday School Union entitled *An Outline for the Study of the Book of Doctrine and Covenants*. In 1904 he wrote a series called *The Study of the Book of*

Doctrine and Covenants. He prepared still another series, *The History and Message of the Doctrine and Covenants,* for the Young Mens Mutual Improvement Association in 1906.

In an article published in the *Improvement Era* in October 1951 detailing the history of the development of the Doctrine and Covenants, A. C. Lambert reported the major changes in the 1921 edition. He noted that it still contained 136 sections but that the Lectures on Faith had been removed. He further noted that it was published "with revised prefaces to the individual sections in double-column pages, and with an index and concordance by John A. Widtsoe."[8] Elder G. Homer Durham reported that "the 'Index and Concordance' of all editions of the Doctrine and Covenants since 1921 is based on this work."[9]

Dr. Widtsoe's work on indexing the Doctrine and Covenants did not end with the publication of this concordance. He continued his card file of cross-references and compiled three large binders totaling 939 pages containing multiple clippings taken from copies of the 1921 edition. Every verse in the Doctrine and Covenants was arranged topically with many verses appearing several times. His devotion to the Doctrine and Covenants is also evidenced in his gospel sermons. A review of scriptural references in all of his conference addresses revealed that he referred to the Doctrine and Covenants almost five times more frequently than he referred to any other book of scripture.

Another indication of his devotion to the Doctrine and Covenants is found in a special calling extended to him during the school year 1935–36. The University of Southern California had invited the Church to send a representative to teach Mormonism for university credit. Elder Widtsoe was sent as a visiting professor for the entire school year. His lectures in the first two quarters were the basis of his book *The Program of the Church.* In the spring quarter he delivered a series of lectures on the teachings of the Doctrine and Covenants. From the actual transcripts of the lectures, and also from Dr. Widtsoe's outline and lecture notes, those lectures were later compiled by Elder G. Homer Durham and published as *The Message of the Doctrine and Covenants.*

While on this assignment Elder Widtsoe taught religion courses to Church members at USC and three other local campuses. In a very real way this assignment of Elder Widtsoe was a forerunner to the institute of religion program in Southern California.[10]

Elder Widtsoe applied himself to understanding the doctrinal teachings of latter-day prophets. He published two books on the teachings of the Prophet Joseph Smith, *Joseph Smith As Scientist: A Contribution to Mormon Philosophy,* and *Joseph Smith: Seeker After Truth, Prophet of God.* He also compiled the *Discourses of Brigham Young,* and *Gospel Doctrine,* the teachings of Joseph F. Smith.

ELDER WIDTSOE'S TEACHINGS ABOUT DOCTRINE AND COVENANTS 76

On 16 February 1832, the Prophet Joseph Smith and Sidney Rigdon were given a remarkable vision of the resurrected worlds. The Prophet recorded descriptions of the sons of perdition, the three degrees of glory, and the characteristics of those who would obtain each of those degrees. Elder Widtsoe's feelings about section 76 were beautifully expressed in his last lecture at USC in the spring of 1936:

"In the sacred literature of the world, there is probably no more beautiful, no more eloquent message than Section 76. It is a jewel, a gem, a scintillating diamond. It is the most beautiful in all our literature, both because of its phrasing, its vision of the future, and the glorious promises to humanity. It is a great chapter in the sacred writ which may be set side by side with the finest in the Bible or Book of Mormon, or the more or less inspired writings of the sages of all times. It bears reading and rereading."[11]

Elder Widtsoe was a scientist. His instinct and training was to be logical and analytical, to probe more deeply than most, and to suggest conclusions from a set of relevant data. He investigated our understanding of God, man, and eternal life much as he did our understanding of the chemistry of life in plants and people. In reviewing his teachings, we should be aware that on some very important points differing views have been taught by equally prominent Church leaders. Some of the views of these other authorities, as well as some explanations, are also included in this discussion. Explanations are, by nature, interpretations. The interpretations I have given are intended to clarify, not replace, the teachings of Elder Widtsoe. Where all things have not been restored, it is wisdom to understand the teachings of several of the best of the Lord's anointed.

SATAN AND THE SONS OF PERDITION

Joseph Smith and Sidney Rigdon were commanded to write that they beheld that Satan "rebelled against God, and sought to take the kingdom of our God and his Christ—wherefore, he maketh war with the saints of God, and encompasseth them round about." (D&C 76:28–29.) The Prophet further recorded that they "saw a vision of the sufferings of those with whom he [Satan] made war and overcame." (D&C 76:30.) In this part of the vision the voice of the Lord described those of the resurrection of damnation. Of them he used the label "the sons of perdition," for they had been overcome by him, they had become "born" unto him (perdition), and thus had become his sons. (D&C 76:31–49.)

From this revelation it can be concluded that the resurrection of damnation refers only to the sons of perdition. All others will be saved in the variety of degrees of glory described in other parts of the vision. The revelation states that neither their end, nor their torment, nor the place thereof has been or will be revealed, except to those "ordained unto this condemnation." (D&C 76:48.) In his lectures at USC, Elder Widtsoe taught that the Lord shut off the vision when he got to the sons of perdition. Of their fate he explained:

"No one understands and I certainly do not understand. Brigham Young offered the opinion in one of his discourses that probably the punishment to be inflicted upon the sons of perdition would be that they would have to start over the long painful journey from the beginning. They would be reduced to the elements from which they started."[12]

As Lucifer was called perdition for rebelling against the knowledge he had acquired, so the sons of perdition qualify themselves through rebelling against their acquired knowledge. They must "know [his] power, and . . . [be] partakers thereof" (D&C 76:31), and they must have received the Holy Spirit and have denied the Only Begotten Son after having that spiritual witness, thereby, "having crucified him unto themselves and put him to an open shame." (D&C 76:35.)

Elder Widtsoe wrote: "It is probable that only personages who have acquired similar full knowledge, who willfully and deliberately deny the truth, when they know it to be the truth, can commit the unpardonable sin and become sons of perdition. . . . They must have had a fullness of knowledge; a testimony which cannot be destroyed. One must be on a high eminence to fall so low; and few in world's history have attained such a height."[13]

He also wrote: "These are the sons of perdition—they who come to a knowledge of the truth, who knew the Father, and understood His will, and then willfully denied the truth. I have come to think that this was the sin of the devil himself. I know of no more damnable sin than to know the truth and then deny it."[14]

And further: "It must be a terrible punishment beyond human comprehension, the greatest conceivable, yet a justified punishment. Since the greatest sin is the unpardonable sin, it would appear that they will forfeit all the gains of the ages of pre-existence and the years on earth. It is no wonder that the heavens wept over Lucifer's rebellion. (D. & C. 76:26)."[15]

Elder Widtsoe taught that the sons of perdition stand as a warning against all "who deal lightly with truth in their lives," and that "though they may not become sons of perdition, [they] must expect a heavy punishment, which often begins in mortality."[16] He further taught that the old notion of hell, a place of unending torture and a flaming cauldron, was erroneous. "The word *hell*, when used in these revelations [D&C 19 and 76], refers to the abode of the devil and his ugly brood. As used in the Bible, it has the same connotation."[17]

UNIVERSAL SALVATION

The final chapter in *The Message of the Doctrine and Covenants* contains the last lecture Dr. Widtsoe gave at USC. It is entitled "Salvation and Eternal Life." He taught that Doctrine and Covenants 76 is the culmination of the message of the Doctrine and Covenants.[18] "Whatever system of truth, whatever gospel is presented, which does not admit all to the plan of salvation if they so desire, can not be of God. The book is emphatic there. The work must be done in temples."[19] On this premise he taught the importance of temple work for the dead, which, he emphasized, had been given to the Latter-day Saints as a special commission. He reasoned that the privileges of salvation are linked to man's obedience to the laws of salvation, which extend through eternity and bridge the bands of death. Salvation is a concern as vital for the dead as for the living and is the chief pursuit of all men through eternity.

In 1906 he wrote a lengthy article on Doctrine and Covenants 2, the priesthood mission of Elijah, fulfilled through the Prophet Joseph Smith. In it he wrote that the plan of salvation was designed to save all of God's children. It was not to be blocked by mortal death but was to reach into the life beyond. Otherwise, the mission of mortality and the efforts of God would have been largely wasted. He held that the opportunity for salvation is always open and that the ordinances required and performed in the mortal world have eternal validity. Said he:

"The promise of salvation is to all individuals who will repent and conform to the ordinances of the gospel, whether they are alive or dead, or whether the acceptance is made today or an eternity from now. The laws of life in the here and the hereafter are not, according to 'Mormonism,' essentially different. . . .

"The plan of salvation was not formulated in order to provide eternal life for a few handfuls of spirits. On the contrary, it was intended for the salvation of a family of spirits numbering many millions of members. The earth-experience was necessary for the development of the spirits towards a God-like state of superiority. The laws of the gospel are eternal and irrevocable. Every spirit to be saved, must believe, repent and be baptized, before he enters properly upon the road to eternal life; yet there can be no justice in withholding salvation from those who died on earth without hearing the gospel, or from those who, at any future time, in the hereafter, may acquire faith, repent, and desire baptism. . . .

"If, now, this work for the dead has not been done at the last day, what shall become of the waiting spirits, who perhaps, on the other side, have declared their willingness to accept the gospel? They are not legal members of the Church; and can not become such unless an earthly ordinance is performed. The purpose of the plan of salvation is blocked; the mission of the earth and her children has not been completed; the efforts of God and righteous men have largely been wasted. Even more terrible is the fact that in such an event the glory of God is obscured, for the Father of All, glories not in saving a few of his children; his joy is full only when the hosts of earth-spirits shout hosannas to the King of kings in gratitude for their citizenship in the Kingdom of Heaven."[20]

In 1931 Elder Widtsoe taught that the restoration through the Prophet Joseph Smith opened man's eyes to the opportunity of salvation in one of the degrees of glory through repentance either here or in the hereafter: "The doctrine of universal salvation grips the hearts of mankind. Seventy-five years ago the greatest theological battle of the centuries was waged with that doctrine as the storm center. Were all men to be saved, or only a few? The vicious doctrine had been preached for generations that only a few men and women were destined to be saved in the presence of God. In that battle, questions were asked. Is there power of repentance beyond the grave? At death does nothing remain of the old life? Is memory blotted out? Is the power of free will then a thing of the past? Around such questions, asked by intelligent men, a great battle was waged. That was after the Lord had turned the key, through the Prophet Joseph Smith, and laid bare the doctrine of universal salvation, which declares that all who repent, either here or in the hereafter, may achieve salvation in one or the other of the great glories that the Lord has prepared for his children."[21]

GRADATIONS AND DEGREES OF SALVATION

Resurrection is a free gift to all the children of God. Individual attainment in the resurrection is determined by the combination of knowledge and works. In Elder Widtsoe's words: "The test is this: the use one makes of his knowledge will determine his place in the hereafter."[22] It is a common practice in the Church to focus only on the celestial degree of glory. As a consequence, many remain confused about the glorious nature of life in the other degrees and how they fit into the resurrection. Many Church members, if asked to describe the telestial kingdom, may likely make it resemble our view of hell more than our view of heaven. To the question, "what do you teach your students about the telestial kingdom?" a colleague answered, "I try to scare them away from it. I try to make it sound so terrible that they will be afraid of anything but the celestial kingdom." Salvation in the other degrees and their place in the overall plan of the Lord is well addressed in Elder Widtsoe's teachings:

"The doctrine is taught by the church that we shall be placed, in the hereafter, 'according to our works.' Here shall be one, there another. Apparently for convenience, to make clear the thing to the human mind, the book tells (D&C 76) of three great divisions—the celestial; the terrestrial; and the telestial. It is made clear that in each one of these degrees or glories there are many divisions. As one reads the book he learns of an infinite gradation, accorded to each as they have done certain kinds of works."[23]

Elder Widtsoe also explained: "As everything in Mormonism tends to be of a rational character, so with the resurrection. First those arise who have earned that right. Then those arise who have earned a later call. Those yonder arise. There is a series of resurrections. There are several calls, for those who have done best, first, and those who have done worst, last. That seems to be a fair procedure from beginning to end. This book [the Doctrine and Covenants] deals in an understandable way with all such problems."[24]

In two addresses given in 1921 Elder Widtsoe taught about gradations of salvation, the means of achieving progression, and their desirability:

"Through obedience to the first principles of the Gospel, and a subsequent blameless life, a person may win salvation for himself. But in God's kingdom are many gradations, which lead to exaltation upon exaltation. Those who hunger and thirst for righteousness and labor for the fulfillment of the promise involved in the gift of the Holy Ghost will advance farther that those who placidly sit by with no driving desire within them."[25]

"There is a graded salvation, within the ultimate reach of every human being, if he cares to accept of it, there can be no deep-seated fear of the hereafter, especially when we have been told that the lowest glory of this graded salvation is entirely beyond the understanding and wildest fancy of man."[26]

Addressing the Liberty Stake Genealogical Convention on the fundamentals of temple doctrine in May 1922, Elder Widtsoe again spoke about graduated degrees of progression. Though there is progression in each kingdom, there is a type of hell that stays through endless ages: to know what might have been, but be restricted in progression to a lower kingdom:

"We are told in section 76 of the Doctrine and Covenants that there are different degrees of glory in the great hereafter. This is indeed simply an emphatic statement of the fact that the judgment passed upon man will be graduated according to the works of man. We do not know much about conditions in the hereafter; but the spirit of revelation known as Section 76, is very clear to all who care to understand. A man shall be judged according to his life; and his place in the hereafter will depend on what he has earned for himself. . . . After reading Section 76 of the Doctrine and Covenants, it seems that hell is to find ourselves in an inferior position and conditions, and to know that we might have been, by our efforts, in a higher and more glorious place, had we exercised our free agency more vigorously for better things. Moreover our punishment stands, at least measurably, throughout the endless ages, because as we go onward, those above us go onward also, and the relative positions remain the same. This is the just but fearful punishment of evil doing. Temple work in its various departments assumes this principle of eternal justice. The Gospel, however, fills human hearts with joy, for it teaches that even in the lowest glory described in Section 76 [v. 89], the place reserved for those who have made the greatest mistakes, who have failed to get beyond the first step, is so glorious as to be beyond the conception of mortal man."[27]

In 1944 a series of radio addresses by Dr. Widtsoe were published as a book under the title *An Understandable Religion*. In an address entitled "Facing the Judgment," he taught that the degrees of salvation are the equitable reward of justice tempered by mercy and the logical consequence of man's earnestness to be faithful to God:

"We do not all strive with equal earnestness to pay the price. What then is the logical consequence? We shall not all attain to the same degree of salvation. Under the law, composed of divine justice tempered with mercy, each one of us will be given a fully equitable reward. All that we have earned will be given us, and the measure will be full to overflowing. But there will be no dead equality of salvation, such as has been painted by churches for generations of men. . . . This really means that salvation is graded . . . And in our day, through Joseph Smith, the Prophet, the more complete understanding of the gradations of salvation has been secured. The document in which this doctrine is stated is one of the most precious in sacred literature [D&C 76]."[28]

In the passages cited above he consistently taught that those who qualify for a greater degree receive a greater reward and advance further than those who do not so qualify. He taught that there is no equality in salvation of those who hunger and thirst after righteousness and those who are less attentive to righteousness and that our punishment stands throughout endless ages. Concerning the differences in the three degrees of glory as revealed in Doctrine and Covenants 76, he taught:

"The revelation details somewhat fully, and with much beauty of language, the conditions that place people in each of these kingdoms. Those of the celestial, the place where God and Christ dwell, have accepted Jesus and the ordinances of his Church. Those of the terrestrial died without the law, or were not valiant in the testimony of Jesus. Those of the telestial kingdom did not receive Jesus but were content to follow falsehood.

"These kingdoms, though very different, are filled with the children of God the Father. Though those of the lower kingdom have not shown themselves worthy of the fulness of salvation, yet the love of the Father envelops them. Even the glory of the lowest, the telestial, 'surpasses all understanding' [D&C 76:89].

"Nevertheless, there remained the punishment that one in the lower kingdoms might by another mode of life have received and enjoyed a higher glory. The eternal memory, though terrible, is a more reasonable punishment than the fiery furnace taught through generations of time by false teachers."[29]

The eternal memory of those in a lower glory indicates that the differences and limitations of a lower degree of salvation remain through eternity. Elder Widtsoe characterized the differences in the progression of those in lower degrees as limitations placed on their capacities such that they could never endure the glory of a higher kingdom.

"Moreover, those who are assigned to the lower kingdoms, have so lived, so misused their opportunities, that they could not adapt themselves to the prevailing conditions in the higher kingdoms. Their capacities, by their own acts, have been changed to fit a lower glory. They would not be happy in a higher kingdom. They are unprepared for association with those whose lives have been in accord with God's truth. As we have made ourselves, so shall our judgment be."[30]

Some of his children have already been denied the capacity for mortal life. Likewise, all who do not achieve exaltation in the celestial glory will be denied the capacity to live as do those who will obtain it. In an essay teaching that it is not possible to progress from one glory to another, Elder Widtsoe wrote:

"They who inherit the celestial glory will dwell in the presence of the Father and the Son. They are kings and priests. From that glory issues the power of God, known to us as the Priesthood of the Lord. In that glory certain conditions of joy belong which are absent in the other glories. They who have inherited the lesser glories will receive a salvation so glorious as to be beyond the understanding of man — that has been revealed to us — but, 'where God and Christ dwell they cannot come, worlds without end' (D&C 76:112)."[31]

Elder Widtsoe's teachings about salvation and progression in the lower degrees of glory are unusually optimistic and cause some to question whether he pictured progression to be on a single continuum, so that in time all the blessings of the highest kingdom may be obtained by those in the lower kingdoms. These teachings raise the question of overlap, or the possibility of progression between the three degrees of glory. The following statement was given in his lectures at USC, to indicate his belief that though there is progression in all the degrees of glory, it is "utterly impossible" to progress from one degree to another.

"The question is frequently asked concerning three men placed in the three glories, can the one in the lower glory, by acceptable living in that glory, be transferred into the next glory, and the one in the middle glory move into the higher glory? If you will stop to think, you will see how utterly impossible that is. Growth, the basis of judgment, means greater power, greater strength. Those who are placed in the highest glory have greater power for, or a greater rate of, increase. They move at the rate of, say, fifty miles an hour, while those in the next glory move at twenty-five miles an hour; and those in the lower have power to move at only ten miles an hour. In the course of time, the one in the lower glory may reach the point that was occupied by the one in the higher, but then the one in the higher glory will be miles and miles ahead. Start three automobiles at the same time moving ten, twenty, and thirty miles an hour, and you will see that every second they are farther and farther apart, yet all are progressing."[32]

This explanation was given to non–Latter-day Saint students. He might not have chosen to characterize it quite so simply to an audience familiar with Latter-day Saint beliefs. The statement and the impression given in the illustration, that in time those in the lower kingdoms "may reach the point that was occupied by one in the higher," is misleading. The logical extension is that in time the slower cars could reach the starting point of the fastest, or that telestial and terrestrial beings may, in time, become celestial. As already indicated, Elder Widtsoe did not believe there could be progression between kingdoms. His explanation was that the capacities of those in lower kingdoms were incompatible with life in the higher degrees and that their progression was confined to their inferior capacity. President Joseph Fielding Smith taught that progression in the different degrees was to be in different directions.

"The celestial and terrestrial and telestial glories, I have heard compared to the wheels on a train. The second and third may, and will, reach the place where the first was, but the first will have moved on and will still be just the same distance in advance of them. *This illustration is not true! The wheels do not run on the same track, and do not go in the same direction. The terrestrial and the telestial are limited in their powers of advancement, worlds without end.*"[33]

ETERNAL LIFE

Elder Widtsoe taught that the best picture we have of eternal life is that given in Doctrine and Covenants 76. The essence of that picture is that eternal life is the highest possible attainment for man:

"Life eternal is a life of action, of development, of growth, of eternal progression. Life hereafter is active, not static. Eternal life is eternal growth according to the Book of Doctrine and Covenants. For that reason, as the book says, the greatest gift of God is eternal life (14:7). There is no greater gift, according to the book, than the gift of being able to increase continually whether upon this earth or in the life to come. There must be growth where there is life. There you have a cardinal doctrine which may be applied to everyday life. . . . The difference between immortality and eternal life is that immortality is eternal existence. But eternal life involves growth."[34]

In 1934 Elder Widtsoe taught about the rich potential and the ultimate value of a soul who may rise to perfected achievement. He explained that eternal progression is the means of obtaining the joy Father Lehi described as the essence of man's existence:

"We are eternal souls, with the inherent power to progress, placed on earth for the purpose of learning better how to go forward under the law of progression, stepping on from one estate to another estate, preparing ourselves for still another estate, all in the line of advancement. The result of such progression, the final purpose of life, has been clearly and definitely stated by the Prophet Lehi: 'Men are, that they might have joy.' . . . And joy can be won in only one way—the joy of which the prophet Lehi speaks, through the definite principle of eternal progress. There can be no joy for a person who stands still; to him, that which seems joy is merely a make-believe, the shell, not the kernel. It is but the savory smell, not the feast itself."[35]

Elder Widtsoe described death as entry into the third estate of man's advancement. He described that estate as an eternal life of progress, of never-ending education and advancement:

"Death must be viewed as a portal to a new and a greater life, in which man, possessed of new experiences and a material as well as a spirit body, may continue eternally the exploration of the inexhaustible universe and gain never-ending education and never-ending advancement. Under the law of progression, the imperishable man may move onward more rapidly and fully than ever before. Every natural power of man on earth will be retained, improved and perfected, with others added. The power to accept or to reject, to gain knowledge and to use it wisely, will be keener than before. This is the Third Estate and the last estate of man. It is an eternal life of action, increase and progress."[36]

In 1922 Elder Widtsoe described eternal progression as the reason for existence, for it encompasses an existence of everlasting achievement and everlasting growth toward our ideal, God. "It is the glory of this Church that it possesses, and the glory of the Prophet Joseph Smith, that he left behind him, for us and for all generations to come, the explanation of explanations, the reason for life and the reason for human existence. Under the inspiration of God, he told us whence we came, what we are doing here and where we are to go. . . . We shall live hereafter — not a quiet, silent, purposeless life, but a life of development and progress, everlastingly achieving, everlastingly growing, everlastingly becoming more and more like the greatest and highest of our ideals."[37]

Several prominent members of the First Presidency and the Council of the Twelve Apostles spoke on the topic of eternal progression at the annual leadership week at Brigham Young University in January 1937. Newspaper accounts record the essence of Elder Widtsoe's remarks. "The speaker [Elder Widtsoe] said also that man was living in a progressive universe, a purposeful universe, and was engaged in an eternal journey of which there were many stages. Progression of man never stops, Elder Widtsoe explained, carrying this thought into an explanation of the three degrees of glory to which man will eventually attain in a state of salvation. Salvation of man is progression, he said, explaining these various degrees of future progress as revealed in modern scriptures."[38]

In 1934 Elder Widtsoe again urged that the purpose of earth life is eternal progress, just "as had been the purpose of all life before and will be the purpose of all life in the hereafter. In the universe of living, intelligent beings, there are many gradations. Some are perfected — we call them gods. God, the Father of all, is beyond our full comprehension in his attributes. No man can comprehend infinity. There are other living beings, here and elsewhere, of lesser and varying intelligence and achievements, all moving forward, upward, to the high destiny of all sentient beings. It is self-evident that those who are lower down in the scale of progression do not know as much as those who are superior in experience and therefore need help from those further advanced. We need ask and receive help from our Heavenly Father. Every man has need of the guidance that comes from a greater intelligence. Therefore we have a plan of salvation."[39]

To better understand Elder Widtsoe's teachings about man's growth toward the ideal of perfection personified in God, it is necessary to know his teachings about God's perfection. He held the view that eternal life is a condition of continual growth that brings the eternal joy Lehi described as man's object. Eternal growth is a characteristic of the eternal life that God enjoys. To acquire eternal life in the highest degree is to acquire the degree of exalted increase that God has acquired. Elder Widtsoe recognized that to man, much about God's nature is incomprehensible, therefore, attempts to describe the finer points of His nature are severely limited. Implicit in his view of God's progressive nature is the recognition that God's nature is consistent with universal laws.

"To determine this relationship between God and man, it is necessary to know, as far as the limited human mind may know, why the Lord is the supreme intelligent Being in the universe, with the greatest knowledge and the most perfected will, and who, therefore, possesses infinite power over the forces of the universe. It must be admitted at once that the mind of man can know God only in part. One thing seems clear, however, that the Lord who is a part of the universe, in common with all other parts of the universe is subject to eternal universal laws. In some manner, mysterious to us, he has recognized and utilized the laws of the universe of which he is the chief intelligence. Therefore, if the law of progression be accepted, God must have been engaged from the beginning, and must now be engaged in progressive development, and infinite as God is, he must have been less powerful in the past than he is today. Nothing in the universe is static or quiescent. While it is folly for man to attempt to unravel in detail the mystery of the past, yet it is only logical to believe that a progressive God has not always possessed his present absolute position. That view does not change his relative position to man. The term infinite is always of relative meaning.

"The supreme Being of the universe transcends the human understanding. His intelligence is as the sum of all other intelligences. There can be no rational discussion of the details of God's life or nature. To him we give the most complete devotion, for to us he is in all respects infinite and perfect. His Godhood, however, is the product of simple obedience to the laws of the universe.

"God, exalted by his glorious intelligence, is moving on into new fields of power with a rapidity of which we can have no conception, whereas man, in a lower stage of development, moves relatively at a snail-like, though increasing pace."[40]

Elder Widtsoe also wrote: "There are those who will protest that there is no growth in heaven. In firm answer, the Church of Jesus Christ of Latter-day Saints asserts that the power of increase or growth is a necessary quality of intelligence. If intelligence remains with us in the hereafter, the power of growth will continue also.

"We can now understand more clearly the real, the ultimate object of life. Growth or progress may be unending. Every onward step, ever so small, is another approach to the ideal of perfection. God is perfect. Therefore, eternally progressing man is ever approaching the likeness of God; ever on the way to perfection. That is the objective of life, here and hereafter, — to approach, eternally, the likeness of our Father in Heaven, on earth, and in the hereafter."[41]

If God himself is forever progressing in a degree of glory beyond man's comprehension, it is a reasonable deduction that man is incapable of being equal to him at any given point in time. To be ever approaching that high ideal in the same degree is therefore a description of exalted attainment. Teachings about the progressive nature of God were more widely taught in Elder Widtsoe's day than in our own. Because they dealt with God's incomprehensible nature, attempts to convey one's impressions were limited by language and interpretation. When studying the teachings of those who addressed this subject, it is often difficult to know whether that person is describing individual advancement or eternal family increase, the latter being more widely accepted today. All who made such attempts seemed to agree that understanding about God's advancing glory is important but can only be approximated. The statements that follow indicate the difficulty of ascertaining what God's progression consists of. The strongest advocate of eternal increase was President Joseph Fielding Smith, who taught:

"Do you not see that it is in this manner that our Eternal Father is progressing? Not by seeking knowledge which he does not have, for such a thought cannot be maintained in the light of scripture. It is not through ignorance and learning hidden truths that he progresses, for if there are truths which he does not know, then these things are greater than he, and this cannot be. Why can't we learn wisdom and believe what the Lord has revealed? . . .

"It is not because the Lord is ignorant of law and truth that he is able to progress, but because of his knowledge and wisdom. The Lord is constantly using his knowledge in his work, and his great work is in bringing to pass the immortality and eternal life of man. By the creation of worlds and peopling them, by building and extending, he progresses, but not because the fulness of truth is not understood by him."[42]

Several favored advancement beyond the increase President Smith described. Elder James E. Talmage gave numerous descriptions of the progressive nature of God, of which the following are typical:

"The fact of man's eternal progression in nowise indicates a state of eventual equality on however exalted a plane; nor does it imply that the progressive soul must in the eternal eons overtake those once far ahead of him in achievement. Advancement is not a characteristic of inferior status alone; indeed, the increment of progress may be vastly greater in the higher spheres of activity. This conception leads to the inevitable deduction that God Himself, Elohim, the Very Eternal Father, is a progressive Being, eternally advancing from one perfection to another, possessed as He is of that distinguishing attribute, which shall be the endowment of all who attain celestial exaltation — the power of eternal increase."[43]

"It is reasonable to believe, in the absence of direct revelation, by which alone absolute knowledge of the matter could be acquired, that, in accordance with God's plan of eternal progression, advancement within each of the three specified kingdoms will be provided for; though as to possible progress from one kingdom to another the scriptures make no positive affirmation. Eternal advancement along different lines is conceivable. We may conclude that degrees and grades will ever characterize the kingdoms of our God. Eternity is progressive; perfection is relative; the essential feature of God's living purpose is its associated power of eternal increase."[44]

Elder B. H. Roberts taught that God's immutability, or unchange-ableness, does not preclude enlargement in his kingdom, nor, perhaps, new thoughts, new vistas, and new experiences:

"His [God's] immutability should be regarded as stability, adherence to principle. . . . But God's immutability should not be so understood as to exclude the idea of advancement or progress of God. Thus, for example: God's kingdom and glory may be enlarged, as more and more redeemed souls are added to his kingdom: as worlds and world-systems are multiplied and redeemed and enrolled with celestial spheres, so God's kingdom is enlarged and his glory increased. . . . An absolute immutability would require eternal immobility—which would reduce God to a condition eternally static, which, from the nature of things, would bar him from participating in that enlargement of kingdom and increasing glory that comes from redemption and progress of men. And is it too bold a thought, that with this progress, even for the Mightiest, new thoughts, and new vistas may appear, inviting to new adventures and enterprises that will yield new experiences, advancement, and enlargement even for the Most High?"[45]

Elder Melvin J. Ballard spoke of the eternal laws, which God obeyed in order to become God, and which govern man's advancement and eternal progression. These laws are as basic as those associated with the fall of Adam, which God could not violate or change:

"We have learned that upon those planets our Father's children dwell in all stages of perfection and advancement. There are those who are infinitely beyond us in eternal progress, who have reached their present degree of perfection by obedience to everlasting and irrevocable law. God Himself can not change that law, no more than He could obliterate the consequence of Adam's fall. He could not be God and violate a law which is eternal, and by obedience to which He became God."[46]

Elder Anthony W. Ivins summarized his views of the law of eternal progression as follows: "All I have to say to you is that we believe in progression, we are a progressive people, and we believe that there will never be an end to it, that we shall continue and must continue, in this life and in the life to come, to go forward, for water that stands still of necessity becomes stagnant."[47]

Elder Charles W. Penrose said, "Progress is the law of the universe, and all beings, all intelligences will have an opportunity of progressing along certain lines."[48]

President Joseph F. Smith described man's eternal life as continual advancement throughout the eternities: "We believe that every man will have his work to do in the other world, just as surely as he had it to do here, and a greater work than he can do here. We believe that we are on the road of advancement, of development in knowledge, in understanding, and in every good thing, and that we will continue to grow, advance and develop throughout the eternities that are before us. That is what we believe."[49]

CONCLUSION

The teachings of the Doctrine and Covenants regarding salvation and eternal life focus on the celestial glory and those things associated with qualifying therefore. By the declaration of section 76, all three degrees of glory surpass our understanding in dominion, might, and glory. Yet, because the Lord has given us this revelation, he intends that we learn much of eternal value from the descriptions therein. Perhaps more revelation restoring doctrinal understanding of the degrees of glory and life associated therewith only awaits our mastery and appreciation of what he has already given us. It is edifying to study the teachings of our great leaders, of whom Elder John A. Widtsoe is but one. They have set an example before us; and as they have sought to understand these great visions, so ought we. In their teachings is the sense that they speak "as one having authority": that in their hearts they comprehend more than their pen is able to write or their mouth to speak. Within us there ought to swell the urging to study these things out in our mind that we might be ready to understand them by the Spirit. The Lord ended section 76 by stating that these things are "only to be seen and understood by the power of the Holy Spirit, which God bestows on those who love him, and purify themselves before him; to whom he grants this privilege of seeing and knowing for themselves." (D&C 76:116–17.)

NOTES

1. Bruce R. McConkie, "The Doctrinal Restoration," in *The Joseph Smith Translation of the Bible* (Provo, Utah: Religious Studies Center, 1984), pp. 1-22.

2. John A. Widtsoe, *In a Sunlit Land* (Salt Lake City: Deseret News Press, 1952), p. 25.

3. Ibid., p. 37.

4. Ibid., p. 50.

5. Ibid., p. 52.

6. An entry in the Journal History, dated 11 April 1898, reads, "Professor J. A. Widtsoe prresented [sic] to the First Presidency the Mss of an elaborate concordance of the Doctrine and Covenants, which he had prepared with great labor and completeness, and offered it as a gift to the church, hoping that it would prove acceptable and useful. The Presidency thankfully accepted the gift in behalf of the Church, and expressed the belief that it would prove very useful."

7. John A. Widtsoe, *A Concordance to the Doctrine and Covenants of The*

Church of Jesus Christ of Latter-day Saints (Salt Lake City: Deseret Sunday School Union, 1906), Preface.

8. A. C. Lambert, "The Book of Doctrine and Covenants," *Improvement Era,* Oct. 1951, p. 714.

9. G. Homer Durham, *The Message of the Doctrine and Covenants* (Salt Lake City: Bookcraft, 1969), p. v.

10. See David B. Rimington, *Vistas on Visions: A Golden Anniversary History of Church Education in Southern California* (Anaheim, Calif.: Shumway Family History Services, 1988), p. v.

11. Durham, *Message,* p. 170.

12. Ibid., pp. 167–68. "President Brigham Young has suggested that the ultimate punishment of the sons of perdition may be that they, having their spiritual bodies disorganized, must start over again, must begin anew the long journey of existence, repeating the steps that they took in the eternities before the Great Council was held. That would be punishment, indeed!" (Widtsoe, *Evidences and Reconciliations* [Salt Lake City: Bookcraft, 1987], pp. 213–14; see also *Journal of Discourses,* 7:57; 2:124.

Elder James E. Talmage gave a similar view in the centennial general conference: "What is it to be damned? Does it mean that all who come under that sentence shall be cast into hell, there to dwell forever and forever? The light of the century, given by the Lord, declares the falsity of that construction. . . . During this hundred years many other great truths not known before, have been declared to the people, and one of the greatest is that to hell there is an exit as well as an entrance. . . . No man will be kept in hell longer than is necessary to bring him to a fitness for something better. . . . The Lord has not abated in the least what he has said in earlier dispensations concerning the operation of his law and his gospel, but he has made clear unto us his goodness and mercy through it all, for it is his glory and his work to bring about the immortality and eternal life of man." (In Conference Report, Apr. 1930, pp. 95–97.)

13. Widtsoe, *Evidences,* p. 212.

14. John A. Widtsoe, "Fundamentals of Temple Doctrine," *Utah Genealogical and Historical Magazine,* 13 (1922): 132.

15. Widtsoe, *Evidences,* p. 213.

16. Ibid., p. 214.

17. Ibid., p. 216.

18. The same teachings had been taught by Dr. Widtsoe in the first two quarters at USC and were published in a textbook, *The Program of the Church.* The title of the book was taken from the course catalog for Religion 60-B1. Several chapters in section IV, "Explanations of the Church," address our teachings about salvation and eternal life, universal salvation, graded salvation, and eternal progression.

19. Durham, *Message,* p. 157.

20. John A. Widtsoe, "The Prophetic Value of Section Two," *Improvement Era,* Aug. 1906, pp. 760, 764–65.

21. John A. Widtsoe, "Genealogical Activities in Europe," *Utah Genealogical and Historical Magazine,* 22 (July 1931): 104–5.

22. Durham, *Message,* p. 167.

23. Ibid., p. 166.

24. Ibid., p. 164.

25. John A. Widtsoe, "Temple Worship," *Utah Genealogical and Historical Magazine,* 12 (April 1921): 55.

26. In Conference Report, Apr. 1921, p. 36.

27. Widtsoe, "Temple Doctrine," p. 132.

28. John A. Widtsoe, *An Understandable Religion* (Independence, Mo.: Zions Printing and Publishing Co., 1944), pp. 84–85.

29. Widtsoe, *Evidences,* p. 199.

30. Ibid., pp. 199–200.

31. Ibid., p. 204.

32. Durham, *Message,* pp. 169–70.

33. Joseph Fielding Smith, *Doctrines of Salvation* (Salt Lake City: Bookcraft, 1955), 2:32.

34. Durham, *Message,* pp. 168–69.

35. John A. Widtsoe, "The Worth of Souls," *Utah Genealogical and Historical Magazine,* 25 (1934): 188.

36. John A. Widtsoe, *Program of the Church of Jesus Christ of Latter-day Saints* (Salt Lake City: Deseret News Press, 1937), pp. 204–5.

37. In Conference Report, Apr. 1922, p. 96.

38. *Deseret News,* 26 Jan. 1937.

39. Widtsoe, "Worth of Souls," p. 189.

40. John A. Widtsoe, *A Rational Theology,* 7th ed. (Salt Lake City: Deseret Book Co., 1965), pp. 24–26.

41. Widtsoe, *Understandable Religion,* p. 38.

42. Smith, *Doctrines of Salvation,* 1:7, 10.

43. James E. Talmage, *The Story of "Mormonism"* (Salt Lake City: Deseret Book Co., 1930), p. 127.

44. James E. Talmage, *The Articles of Faith* (Salt Lake City: The Church of Jesus Christ of Latter-day Saints, 1959), p. 409.

45. B. H. Roberts, *Seventies' Course in Theology, 4th Year, Atonement* (Salt Lake City: Deseret News, 1911), pp. 69–70.

46. In Conference Report, Oct. 1912, p. 106.

47. In Conference Report, Oct. 1912, p. 100.

48. In Conference Report, Apr. 1915, p. 37.

49. In Conference Report, Apr. 1912, p. 8.

CHAPTER SIXTEEN

The New and Everlasting Covenant

Chauncey C. Riddle

Professor of Philosophy
Brigham Young University

I begin with a word about speaking. Realities are wholes. Human words can never capture wholes; thus, human descriptions always fall short of being true to the reality they attempt to describe. The best we human speakers can do with words is to paint broad brush strokes that indicate some basic relationships and hope that each recipient will gain inspiration from that painting, partial and incomplete though it be, and that each hearer will then search for the truth of the matter through the Holy Spirit.

I propose to paint for you a picture of the new and everlasting covenant. I do not suppose that I can or will say everything necessary to do justice to this topic, but I will attempt to express what I feel to be certain key concepts and ideas that are important. I ask you to compare these with your own picturings of the reality of things in the hope that we may each move one step closer to understanding those things which are eternally important. I therefore bear the following witness.

THE GODS

We begin with the concept of our God. We know of three beings who are our God: the Father, the Son, and the Holy Ghost.[1] These three are individuals, yet they are also one, and furthermore, they invite every human being to become one with them.[2] The good news of the restored gospel of Jesus Christ is that God is our Father and invites us to become as he is and to become one with him through his son Jesus Christ.[3]

Though there be gods and lords many, there is but one God,[4] and that God is the priesthood-ordered community of all the righteous, exalted beings who exist.[5] To be invited to join them by hearing the gospel of Jesus Christ is to receive the greatest message in the universe; to be enabled to join them by receiving the new and everlasting covenant is to have the greatest opportunity in the universe; to be joined with them is the greatest gift in the universe, which gift is life eternal, sharing with them all the good they have and are.[6]

This good that they share is righteousness. Righteousness is that necessary order of social relationships in which beings of knowledge and power must bind themselves in order to live together in accomplishment and happiness for eternity. They bind themselves to each other with solemn covenants to become predictable, dependable, and united so that they can be trusted. They bind themselves to be honest, true, chaste, and benevolent so that they can do good for all other beings, which good they do by personal sacrifice to fulfill all righteousness.

The contrary of this good is evil. Evil is departing from God's order of righteousness by twisting and/or diminishing it. Evil enables one being in a social order to fulfill his own personal desires at the expense of others, thus to be a law unto himself.[7]

MAN

We, the children of God, as we are found in our natural and evil state upon the face of this earth, are called by the scriptures "natural man" or sometimes simply "man."[8] The natural man is without God and Christ in the world and by default is carnal, sensual, and devilish.[9] We are carnal insofar as we pay more attention to information that comes through our flesh than to that that comes directly to our spirit. We are sensual insofar as we delight more in the pleasures of the flesh and of the world than we delight in doing good. We are devilish insofar as we would rather yield to the temptations of Satan and be selfish than perform the sacrifices necessary to do good for others. Such a natural man tends to continue in his inertial path of choosing first good and then evil, as he pleases, until he is jarred out of his complacency by a divine witness. The witness is that to become righteous, he must repent of choosing evil and accept the godly order of choosing good. Those who accept that jarring are the honest in heart.[10] Those who will not accept the jarring harden their hearts by that rejection, moving themselves further from righteousness.[11]

The honest in heart who hear the restored gospel are taught that Father is Man of Holiness, who cannot look upon sin with the least degree of allowance.[12] They are also taught that Father so loved his children of this world that he gave his Only Begotten Son as a sacrifice so that every human soul might be redeemed both from the effects of the fall of Adam and from the effects of his own sins and weaknesses. They are taught that because of the Fall, man's nature is to be evil continually[13] and that only through striving to accept the merits and mercy of the Son of God can any human be rescued from being and doing evil.[14]

SALVATION

The rescue process is called salvation. To be saved is to be placed beyond the power of one's enemies.[15] The great enemy of each human being is himself, for in our weakness and selfishness we are and do evil. We as individuals or as collective humanity cannot help ourselves or each other fully to overcome weakness or selfishness.[16] That overcoming is possible only if we fully cooperate with Jesus Christ in fulfilling Father's plan of salvation. That cooperation enables each human being also to become a person of holiness, which is to be completely righteous, perfect in good, even as the Father is, even as the Son is.[17]

Such salvation comes only by covenant with God, never by accident or by natural or human process.[18] Man must first understand and then desire the proffered transformation of his own eternal nature when it is proffered.[19] Before it is too late,[20] man must cooperate with Christ to the fullest extent of his considerable human powers to do better,[21] and he must then fully submit to the incomparable divine power of Jesus Christ to create for him and of him a new creature, remade in every aspect of being.[22] Thus human beings may become good and gods.[23]

There are two covenants whereby a human being may attain complete good and thus become an exalted being as God is. These two covenants were established by Father in the beginning for the salvation of his children. The first of Father's covenants is a covenant of justice; the second is called the new and everlasting covenant and is a covenant of mercy.

THE FIRST COVENANT

The first covenant, the covenant of justice, was discussed in the council of the gods held before this world was, as is recorded in the book of Abraham: "God saw these souls that they were good, and he stood in the midst of them, and he said: These I will make my rulers; for he stood among those that were spirits, and he saw that they were good; and he said unto me: Abraham, thou art one of them; thou wast chosen before thou wast born.

"And there stood one among them that was like unto God, and he said unto those who were with him: We will go down, for there is space there, and we will take of these materials, and we will make an earth whereon these may dwell;

"And *we will prove them herewith, to see if they will do all things whatsoever the Lord their God shall command them;*

"And they who keep their first estate shall be added upon; and they who keep not their first estate shall not have glory in the same kingdom with those who keep their first estate; and they who keep their second estate shall have glory added upon their heads for ever and ever." (Abraham 3:23–26; italics added.)

The conditions of the first covenant, the covenant of justice, were these:

1. Father would give his children instruction and commandments.

2. Any child who would believe Father and obey his every commandment, without exception, would in that obedience grow to attain and maintain all the good that Father is and does, which is exaltation.

3. Any child who disobeyed any single commandment of Father, would, without exception, immediately die spiritually, which spiritual death is to be cut off from Father's presence, no longer to be able to grow in his order of good.[24]

4. For every transgression of a commandment of Father, the offender must suffer for that sin and make full restitution for that sin, this suffering and restitution being at least equal to the suffering and loss caused to the person(s) against whom the transgression was committed.[25]

It is possible that the covenant of justice, or the first covenant, is the order of heaven spoken of in the Lord's prayer.[26] If so, it would have been the abrogation of that covenant by which the third of the hosts of heaven fell in the premortal war in heaven.[27] That speculation aside, it is quite plain that this covenant of justice was understood by Adam in the Garden of Eden, for he was determined to and intended to keep all of Father's commandments.

But Adam transgressed the first covenant, and by so doing he immediately brought upon himself and upon all of his posterity the promised spiritual death.[28] In this condition, if there were no intervention, Adam and his posterity would have been lost and fallen forever.[29] Upon mortal death every soul would have passed fully into the power of Satan, to become angels to Satan forever.[30]

The fall of Adam was necessary. It was necessary because every child of Father needs to be out of Father's presence, to have forgotten the premortal existence, thus to be thrust into a strange world where he would be forced to choose between good and evil according to the desires of his own heart.[31] It is a proving of the heart of each person whereby each person may see for himself whether or not he will choose good over evil and thus be able to stand the opportunity of wielding Father's unlimited knowledge and power.[32] But if the Fall was necessary, so was it necessary to have a means of reclaiming man from the Fall should any man desire to choose good and only good. Father in his goodness and omniscience had already provided before the Fall for a second covenant.[33]

THE SECOND COVENANT

The second covenant is a covenant of mercy and is the new and everlasting covenant. It is new because it is the second covenant,[34] and it is everlasting because "Everlasting" is one of the names of him in whose name we must learn to do all things.[35] We make this covenant with the Father, with the Son, and with the Holy Ghost, but we receive all of the blessings of this covenant through the Son, who is Everlasting. Through him and only through him may any fallen creature claim blessings that are everlasting.[36]

The new and everlasting covenant has two basic parts. Part one is the covenant of baptism, being born of water and of the Spirit. The covenant of baptism is our pledge to seek after good and to eliminate all choosing and doing of evil in our lives, and it is also our receiving the power to keep that promise.[37] Part two of the new and everlasting covenant is the oath and covenant of the priesthood. The work of part two is to receive the power and authority of God and to become perfect in using that power and authority to minister to other beings to bring about their happiness.[38] The intent of both of these parts is to enable a human being to lay hold on every good and godly thing in both time and eternity.[39] They enable us to do all that we can do towards our own salvation and also to receive and rely upon the fulness of the grace of God, that we might be fully transformed from the weak, natural creature that we were into one like unto God himself, unto the measure of the stature of the fulness of Christ.

Please do not mistake: we here consider parts one and two of the covenant as separate only because it helps us to see the whole better by analysis. Analysis reveals distinctions, but these distinctions are artificial and illustrative only. The new and everlasting covenant is one living whole; the two parts intertwine and enable each other in every way, even as the intertwining of body and spirit make the living, acting, breathing human soul, indissoluble in function but separable in understanding.

The formal nature of part one of the new and everlasting covenant is initiated in the covenant of baptism and is progressively renewed and strengthened in partaking of the symbols of the flesh and blood of our Savior in the sacrament. Part two of the new and everlasting covenant is initiated by ordination and is enlarged by the ordinances of the temple.

BAPTISM

The light of Christ is given to every man who comes into the world, that he may know the good, as opposed to the many varieties of evil that are promoted by Satan in this world.[40] The essence of human living is to make many choices between good and evil each day.[41]

We choose so that we can demonstrate what we really desire. If we desire the good, we show that our nature is compatible with Father's and that we would enjoy doing the work of righteousness in time and eternity. If we desire evil, we show that we cannot be trusted with any great power, for we would tend to use it for our personal advantage rather than for the great work of righteousness in which all of the gods participate.[42]

Every soul who comes to accountability is thus forced to wrestle with good and evil and to make choices. He who chooses good will discover that he also chooses evil, for all of us sin and go out of the way.[43] To every sinner there eventually comes a new light, the Holy Ghost. This new light bears witness of Jesus Christ and tells him that if he will put his trust in Christ, Christ will become his Savior and help him to stop choosing evil. Those who desire to stop choosing and doing evil find this message most enticing, so much so that they are willing to try the experiment to see if the promise is true.[44]

Each soul is instructed that if he wishes to try the experiment, he must believe and trust in the Son of God and begin to eliminate each evil thing from his life. These steps are called faith and repentance. The promised consequence of taking these two steps is that the Holy Spirit, which guides and enables these two steps, will then come in even greater abundance and will reward the experimenter with increased understanding and power to have even more faith and to repent of more sins.[45] If the experimenter is pleased with that result, then a new proposal is made to the experimenter: Would you be willing to enter into a covenant with God that would enable you to have full faith in Jesus Christ, to strengthen your repentance by enabling you to have the constant companionship of the Holy Spirit? Those who accept this message are given the opportunity to enter into the new and everlasting covenant by being baptized.[46]

The candidate for baptism must promise three things:[47]

1. The recipient must be willing to take upon himself the name of Jesus Christ. Taking the name of the Savior begins in the waters of baptism whereby we accept Jesus Christ as our new spiritual father and are willing to be known as his children before all people at all times and in all places. But it is also an expression of the willingness to take upon us all of the names of Jesus Christ, even until we receive a fulness of what he is and has. This willingness then is the willingness to go on to receive the second part of the new and everlasting covenant, which is to receive the oath and covenant of the holy priesthood.[48]

2. The covenanter additionally promises always to remember his new father, Jesus Christ. This promise seems to mean to think upon him, yearn for him, pray continually in his name, be anxious for the success of his great work of salvation among the children of men.[49]

3. The recipient of the covenant of baptism must also affirm his willingness to abide and obey every instruction that his new father will give to him. Only in so doing can the covenanter come to avoid choosing and doing evil, for righteousness in this world is only of Christ, he being the sole fountain of this rare reality.[50]

This requirement of total obedience of the second covenant[51] is much like the requirement of total obedience of the first covenant; indeed, it is identical with it. There is a difference in that in the second covenant there is the possibility of salvation and exaltation, even if the promise of obedience is not entirely kept at first. That is to say, there is provision for salvation, even if one is weak and sins after taking the covenant. But the covenant also provides that the covenanter cannot suppose that the provision for sinning will allow him an escape forever; the escape is strictly temporary, and while yet in mortality the person must learn firmly and determinedly to keep this promise to obey fully and faithfully every single instruction the Savior gives him, without error or omission, which means a complete cessation of sinning.[52]

The immediate reward to the covenanter for making these three promises of the covenant of baptism is that hands are then laid upon the person's head, he is blessed with the right to the constant companionship of the Holy Spirit, and he is commanded to receive that companionship unto himself.[53] Only with the help received through that constant companionship can any individual keep the promises made in the waters of baptism. And only by the covenanter's keeping the promises he made will the Holy Spirit remain with him. If one willfully disobeys the promptings to do good which the Holy Spirit brings, one is no longer entitled to nor can stand the continuing presence of the Holy Spirit, and the Holy Spirit then mercifully departs.[54]

Receiving the constant companionship of the Holy Spirit is the baptism of fire which normally follows the baptism of water and is the occasion for the person receiving a remission of the penalty due for the sins which he has previously committed but has now repented of.[55] The presence of the Holy Spirit then enables the person to go forth in the knowledge and power of God on the straight and narrow path of righteousness. As long as the person is obedient to the Savior's instructions as received through the Holy Spirit, he will retain that forgiveness of sins and will enjoy the continued blessed presence of that companionship. Willful disobedience, however, brings a loss of both.[56]

By receiving the baptism of water and of fire, the covenanter has now entered upon the strait and narrow path that leads to the end, which is eternal life.[57] But he is by no means there yet.[58] What he has gained is a fighting opportunity to win the battle between good and evil in his life. If he will do all he can to keep the covenant of baptism, surely and firmly evil will be eliminated from his life, replaced in every particular by the righteousness of God. Thus the person triumphs over worldliness and evil in his own person. Until this triumph of good over evil is an accomplished fact in his life, little can be done with the second part of the new and everlasting covenant.[59]

THE OATH AND COVENANT OF THE PRIESTHOOD

As the first part of the new and everlasting covenant focuses on the triumph of the covenanter in the battle to replace evil with good in all things, so the focus of the second part, the oath and covenant of the holy priesthood, focuses on the training of the individual to function for good in the power of the Holy Priesthood of the Son of God and to use that power correctly and advantageously in the callings of God to promote the eternal work of righteousness. The challenge of receiving the holy priesthood is this: Now that you have shown that you can overcome evil for yourself, let us see if you can go further, to wield the power of God, in righteousness, to help others to overcome evil.[60]

There are three stages by which one takes upon himself the oath and covenant of the holy priesthood and receives the power and authority of the Son of God.[61] The first stage is to receive the priesthood, which one does by receiving ordination, being set apart to a calling, and by functioning faithfully in that calling under the guidance and instruction of the Holy Spirit. Those who thus function carry out the mind and the will of God. If they do this faithfully, they will be given progressively greater power and responsibility in their stewardships, but this does not necessarily mean church position.[62] To receive the priesthood does mean that one fully accepts the priesthood authority of The Church of Jesus Christ of Latter-day Saints and that one will be subject to those who preside over him in that priesthood.

The second stage of receiving the oath and covenant of the holy priesthood is to receive one's personal endowment in the holy temple of God. First, the endowment consists of special blessings that are given to the person so that he can bear the power of God in this world without being destroyed by the abundant evil that will confront and oppose his labors to do the work of God in the power of God. Second, the endowment is a set of instructions and understandings that assist the person to understand mortality and his role therein. Third, the endowment involves covenants that the person makes, special promises to bear the burden of the work of the Lord in righteousness and purity. These promises are covenants of the oath and covenant of the priesthood.[63] The oath is action taken by God, who cannot lie nor sin in any way. Men, who can and do sin and lie, make covenants with God that they might escape sinning altogether and wield the power of God in righteousness, and they do this altogether for the glory of God, as part of their worship of him for his goodness, for his righteousness.[64]

The third part of the oath and covenant of the holy priesthood is to receive the covenant of marriage in the temple. This is God's marriage, eternal marriage, the establishment of a new eternal kingdom in the pattern of godliness, to do the supreme work of godliness eternally. Blessings are bestowed, covenants are made, and power and authority to act in the priesthood roles of husband and wife, father and mother, are given.[65]

To receive the oath and covenant of the Holy Priesthood of the Son of God is to affirm a desire to take one's place in the divine order of righteousness. To be received into that order is, as it were, to be brought into a harness.[66] The harness is a great eternal set of bindings that link husbands to wives, parents to children, men to God. To be worthy of the harness, one must pull one's assigned weight in one's assigned priesthood labors to further the eternal work of righteousness using the gifts and powers of God. One enters that place in the harness by free will, accepts the burden of the position by free will, and endures to the end by free will. The harness is not imposed upon anyone against his desires. Rather it is gained only by much pleading and repentance and is fulfilled only in sacrifice and obedience.[67] It is true that the outward forms of the priesthood are seemingly imposed upon some in their ignorance, unwillingness, or disobedience; but such an imposition is but a temporary thing of this world. Unless they repent, such persons have no power to bind or to act for God in this world, nor have they any claim on the power of God for the next world.[68]

The net sum of the new and everlasting covenant is that it is the power by which a human being learns to love God with all of his heart, might, mind, and strength and to establish God's righteousness here on earth.[69] This is another way of saying that we are thereby enabled to love our Savior and our neighbor in exactly the same manner in which our Savior loves us.[70] The work of the Aaronic Priesthood is to set into the godly order of righteousness affairs that pertain to the subduing of the earth and civil governing. The work of the Melchizedek Priesthood is to promote the spiritual welfare of souls through missionary work, genealogy and temple work, and the perfecting of the Saints unto the establishment of Zion. The highest focus of the Melchizedek Priesthood is the perfecting of the bonds of love between a husband and wife that binds them to the Savior and their children to them in the drawing power of that perfect love which we can receive only from our Savior and only as we abide the promises we make in the new and everlasting covenant.

THE ATONEMENT OF JESUS CHRIST

Hitherto we have concentrated almost solely on what human beings need to do to fulfill their opportunities and responsibilities in the new and everlasting covenant. I wish now to turn our attention to our Savior's role in this grand pattern of salvation for mankind. We have been discussing the necessary human 1 percent of the work of the covenant. Now we turn to the divine 99 percent, the grace of God whereby we are saved. We are and can be saved by that 99 percent only if and as we fully do our 1 percent.[71] I turn now to the atonement of Jesus Christ.

When we examine the etymological roots of the word *atonement,* we find that in Old English there was a regular expression used to say that people became "at one." This was sometimes spelled as two words, sometimes as one. The concept was a bringing together, an arranging of agreement, a uniting of hitherto estranged parties. The process by which this uniting was achieved was in English appropriately denominated "at-one-ment." When a word was desired to express what our Savior accomplishes in our behalf, no better word could be found than the word "at-one-ment," which we have come to pronounce *atonement.* This English word is the translation of the Hebrew *kaphar,* which means, among other things, to cover, and the Greek word *katallag,* which means to change in an intensive way and also to reconcile. The Savior's atonement does cover our sins, and change our nature, and reconcile us to the Father.

My understanding is that our Savior's atonement is the general descriptive term that covers all of his labors to exalt mankind from the moment he said, "Father, thy will be done, and the glory be thine forever,"[72] to the great and last day when he will present his children spotless before Father for Father's acceptation unto exaltation.[73] As it is the task of men to learn to love God with all their heart, might, mind, and strength,[74] so we can see that it is the task of our Savior's atonement to enable men to love God with all their heart, might, mind, and strength. We will describe the atonement in these four aspects.

JUSTIFICATION

The process by which our Savior enables men to love God with all of their minds is termed in the scriptures "justification." Our Savior helps us to become just, which is to say righteous, by teaching us the truth we need to understand about God, about righteousness, about ourselves, and about the nature of our mortal probation. That teaching is essentially accomplished through the teaching and preaching of the gospel of Jesus Christ. This gospel was given to our father Adam and will be yet taught to every child of Adam. Jesus Christ is the truth,[75] and only in truth can man act correctly to be saved. Thus our Savior has worked since the beginning to make sure that every human person has access to enough truth to take advantage of the opportunity to be ennobled in righteousness, to be redeemed from the fall of Adam, and to be reunited with Father.[76]

But truth of itself does not fulfill righteousness. The understanding of *what is* must be supplemented by correct principles that tell us what *ought to be* and by specific instructions about how to implement those correct principles within the framework of the true reality that has been revealed. Thus our Savior also reveals correct principles and specific directions as to how to act wisely for righteousness. These principles and directions are called in the scriptures "light," and together with truth, they constitute intelligence, or the glory of God. Enabling his children to have his light and truth as the basis of all of their understanding, choosing, and acting is the purpose of the Savior's process of justification of his children, thus to assist each of them to become just beings.[77] This mission of justification of his children the Savior does largely through his agent, the Holy Ghost.[78] The receiving of the constant companionship of the Holy Ghost is the means by which our new father, Jesus Christ, teaches each of his children to walk in light and truth, giving each of us line upon line and precept upon precept until that great day when, through complete faith in him, each of his children is glorified in light and truth,[79] even as he, our Savior, has been so glorified by his Father.[80]

In behalf of justification, the prophets have labored in each dispensation to explain to men the basic outlines of truth and righteousness and have hoped that men would rejoice in those outlines, desire to become more righteous, and enter into the new and everlasting covenant to receive a fulness of righteousness. In behalf of justification, the scriptures have been written that men might better understand the witness of past generations and see that God and righteousness are the same today, yesterday, and always. The scriptural epitome of what it means to be just, to have received the justification of Christ, is given in the Sermon on the Mount. The Book of Mormon is the scripture that lays out justification both as a process and a product with greatest clarity.[81] The scriptures testify that justification through our Lord and Savior Jesus Christ is indeed just and true.[82]

PURIFICATION

As the new children of Christ bask in the light and truth of our Savior's power of justification, it gradually dawns on each of us that to pour light and truth into the human vessel is not enough. As a child of Christ attempts to love the light and truth that come to him by his new father's gift, each becomes aware of an alarming fact: having light and truth is no guarantee of being able to do what is right. Sometimes we know full well what our Savior would have us do, but we yet deliberately do that which is evil because we want to. If a person has indeed begun to love God and his neighbor, this revelation of the impurity of one's own heart is horrifying. It means that at any time one is able to and apt to kick over the traces of the priesthood harness and consort with the evil powers in this world to gain some short-term personal advantage. It is this realization that makes even the prophets to weep and to mourn because of their iniquities and weaknesses.[83]

Providentially, the Savior has a cure for this malady of heart, this willingness to choose evil over good. The Savior's cure is denominated in the scriptures as "purification."[84] Being the Lord God Omnipotent, the creator of heaven and earth and all things that in them are, being fully invested with the power of Father, our Savior can reach into our bosom and give each of us a new heart, a pure heart. He tells us that he will not do that merely upon some incidental request but only after we have done literally all we can do to repent and conform to the standards of godliness with the powers and opportunities he has already given to us. If we have repented of every sin we can repent of, have made fourfold restitution as far as we are able,[85] and have been reconciled to our brother,[86] we may present ourselves at the altar with a broken heart and a contrite spirit[87] and plead in mighty prayer for this change of heart.[88] Then and only then will our Savior reach in and give us a new heart.

The new heart will be a pure heart, one that has no selfish desires, one that is willing to do the right thing. It will choose to do the will of God at all times and places, no matter what the opposition or the sacrifice involved. This new heart is made in the image of that of Jesus

Christ, that same heart that enabled our Savior to say, "Father, not my will, but thine be done," that same heart that enabled him to live a sinless life, that same heart for which he was chosen to be the Firstborn and to be the Only Begotten.

To be purified is to become literally a new creature in Christ, to die as to the old person that we were, literally to become of the heart and mind of our new father. The scriptures promise great rewards for those who qualify and take this step. The scriptural name for this new heart is "charity."[89] Charity is to have a heart that loves with the pure love of Christ. Without that charity, we are literally nothing. Thus is the heart of a person saved. Then becomes possible for the person to be redeemed from the Fall,[90] to see God,[91] and not to need to be further protected from the tree of life by those helpful cherubim.[92]

RESURRECTION

The strength of the mortal tabernacles of men was rendered temporary and relatively impotent by the fall of their mortal father, Adam. This fallen and mortal state of man's body is a blessing because, being temporary, it does not have to be endured forever. Pain, illness, hunger, aging, and other kinds of physical distress are able to serve their useful, temporary purpose in educating and strengthening the spiritual aspect of individuals while allowing an anticipated surcease.[93]

Permanent physical death would not be an improvement. Were mortal death to be the end of being tabernacled in flesh, every human would be at a serious disadvantage, because only when one is clothed in flesh can there be a fulness of joy.[94] Because of the circumstances in which Adam fell, he became subject to Satan, and that subjection would have been complete and final had not the Savior a most important part to play relative to our physical tabernacles.

Our Savior is God for every living creature, for he created all of us physically and is charged with fostering our eternal welfare. All the while that he is offering truth and righteousness for our minds and hearts through the light of Christ and through the covenant processes of justification and purification, he is also entirely mindful of the physical circumstances of each being on earth. Not a sparrow nor a hair of our heads falls to earth unnoticed by him.[95]

For his eternal purposes our Savior suffers to transpire much that we humans call evil. But he also prevents much evil from occurring and transmutes all of what evil he does allow into the possibility of becoming a blessing. For that behind-the-scenes love for us he gets precious little credit. But he gives that love in spite of the unknowing and selfish complaining of his reluctant charges.

Persons of the world pay a good deal of attention to creature comforts. In fact, some spend most of their time in acquiring, comparing, and consuming the delights of the flesh. Worldly wisdom has it that a pleasure in hand is worth two hundred in the heavenly bush. Worldly wisdom also has it that the end justifies the means in acquiring said carnal delights, especially when taken at the expense of one's enemies.

But for his faithful covenant children, those who have hearkened to the spiritual call to truth and righteousness, the Savior recommends sacrifice and selective denial of the flesh.[96] Those of his children who are faithful to his recommendations then receive special physical blessings through the power of his holy priesthood and his Holy Spirit, so that illness, accident, genetic disorders, and death take no more than their exact allotted toll. As is appropriate in his wisdom, his faithful servants are renewed in the flesh,[97] so that their earthly mission cannot be shortened by natural processes. He intervenes when appropriate when their enemies would destroy them.[98] And when the time does come for the beneficial suffering of death, his faithful children are accompanied at each step by his Holy Spirit and foreknow his will in these matters. They know that they are not left alone.[99]

When they do die as to the flesh, it is our Savior who welcomes them to the eternal worlds and assigns them to new labors in his order of priesthood.[100] He ministers salvation in the spirit world through them, even as he does on earth, that all former mortals might know of and partake of the gifts he has to give.[101]

When our Savior took upon himself the role of Messiah, descending below all things to become flesh and blood on this earth and in this fallen world, he brought with him a special advantage. Being born of and fully empowered by an immortal Father, he had the power to choose not to die and also the power to raise himself from the dead should he choose to die. Being born of a mortal mother, he inherited the power to die. Not needing to die, he voluntarily gave up his possibly unending mortal life and all he could have accomplished in that sojourn for a greater purpose.[102] By dying voluntarily he performed the sacrifice of the Atonement, and by that sacrifice seized the keys of death and hell from Satan, who had gained them in the Fall, and thus prepared the way for the resurrection of all mankind.[103]

Thus, after all, probation has been extended, after each human creature has chosen the law by which he desires to be governed,[104] after all things are set in order and there is no further need of the special change known as repentance, then our Savior extends the opportunity of resurrection to each human being through his priesthood order. Every soul will receive again a tabernacle of flesh and bone, nevermore to die.[105] His righteous children receive a tabernacle of his own order, a celestial body, having the same powers that he inherited from his Father in becoming the Only Begotten. Thus our Savior draws us into the same order of flesh and bone as that which he and Father enjoy. Thus in one more way we may become one with Father through the atonement of Jesus Christ.

SANCTIFICATION

Coming into this world already just and pure, our Savior was able to live in mortality without sinning. This astounding achievement was not automatic. He knew full well that he had the power to sin, and he could easily have stepped off the path in either direction at any time. But because he loved Father with all of his heart, might, mind, and strength, he refused to sin. In that love he also loved us, his neighbors, with that same pure love with which Father loves him. Thus our Savior was the perfect model of righteousness, truly our total exemplar.[106]

By not sinning even once our Savior demonstrated that he was indeed the Son of God. Not only did he show us the way, the truth, and the life, but he also made it possible by his sinlessness to suffer for our sins, which is the fourth and final aspect of his atonement.

The need for the suffering of the Atonement came from the nature of human sin. Sin is transgression of the law of God.[107] The law of God is not arbitrary but is established upon eternal principles of righteousness. That righteousness, by way of justice, demands that when one being hurts another without cause and permission, that hurt must be matched by a similar suffering on the part of the perpetrator of the injury. Not only that, but restitution must be made so that the injured person is at least as well off after the injury as he was before the injury. Only as both of these conditions — suffering and restitution — are fully satisfied can any sinner stand blameless before Father and endure his presence.[108]

Having given men the opportunity to sin after having created them, our Savior also provided that the individual might not be eternally damned for having sinned if he were truly sorry.[109] The appropriate measure of sorrow is that the sinner confess the sin, forsake sinning completely by turning to do only the Savior's will,[110] and make whatever partial restitution he can, which is repentance. Repentance indeed removes sinning, thus sparing the one-time sinner from further jeopardy, but repentance does not absolve the former sinner of the debt previously incurred. Only our Savior can make a sufficient suffering and restitution to render the sinner clean enough that that person could ever again live with Father.

So when an individual has done all he can to repent of sinning and to make restitution for his sins through partaking of the new and everlasting covenant, our Savior then assumes responsibility for the remainder of the obligation, saving men by his grace, but only after they have done all they can do.[111] The restitution he does through his role as Jehovah, the Father of heaven and earth, he who is able to reach into eternity and remove the everlasting eddies of the sins that men commit. He is able to stop the otherwise inexorable eternal consequences whereby evil is propagated through time and space by cause and effect. Thus he is able to leave each resurrected being in a condition in which he suffers no eternal consequence for any evil done to him in mortality by any other mortal.[112] Thus our Savior satisfies part of the demands of justice. It yet remained for him to suffer for the sins of all mankind, those sins past, present, and future to his mortal sojourn.

The occasion of the suffering of the Atonement was but one day of his life, the final day of his mortality. In Gethsemane and through the time on the cross, our Savior trod the winepress alone,[113] suffering the debt of sin, suffering a total suffering equal to all of the sinning that ever had or ever would be done.[114] Having paid the debt of sinning for the sins of all men, he can invite all of us to come to him and to learn of his ways and to partake of his forgiveness.[115]

Through his suffering our Savior made it possible for men not to need to suffer for their own sins, and thus he also made it possible for them to be acceptable again to Father. Our Savior offers to all men the cleansing of their might, that their power and priesthood in time and eternity might not need to be shortened because of blood and sin. He cleanses their garments, their power, that he then might make them perfect, complete, in all good things, even as Father is. Thus his divine restitution and suffering constitute a great work of atonement, enabling

men to be one with Father in might, thus enabling men to share all
that Father and he have.[116]

CONCLUSIONS

Human beings are saved by the grace of Christ, but only after each
does all he can do to perfect, purify, and ennoble himself. The saving
grace of Christ is his new and everlasting covenant and his power of
atonement, which are made possible by his righteousness and perfect
faith in his Father.

Thus human beings may be saved only by binding themselves to
Christ. It is as if our task were to stand straight and tall before Father,
but because of the Fall, we are broken and twisted. The Savior is our
straight and tall splint. If we bind ourselves to him, wrap strong covenants around us and him that progressively draw us up into his form
and nature, then we can become righteous as he is and can be saved.
But without him we are nothing.[117]

Thus "the righteous" spoken of in the scriptures are not human
beings who are or can become righteous by themselves. The righteous
are only those who have bound themselves to Jesus Christ by the
promises of the new and everlasting covenant and who then keep those
promises.[118] Only in him and by him are they able to do any good thing.
The righteous acts they do are not strictly their own acts; therefore
they take no credit for them. Rather do they give the glory to God.
They know that their righteous acts are acts of Christ, chosen by the
pure heart given by Christ, understood by the just mind given by Christ,
carried out by the new strength given by Christ, redounding to the
blessing of others in the priesthood might of Christ. Thus in Christ
the righteous move, and live, and have their being.[119]

If a human being endures to the end in the new and everlasting
covenant, until he is literally transformed into the stature of Christ in
heart, might, mind, and strength, then he may love God with all of his
heart, might, mind, and strength. And if he then endures to the end of
mortal life in that same condition, unfailingly enacting that same love,
that new nature will become his eternal nature. He becomes one with
God, part of God, also to work for the immortality and eternal life of
man forever, as gods.[120]

Thus the purpose of the new and everlasting covenant is to provide
a means whereby every human being may come to be able to fulfill
the first covenant, to do all things whatsoever their God commands

them. But the first covenant cannot be fulfilled by one who has sinned. Therefore it is only through living vicariously in Christ that any mortal fulfills the first covenant and thereby is enabled to become exalted. Thus Christ wrought eternal life for us in love by satisfying justice for us vicariously. He extends mercy to all who will learn to love until their love can satisfy the demands of Father's justice. The new and everlasting covenant is our detour whereby our Savior strengthens us until we can tread the narrow way of justice and mercy on our own.

Thus the new and everlasting covenant is a special case of the first covenant, that which enables sinners to yet claim the blessing of exaltation in eternity, even though they themselves, by themselves, do not merit such blessings and are at first unable to receive such blessings. Only in and through Christ may they inherit, through his worthiness.

Our Savior kept the first covenant and was exalted by it. Had he sinned, there could have been no one to at-one him with Father. Because of his faithfulness in the first covenant, the second, or new and everlasting, covenant was made possible, that all of us may share his blessings with him for all eternity.[121]

NOTES

1. D&C 20:28.
2. John 17:21.
3. D&C 20:59.
4. 1 Corinthians 8:5–6.
5. D&C 124:123; 76:50–60; Alma 13:1–16.
6. D&C 14:7.
7. D&C 88:21–35.
8. Mosiah 3:19.
9. Moses 5:13.
10. D&C 8:1–3.
11. Alma 10:6; 12:10, 35.
12. Moses 6:57; D&C 1:31.
13. Genesis 6:5; Ether 3:2; Moroni 7:8.
14. Moroni 6:4; D&C 3:20.
15. Joseph Smith, *Teachings of the Prophet Joseph Smith*, sel. Joseph Fielding Smith (Salt Lake City: Deseret Book Co., 1938), p. 305.
16. Acts 4:12.
17. 3 Nephi 12:48; 27:27.

18. "Where there is no kingdom of God there is no salvation.What constitutes the kingdom of God? Where there is a prophet, a priest, or a righteous man unto whom God gives his oracles" to eventuate in the administration of the new and everlasting covenant. (Smith, *Teachings of the Prophet Joseph Smith*, p. 272.)

19. "A man is saved no faster than he gains knowledge." (Smith, *Teachings of the Prophet Joseph Smith*, p. 217.)

20. D&C 45:6.

21. 2 Nephi 25:23.

22. 2 Corinthians 5:17; Galatians 6:15.

23. D&C 132:19–20.

24. Alma 42:14.

25. Alma 42:22–28.

26. 3 Nephi 13:10.

27. Moses 4:1–2; Revelation 12:7–11.

28. 1 Corinthians 15:22.

29. Alma 42:14.

30. 2 Nephi 9:7–9.

31. Psalm 37:4; Mosiah 11:2; Joseph Smith–History 1:15.

32. Psalm 24:3–5.

33. 1 Nephi 10:18.

34. Moses 6:56.

35. Genesis 17:7–8.

36. D&C 132:19.

37. Ephesians 4:11–13.

38. D&C 121:41–46.

39. Moroni 7:9.

40. John 1:9.

41. 2 Nephi 2:26; Alma 5:41.

42. D&C 121:34–40.

43. Romans 3:12; 2 Nephi 28:11.

44. Alma 32:28–32.

45. Alma 32:34.

46. Mosiah 18:8–10.

47. Moroni 4:3.

48. Dallin H. Oaks, "Taking Upon Us the Name of Jesus Christ," *Ensign*, May 1985, pp. 80–83.

49. Alma 34:17–27.

50. Ether 8:26; 12:28.

51. John 14:15.

52. Alma 22:16.

53. John 20:22; 2 Nephi 31:13; D&C 39:23; 76:52.

54. Alma 7:21.

55. 2 Nephi 31:17.

56. D&C 82:7.

57. 2 Nephi 31:18.

58. 2 Nephi 31:19–21.
59. D&C 121:36.
60. Mosiah 8:15–18.
61. D&C 68:2–4.
62. Matthew 25:14–30.
63. D&C 84:39.
64. D&C 82:19.
65. D&C 131:1–4.
66. Alma 13:6–9.
67. D&C 97:8.
68. D&C 121:34–37.
69. 3 Nephi 13:33.
70. John 13:34.
71. 2 Nephi 25:23; Mosiah 2:21.
72. Moses 4:2.
73. D&C 76:107.
74. D&C 59:5.
75. John 14:6.
76. 2 Nephi 2:3.
77. D&C 93:28.
78. Moses 6:60.
79. D&C 76:69.
80. D&C 93:11–14.
81. Alma 5.
82. D&C 20:30.
83. 2 Nephi 4:27; Isaiah 6:5.
84. Malachi 3:3; James 4:8; D&C 112:28.
85. D&C 98:44; Luke 19:8.
86. Matthew 5:23–24.
87. 2 Nephi 2:7.
88. Mormon 7:48; Mosiah 4:2.
89. Moroni 7:47.
90. Ether 3:13–14.
91. 3 Nephi 12:8.
92. Alma 12:21.
93. 2 Nephi 9:15.
94. D&C 93:33–34.
95. Luke 12:6–7.
96. Moroni 10:32.
97. D&C 84:33.
98. 2 Nephi 4:33.
99. John 14:18.
100. 2 Nephi 9:41.
101. D&C 138:30.
102. John 10:18.

103. 2 Nephi 9:10–12.
104. D&C 88:23–37.
105. Alma 11:41–44.
106. John 14:6.
107. 1 John 3:4.
108. D&C 4:2; D&C 84:24.
109. Mosiah 26:23.
110. D&C 58:43.
111. 2 Nephi 25:23.
112. Matthew 19:29.
113. Isaiah 63:3.
114. D&C 19:16–17.
115. 3 Nephi 27:13–22.
116. Alma 34:12–17.
117. John 15:1–5.
118. Alma 9:28.
119. Acts 17:28.
120. D&C 132:19–20.
121. D&C 88:107.

CHAPTER SEVENTEEN

Eyes That See Afar

S. Michael Wilcox

Assistant Professor of Ancient Scripture
Brigham Young University

On the day the Church was organized, the Lord revealed to Joseph Smith the instructions recorded in Doctrine and Covenants 21. It has one theme: follow the prophet. I do not think it is coincidental that this exhortation was given on 6 April 1830. The Church was given the following commandment, stated in words traditionally associated with a commandment — "thou shalt":

"Wherefore, meaning the church, thou shalt give heed unto *all his words and commandments* which he shall give unto you as he receiveth them, walking in all holiness before me;

"For his word ye shall receive, as if from mine own mouth, in all patience and faith.

"For by doing these things the gates of hell shall not prevail against you; yea, and the Lord God will disperse the powers of darkness from before you, and cause the heavens to shake for your good, and his name's glory." (D&C 21:4–6; italics added.)

Notice that the Lord instructed the Church to give heed to *all his words,* not just to his commandments. The Lord promised that the powers of darkness and the gates of hell would disperse and not prevail. Verse 7 indicates that God "inspired" Joseph Smith "to move the cause of Zion in mighty power for good." In the early days of the Church, the Saints were eagerly anticipating the building up of a Zion people in the land of Missouri. With enthusiasm and zeal, they migrated to Missouri and began the grand enterprise. Within a few years all was in disarray.

The persecution they suffered is a large part of our heritage and legacy. If the early Saints had given "heed to all his words and commandments," Joseph Smith would have led them to "move the cause of Zion." (D&C 21:4, 7.) Time and time again he warned them of the enemy he saw "afar off" and gave counsel (D&C 101:54), but in its infant stage the early Church would not follow. They trusted their own counsel.

We must not be too judgmental of those wonderful early Saints. We have the advantage of hindsight and easy access to the scriptural record. Gratitude for their experiences should be our response. We can learn from them the crucial lesson that every word spoken by a seer should be attended to with great solemnity.

In December 1830 Joseph Smith received the revelation we know as Moses 7. It is a very beautiful chapter dealing with Enoch and his city, who are described as being "of one heart and one mind, and dwelt in righteousness; and there was no poor among them." (Moses 7:18.)

This revelation led directly to Doctrine and Covenants 38 and others that followed. The date of section 38 is 2 January 1831. It is the foundation for the law of consecration, which the Saints were expected to live if they were to become a Zion people. Those principles are, first, "all flesh is mine, and I am no respecter of persons" (D&C 38:16); second, "I have made the earth rich" (D&C 38:17)—later the Lord revealed, "the earth is full, and there is enough and to spare" (D&C 104:17); third, "let every man esteem his brother as himself, and practise virtue and holiness before me" (D&C 38:24); fourth, "it must needs be that the riches of the earth are mine to give" (D&C 38:39); and fifth, "I give unto you a commandment, that every man, both elder, priest, teacher, and also member, go to with his might, with the labor of his hands, to prepare and accomplish the things which I have commanded" (D&C 38:40). Upon these five pillars a Zion people could be built through obedience to the law of consecration.

A month later, on 4 February 1831, Joseph Smith received another revelation. He had moved from Fayette to Kirtland. Some "false spirits had crept in among" the Saints, and the Lord gave the following warning. Although it deals with the situation at Kirtland, its implication for the future Saints in Missouri cannot be denied. "Hearken and hear, O ye my people, saith the Lord and your God, ye whom I delight to bless with the greatest of all blessings, *ye that hear me;* and ye that hear me not will I curse, that have professed my name, with the heaviest of all cursings." (D&C 41:1; italics added.)

The Lord promised the Saints he would give them his "law" that they might "have all things right before" him, and he warned, "see that my law is kept." (D&C 41:4.) Those who would not keep it were not his disciples and would be "cast out." (D&C 41:5.) It was "not meet that the things which belong to the children of the kingdom should be given to them that are not worthy." (D&C 41:6.) The Lord's final words prior to revealing his law—the law that would govern Zion— were: "These words are given unto you, and they are pure before me; wherefore, beware how you hold them." (D&C 41:12.) The promised "law" was given five days later, on 9 February 1831, and is recorded in Doctrine and Covenants 42. There the care of the poor and the building up of Zion through the consecration of the Saints is described.

In May 1831 more information concerning the law of consecration was revealed. The members were instructed to "deal honestly and be alike . . . , and receive alike, that ye may be one." (D&C 51:9.) They were also told that God was granting them the "privilege of organizing themselves according to [his] laws." (D&C 51:15.) During this time Oliver Cowdery and three others were serving a mission among the Indians in western Missouri. Joseph Smith wrote that "the mission to western Missouri and the gathering of the saints to that place was the most important subject which then engrossed the attention of the church." (*History of The Church of Jesus Christ of Latter-day Saints,* 2d ed. rev., ed. B. H. Roberts [Salt Lake City: The Church of Jesus Christ of Latter-day Saints, 1932–51], 1:182.)

On 7 June 1831, Joseph was commanded to hold the next conference of the Church in Missouri. (D&C 52:2.) He was promised that the land of Zion would be "made known unto them." (D&C 52:5.) At the conclusion of this revelation, the Lord issued a subtle warning: "Remember in all things the poor and the needy, the sick and the afflicted," he said, "for he that doeth not these things, the same is not my disciple." (D&C 52:40.)

Before starting on his journey to Missouri, Thomas B. Marsh went to Joseph Smith to inquire of him. He had earlier been commanded to fill a mission, and his companion Ezra Thayre was not ready to go. In the revelation the Prophet received came a final warning from the Lord regarding covetousness and the corrupting influence of wealth. This worldly attitude would stand in the way of building Zion. It was the last revelation given before Independence, Missouri, was named as the spot for the modern city of Enoch.

"Behold, thus saith the Lord unto my people—you have many things to do and to repent of; for behold, your sins have come up unto me, and are not pardoned, because you *seek to counsel in your own ways.*

"And your hearts are not satisfied. And ye obey not the truth, but have pleasure in unrighteousness.

"Wo unto you rich men, that will not give your substance to the poor, for your riches will canker your souls; and this shall be your lamentation in the day of visitation, and of judgment, and of indignation: The harvest is past, the summer is ended, and my soul is not saved!

"Wo unto you poor men, whose hearts are not broken, whose spirits are not contrite, and whose bellies are not satisfied, and whose hands are not stayed from laying hold upon other men's goods, whose eyes are full of greediness, and who will not labor with your own hands!" (D&C 56:14–17; italics added.)

This revelation also contains a warning to the "rebellious" who "profess my name": "I, the Lord, command; and he that will not obey shall be cut off in mine own due time, after I have commanded and the commandment is broken. Wherefore I, the Lord, command and revoke, as it seemeth me good; and all this to be answered upon the heads of the rebellious, saith the Lord." (D&C 56:1, 3–4.)

After receiving this revelation, Joseph journeyed to Missouri. On 20 July 1831 the Lord revealed, "This is the land of promise, and the place for the city of Zion." (D&C 57:2.) He also designated the spot for the building of a great latter-day temple. The principles, laws, and warnings had already been given by which Zion could flourish. With eagerness the early Saints began to purchase lands, build cabins, plant crops, and set about laying the foundation of Zion. A few days after Joseph's arrival, the Colesville branch of the Church arrived. At the same time, the first of a series of revelations warning of the coming persecution was given. From these revelations we find evidence that clearly demonstrates the nature of a seer. Whether or not those early Church members understood the significance of Joseph's words we are left to ponder, but with our advantage of hindsight, the words are plain. As the first logs were being laid for the cabins, the Lord spoke of tribulation: "He that is faithful in tribulation, the reward . . . is greater in the kingdom of heaven.

"Ye cannot behold with your natural eyes, for the present time, the design of your God concerning those things which shall come hereafter, and the glory which shall follow after much tribulation.

"For after much tribulation come the blessings. Wherefore the day cometh that ye shall be crowned with much glory; the hour is not yet, but is nigh at hand.

"Remember this, which I tell you before, that you may lay it to heart, and receive that which is to follow." (D&C 58:2–5; italics added.)

Immediately after these somewhat ominous words, the Lord gave counsel on how to avoid the eventual loss of the land of their inheritance. "I have sent you—that you might be *obedient."* (D&C 58:6; italics added.) But the Lord did not want just obedience; he wanted a people "anxiously engaged in a good cause," people who would "do many things of their own free will." (D&C 58:27.)

Then the Lord issued another warning. In light of what happened in Missouri, the words are prophetic:

"Who am I that made man, saith the Lord, that will hold him guiltless that obeys not my commandments?

"Who am I, saith the Lord, that have promised and have not fulfilled? . . .

"Then they say in their hearts: This is not the work of the Lord, for his promises are not fulfilled. But wo unto such, for their reward lurketh beneath, and not from above." (D&C 58:30–31, 33.)

Six days after this revelation, the Lord gave Joseph the revelation recorded in section 59. It is a companion revelation to Doctrine and Covenants 42—an addition to the law of the Lord, except in this case the laws are made "especially applicable to the saints in Zion." (D&C 59, headnote.)

Late in August Joseph returned to Kirtland. There he received the revelation recorded in Doctrine and Covenants 63. Prefacing this revelation in his history, the Prophet wrote, "In these infant days of the Church, there was great anxiety to obtain the word of the Lord upon every subject that in any way concerned our salvation; and as the land of Zion was now the most important temporal object in view, I inquired of the Lord for further information upon the gathering of the Saints." (*History of the Church,* 1:206–11.) The revelation starts with the Lord's call to his Saints to "hearken . . . ; and listen, you that call yourselves the people of the Lord." (D&C 63:1.) He stated that his "anger is kindled against the . . . rebellious" and that he can "take even them whom he will take, and preserveth in life them whom he will preserve; [he] buildeth up at his own will and pleasure; and destroyeth when he pleases." (D&C 63:2–4.) He ended his introduction to the revelation concerning Zion with the words, "I, the Lord, utter my voice, and it shall be obeyed." (D&C 63:5.)

These words take on added significance in light of what happened in Missouri. After giving instruction and intelligence, the Lord spoke directly of the coming storm of persecution, but remember the introductory verses of this section: he could preserve whom he liked if they would be obedient. "Behold, the land of Zion — I the Lord, hold it in *mine own hands.*" (D&C 63:25; italics added.) These are comforting words. The Lord then continued:

"For Satan putteth it into their hearts to anger against you, and to the shedding of blood.

"Wherefore, the land of Zion shall not be obtained but by purchase or by blood, otherwise there is none inheritance for you.

"And if by purchase, behold you are blessed;

"And if by blood, as you are forbidden to shed blood, lo, your enemies are upon you, and ye shall be scourged from city to city, and from synagogue to synagogue, and but few shall stand to receive an inheritance." (D&C 63:28–31.)

All of the revelations recorded in Doctrine and Covenants 58 through 63 were received within a month of the Saints' establishment in Zion. At this point, I am sure, they did not know what was coming. Perhaps even Joseph Smith was not fully aware of the import of his own words.

The headnote to Doctrine and Covenants 64 tells us that this revelation was given while a company of brethren were making preparations to leave for Missouri in October. It speaks of the need for all to forgive their brethren their trespasses and not to seek "occasion against one another." (D&C 64:8.) The importance of this counsel becomes much more apparent in light of the Lord's words to the Saints after the expulsion. He chided them for their "jarrings, and contentions, . . . and strifes." (D&C 101:6.) The Lord encouraged his Saints to pay their tithes and "labor while it is called today." (D&C 64:23–25.) He gave counsel concerning debt and then, speaking of Zion, he once again issued counsel that hinted at the coming troubles and the means of their prevention:

"And behold, I, the Lord, declare unto you, and my words are sure and shall not fail, that they shall obtain it.

"But all things must come to pass in their time.

"Wherefore, be not weary in well-doing, for ye are laying the foundation of a great work. And out of small things proceedeth that which is great.

"Behold, the Lord requireth the heart and a willing mind, and the willing and obedient shall eat the good of the land of Zion in these last days.

"And the rebellious shall be cut off out of the land of Zion, and shall be sent away, and shall not inherit the land.

"For, verily I say that the rebellious are not of the blood of Ephraim, wherefore they shall be plucked out." (D&C 64:31–36.)

The promise of a flourishing Zion is given, a Zion filled with the glory of the Lord, but Zion must also serve as an "ensign" to the people, a light to the world. (D&C 64:41–42.) The Lord's people can be a light only if they are different from the world. They must be a peculiar, holy people, or the ensign cannot stand high enough for the nations to flow unto it. A people who are to serve as an ensign must be obedient, not rebellious, anxiously engaged, unified, and so forth. In short, they must follow the counsel given by the Lord through Joseph Smith in the revelations already discussed.

In November 1831, about three and one-half months after the Saints first began to establish themselves upon the land of Missouri, a revelation was given in which the first indications of trouble and disobedience are spoken of. General counsel was given to the inhabitants of Zion that apply to all of her stakes. They were to teach their children, observe the Sabbath, pray, walk uprightly, and remember their labors. The Lord then directly said of the "inhabitants of Zion" that he was "not well pleased" with them, "for there are idlers among them; and their children are also growing up in wickedness; they also seek not earnestly the riches of eternity, but their eyes are full of greediness. These things ought not to be, and must be done away from among them; wherefore, let my servant Oliver Cowdery carry these sayings unto the land of Zion." (D&C 68:31–32.) Though the Saints in Missouri did not receive this revelation until Oliver Cowdery arrived, its importance relative to the coming storm cannot be denied.

In November and December 1831, further refinements to the law of consecration were given. Doctrine and Covenants 70 and 72 speak of the principle of stewardship and the accounting that must be made in both time and eternity. In these revelations the Lord once again spoke of the members of the Church who were "*privileged* to go up unto Zion." (D&C 72:24; italics added.) Obviously the Lord felt the opportunity to live his laws upon his promised land was a blessing worthy of the Saints' obedience, righteousness, and anxious engagement in his cause.

For a few months the revelations directly concerning Zion halted. The Lord watched the Saints to see if they could live the laws he told them they were "privileged" to receive. In March 1832, it was revealed to Joseph Smith that he, Sidney Rigdon, and Newel K. Whitney should sit in counsel with the Saints in Zion. "Otherwise," they were told, "Satan seeketh to turn their hearts away from the truth, that they become blinded and understand not the things which are prepared for them." (D&C 78:10.) On 26 April 1832, Joseph Smith, having arrived once again in Missouri, received a revelation instructing them concerning their duty. "There are those among you who have sinned exceedingly," the Lord began, "even all of you have sinned; but verily I say unto you, beware from henceforth, and refrain from sin, lest sore judgments fall upon your heads. For of him unto whom much is given much is required; and he who sins against the greater light shall receive the greater condemnation." (D&C 82:2–3.)

It is a great responsibility to have the truth of the gospel. We must remember the Lord used the word *privilege* when referring both to his land and to his laws. The Lord had graciously given to his Saints the "riches of eternity," meaning his revelations. They were bound to live and act according to their directions:

"Ye call upon my name for revelations, and I give them unto you; and inasmuch as ye keep not my sayings, which I give unto you, ye become transgressors; and justice and judgment are the penalty which is affixed unto my law.

"Therefore, what I say unto one I say unto all: Watch, for the adversary spreadeth his dominions, and darkness reigneth." (D&C 82:4–5.) The last phrase once again hints at the growing discontent and spirit of mobocracy that was present in Missouri.

In the next verses the Lord forgave his people and added a charge that they "sin no more" or their "former sins return." (D&C 82:7.) He then gave counsel concerning the law of consecration and the cause of the poor. With this instruction came a call that Zion must "arise and put on her beautiful garments." (D&C 82:14; in Revelation 19:7–8 we learn that Zion's beautiful garments are her righteous acts of obedience and dedication.) An assurance was given that "the kingdom is yours, and shall be forever, if you fall not from your steadfastness." (D&C 82:24.) Part of that steadfastness was the unity required of a Zion people, who were of one heart and one mind, with every man seeking the interest of his neighbor, and doing "all things with an eye single to the glory of God." (D&C 82:19.) After strengthening the Church members and delivering this message, Joseph Smith returned to Kirtland.

No revelations are recorded as having been received between April and September of 1832. Again a period of probation was granted. Would the Saints respond to the Lord's forgiveness and counsel? Section 84 is one of the key sections in the Doctrine and Covenants. In the middle of this revelation the Lord corrected the Church and explained to them why they were under condemnation. He spoke specifically about those children of Zion who were on his "holy land." (D&C 84:59.) The words of this revelation should have special meaning to us today, for they are words we have often heard President Ezra Taft Benson apply to our own situation:

"And your minds in times past have been darkened because of unbelief, and because *you have treated lightly the things you have received* —

"Which vanity and unbelief have brought the whole church under condemnation.

"And this condemnation resteth upon the children of Zion, even all.

"And they shall remain under this condemnation until they repent and remember the new covenant, even the Book of Mormon and the former commandments which I have given them, not only to say, but to do according to that which I have written —

"That they may bring forth fruit meet for their Father's kingdom; otherwise there remaineth a scourge and judgment to be poured out upon the children of Zion.

"For shall the children of the kingdom pollute my holy land? Verily, I say unto you, Nay." (D&C 84:54–59; italics added.)

The intent of these words is clear. The Lord had spoken before of the importance of heeding his revelations and not treating them lightly. If the Saints in Zion wanted to prevent the "scourge," they needed to give stricter heed to the words of Joseph Smith, particularly the Book of Mormon, which was and still is the most important and critical latter-day revelation.

It is hoped that some of the parallels to our own time have become apparent, for many of us have also covenanted to live the law of consecration. We too are urged to give strict heed to our prophet's counsel. We also are encouraged to spread the message of the kingdom to all the world. Although we are not as a people gathered upon the land of Missouri, we are endeavoring to establish Zion in all her stakes. Therefore, the lessons and experiences of our ancestors as they endeavored to build Zion in their own day should be looked to by our generation with great interest. The last revelation found in section 84 contains one of the last clear warnings of the coming struggle. The next time the Lord spoke about Missouri, the conflict had already started. It erupted in the summer of 1833. But it is easily seen that the Lord through his prophet told the people what he saw "afar off" and how to be ready for it. Zion requires great efforts of obedience and righteousness. It requires selflessness, zeal, and brotherly love. Pride must be destroyed along with envy and contention. We are not free of these things today in spite of more than one hundred fifty years of experience.

On 8 March 1833, the revelation recorded in Doctrine and Covenants 90 was given. This section deals primarily with the establishment of the First Presidency. In the opening verses the Lord forgave Joseph Smith of his sins and told him his prayers were heard. He promised Joseph that the keys he held "shall never be taken from" him. (D&C 90:3.) Then, speaking to the Church, the Lord explained how we should receive the oracles of a prophet. His words magnify a recurring theme of the Doctrine and Covenants:

"And all they who receive the oracles of God, let them beware how they hold them lest they are accounted as a *light thing*, and are brought under condemnation thereby, and stumble and fall when the storms descend, and the winds blow, and the rains descend, and beat upon their house." (D&C 90:5; italics added.)

Within a few months, for the Saints in Missouri, a storm of tremendous fury would beat upon them. Yet even during the storm, counsel from the Prophet was given, which, if it had been obeyed, would have prevented the storm from mastering the people of Zion.

On 2 August 1833, the revelation recorded in Doctrine and Covenants 97 was given. The persecutions were already in full force. On 23 July 1833, the leaders of the Church in Missouri had been forced to sign an agreement to leave Jackson County.

Section 97 begins with words of hope and encouragement. Many of the brethren were "truly humble" and "seeking diligently to learn wisdom and to find truth." (D&C 97:1.) The Lord spoke of his pleasure with the School of the Prophets in Missouri and with its teacher, Parley P. Pratt. The Lord then spoke of his people as fruit trees, warning that the "ax is laid at the root" of those who will not bring forth "good fruit." (D&C 97:7.) The key to bringing forth acceptable fruit was given in verse 8. Those who are "willing to observe their covenants by sacrifice—yea, *every sacrifice* which, I, the Lord shall command—they are accepted of me." (D&C 97:8; italics added.) This attitude will make them as fruitful as a tree "planted in a goodly land by a pure stream." (D&C 97:9.)

The Lord had a specific sacrifice in mind. He commanded the Saints in Zion to build a temple to him "speedily, by the tithing of my people. . . . this is . . . the sacrifice which . . . the Lord, requires at their hands." (D&C 97:11–12.) As in almost all commandments the Lord extended a promise. "If Zion do these things she shall prosper, and spread herself and become very glorious, very great, and very terrible." (D&C 97:18.) Now, obviously these promises have a broader application than just to the Saints in Jackson County in 1833; however, the implication for those Saints remains clear. The Lord continued his promise to Zion by quoting what the nations of the earth would say of her: "Surely Zion cannot fall, neither be moved out of her place, for God . . . [would be] her high tower." (D&C 97:19–20.)

The revelation ends in the Lord's prediction of a "scourge" that awaits the wicked. "Nevertheless," the Lord stated, "Zion shall escape if she observe to do all things whatsoever I have commanded her.

"But if she observe not to do whatsoever I have commanded her, I will visit her according to all her works, with sore affliction, with pestilence, with plague, with sword, with vengeance, with devouring fire.

"Nevertheless, let it be read this once to her ears, that I, the Lord, have accepted of her offering; and if she sin no more none of these things shall come upon her." (D&C 97:25–27.)

It seems a strange thing, perhaps, that the Lord would choose this time to emphasize the building of the temple, especially in light of the agreement already reached by the Church leadership in Missouri to move. It would require great faith and unity among the Saints and an unquestioning sense of obedience to a prophet's counsel. It would also require the purity of heart that the Lord gave as a definition of Zion in this same section. The Saints did not rise to the challenge; nothing was done for the building of a temple. In the meantime, the persecution increased. Four days later Joseph Smith gave counsel to the persecuted Saints that in essence told them not to retaliate or seek revenge for their treatment at the hands of the mobs. Shortly after this revelation was given, Joseph Smith, in company with Sidney Rigdon, went to New York. They had been away from their families for a while and felt concern for their welfare. On 12 October 1833, the revelation recorded in Doctrine and Covenants 100 was given to ease their minds concerning their families. It is obvious from the revelation that Joseph also felt considerable anxiety for his brethren in Missouri. The Lord addressed those concerns in the last verses of section 100: "Now I give unto you a word concerning Zion," the Lord declared. "Zion shall be redeemed, . . .

"Therefore, let your hearts be comforted; for all things shall work together for good to them that walk uprightly, and to the sanctification of the church.

"For I will raise up unto myself a pure people, that will serve me in righteousness." (D&C 100:13, 15–16.) The emphasis is still positive and filled with hope, but the hope is contingent upon the purity and righteousness that define a Zion society. This is the last revelation given about Zion before the actual expulsion. By December 1833 the Saints were driven to neighboring Clay County after suffering great loss.

On 16 December the Lord revealed to Joseph Smith the reasons for this final treatment. These reasons are not inclusive. Many historical factors caused friction between the Saints and the old settlers, but these could have been overcome by the influence of the Lord had his people obeyed his counsel—the counsel they had been given since day one of their settlement. In a single sweeping statement beginning Doctrine and Covenants 101, the Lord states the problem:

"I, the Lord, have suffered the affliction to come upon them, wherewith they have been afflicted, in consequence of their transgressions; . . .

"For all those who will not endure chastening, but deny me, cannot be sanctified.

"Behold, I say unto you, there were jarrings, and contentions, and envyings, and strifes, and lustful and covetous desires among them; therefore by these things they polluted their inheritances.

"They were slow to hearken unto the voice of the Lord their God; therefore, the Lord their God is slow to hearken unto their prayers, to answer them in the day of their trouble.

"In the day of their peace they esteemed lightly my counsel; but, in the day of their trouble, of necessity they feel after me." (D&C 101:2, 5–8.)

In spite of these words, the Lord loved his people, and section 101 is full of hope and a promised redemption. The Lord, however, wanting the lesson of their failure to stand forever, related a parable. He introduced it with a reference to a teaching he gave in the Sermon on the Mount — that of the salt of the earth. Those who bind themselves to the Lord in the everlasting covenant are the salt of the earth and the "savor of men." But when they lose that savor, they are "cast out." The Lord then gave the parable concerning Zion.

We can glean many insights from this parable. The basic elements are plain. The nobleman is Christ, the choice piece of land is Missouri, the servants are the Saints, the watchman is the Prophet Joseph Smith. The tower is, in all probability, the temple they were commanded to build but which they never started. The following phrases taken from the parable carry a strong message and explain both the attitude of the Lord and the attitude of the Saints:

"What need hath my lord of this tower?" (D&C 101:47.) In reality, the Lord did not need the tower; the servants did.

"And [the servants] consulted for a long time, saying among themselves: What need hath my lord of this tower?" (D&C 101:48.) Notice they consulted among themselves instead of with the watchman or the Lord.

"And while they were at variance one with another they became very slothful, and they hearkened not unto the commandments of their lord." (D&C 101:50.) Two of the cornerstones of a Zion society are obedience to commandments and a unified people who are of "one heart and one mind." (Moses 7:18.)

The result of disobedience, disharmony, and consulting among themselves (or heeding their own counsel) was the loss of the choice piece of land and the olive trees, when "the enemy [Satan]" came. The lesson the Lord drew from this parable is plainly explained in verses 53 and 54. The Lord asked of his Saints a question and then supplied the answer. "Ought ye not to have done even as I commanded you?" (D&C 101:53.) If they had followed his counsel, "the watchman upon the tower would have *seen* the enemy while he was *yet afar off*; and then *ye could have made ready* and kept the enemy from breaking down the hedge thereof, and saved my vineyard from the hands of the destroyer." (D&C 101:54; italics added.)

Even at this point the Lord held out hope for the Saints. Zion could still be redeemed, if they had finally learned the lesson of obedience. Counsel was again given. The Saints were to gather together all the means they could and continue to purchase lands in Jackson County. The persecution of the Saints made this counsel appear unwise. Nevertheless, it was given. A command was also given to the Church members in the east. They were to gather funds for the redemption of Zion. The Lord instructed his Saints that "there is even now already in store sufficient, yea, even an abundance, to redeem Zion, and establish her waste places, no more to be thrown down, were the churches, who call themselves after my name, willing to hearken to my voice." (D&C 101:75.) A hint of the attitude of many of the Saints toward obeying the Lord's counsel through his prophet is easily seen in the last words of this verse. The Saints were also counseled to use the legal system of the American government to seek redress.

The rest of the Lord's counsel was given on 24 February 1834, several months later, in Doctrine and Covenants 103. The Lord reiterated the reason for their suffering: "They did not hearken altogether unto the precepts and commandments which I gave unto them." (D&C 103:4.)

"By hearkening to observe all the words which I, the Lord their God, shall speak unto them, they shall never cease to prevail until the kingdoms of the world are subdued under my feet, and the earth is given unto the saints, to possess it forever and ever.

"But inasmuch as they keep not my commandments, and hearken not to observe all my words, the kingdoms of the world shall prevail against them.

"For they were set to be a light unto the world, and to be the saviors of men;

"And inasmuch as they are not the saviors of men, they are as salt that has lost its savor, and is thenceforth good for nothing but to be cast out and trodden under foot of men." (D&C 103:7-10.)

Joseph Smith was instructed to gather together the "young men and the middle aged" and march to Missouri to the aid of the Saints. The Lord wanted five hundred men to go, but knowing the disposition of his Saints, he told Joseph Smith: "If you cannot obtain five hundred, seek diligently that . . . you may obtain three hundred. And if ye cannot obtain three hundred, . . . peradventure ye may obtain one hundred." (D&C 103:32–33.) Even in this counsel the Lord gave a hint to his

Saints concerning their obedience: "Behold this is my will; ask and ye shall receive; but men do not always do my will." (D&C 103:31.) As a result of this revelation, Zion's Camp was organized. They did not obtain five hundred or even three hundred.

The Zion's Camp members marched to Missouri, but the march proved to be a testing ground for the Lord's future leaders, not a redemptive effort to reclaim Jackson County. When Zion's Camp arrived in Missouri and were camped on Fishing River, the last revelation concerning the first latter-day effort to build up the New Jerusalem was given on 22 June 1834. Even though it concludes that theme in the Doctrine and Covenants, this revelation should be read as the preface to the future building up of Zion. It is a revelation given especially to us, for in it are the keys to our own efforts. We should learn from those early Saints' attempt and avoid the pitfalls they were not able to overcome.

"Behold, I say unto you, were it not for the transgressions of my people, speaking concerning the church and not individuals, they might have been redeemed even now.

"But behold, *they have not learned to be obedient* to the things which I required at their hands, but are full of all manner of evil, and do not impart of their substance, as becometh saints, to the poor and afflicted among them;

"And are *not united according to the union* required by the law *of the celestial kingdom;*

"And *Zion cannot be built up unless it is by the principles of the law of the celestial kingdom;* otherwise I cannot receive her unto myself.

"And my people must needs be chastened until *they learn obedience,* if it must needs be, by the things which they suffer." (D&C 105:2–6; italics added.)

It is difficult to live the principles of the celestial kingdom in a fallen telestial world, but that is what the Lord expects. Therefore "it is expedient . . . that mine elders should wait for a little season for the redemption of Zion—that they themselves may be prepared, and that my people may be taught more perfectly, and have experience, and know more perfectly concerning their duty, and the things which I require at their hands." (D&C 105:9–10.) Part of that perfect teaching was to come, and it can still be had in the temples of the Lord. As a people we are gaining the necessary experience. We have a much better appreciation of prophets, seers, and revelators because of our heritage and the lessons those wonderful Missouri Saints left us. The hope and the promise of Zion are still the driving motivation of the Church, but it is a hope that must be supported by hearkening to the voice of our seer. "And inasmuch as *they follow the counsel* which they receive, they shall have power after many days *to accomplish all things* pertaining to Zion." (D&C 105:37; italics added.)

It may be well for us today when we hear the First Presidency and the Twelve give their counsel to realize that they are the modern watchmen upon the tower. We may then avoid the pitfalls to which the Doctrine and Covenants so pointedly testifies.

CHAPTER EIGHTEEN

The Articles and Covenants of the Church of Christ and the Book of Mormon

Robert J. Woodford

Instructor, Salt Lake Institute of Religion
Salt Lake City, Utah

In 1959 Brenda Daily and her brother Bill attended the Ravenna High School in Ravenna, Ohio. They had recently moved there with their family from the Canal Zone where their father, William D. Daily, served in the military. While in the Canal Zone, these two young people had learned conversational Spanish. They were anxious to study the language at their new school. Unfortunately the school was not large enough for a regular Spanish class; however, the principal, Wayne E. Watters, had experience teaching Spanish. He was willing to teach a class before school if Brenda and Bill could also get some other students to attend. They found several willing classmates, and soon they had an enthusiastic class functioning.

During the year, Mr. Watters found out that Bill and Brenda were Latter-day Saints. Once he knew that, he had several discussions with them about the Church. On one occasion he mentioned that his wife's father had an early document of the LDS Church in his possession. He told them that the family had preserved it through four generations. His wife's maiden name is Virginia Ryder, and she is a great-great-granddaughter of Symonds Ryder. He was an 1831 convert to the Church from Hiram, Ohio.[1] Somehow Symonds Ryder obtained this document, but there are no historical records that relate how he obtained it.

Later in the year, during a serious illness, Wayne and Virginia Watters feared her father would soon die. They thought that he had no more use for the document, and so they gave it to Brenda.[2] They felt it would be of greater value to a member of the Church than it was to them. Brenda took it to her father, and he immediately realized that it was a record of some worth. He conveyed it to the mission president in Ohio, who sent it to Church headquarters with the next missionary returning to Utah. The Church Historian placed it in the archives of the Historical Department of the Church, where researchers can have access to it today.

This document is in the handwriting of Oliver Cowdery[3] and is three pages in length. It begins: "A commandment from God unto Oliver how he should build up his Church & the manner thereof." It ends: "Written in the year of our Lord & Saviour 1829—A true copy of the Articles of the Church of Christ. O.C."

The body of the document is composed of scriptures from the Book of Mormon and the Doctrine and Covenants interspersed with commentary by Oliver Cowdery.[4] Through these, Oliver Cowdery established several important doctrinal truths. First, because the world is becoming a more wicked place, there is a great need to repent and be baptized. He then explained the procedures for proper baptism.

Second, he established that men are to be ordained to the priesthood, and he demonstrated the proper method of performing these ordinations. Those who are so ordained are to pray for the Church and teach the members the truths of the gospel.

Third, he explained the doctrine concerning the sacrament. The members are to meet together often to partake of it. He related from the scriptures the form of the ordinance, including the prayers that should be said. He also included the warning from 3 Nephi about partaking of the sacrament unworthily.

Fourth, he taught that the Church members should meet together often to tell each other of their progress toward eternal life, and he explained a standard of moral conduct which every member should live. He also explained that those who will not repent must be cast out of the Church.

Finally, he issued a call for all people to come to Christ and take his name upon them. If they will walk uprightly before the Lord, then his grace is sufficient for them.

There is a close connection between this 1829 manuscript of Oliver Cowdery and section 20 of the Doctrine and Covenants. The title of section 20 in the other surviving manuscripts is "The Articles and Covenants of the Church of Christ." The title of section 20 as it was published in *The Evening and the Morning Star* is the same, and it is very similar to the title of Oliver Cowdery's manuscript. Section 20 also contains most of the Book of Mormon scriptures quoted by Oliver Cowdery in his manuscript. Oliver Cowdery's manuscript is probably an early draft of section 20. The following is an attempt to reconstruct the events leading to the composition of both this document and our present Doctrine and Covenants 20.

In section 20 are short statements about the origin of the Church, the basic doctrines, and the ordinances. There are also statements about the duties of members and priesthood bearers. The intent of the articles and covenants was to provide members and investigators with a summary about the Church. In one short reading they could gain a comprehensive overview of the whole Church.[5] The Lord may have inspired Joseph Smith to assign Oliver Cowdery to write this "constitution for the Church."[6]

Oliver Cowdery had wanted to know what material to put into the articles and covenants and approached the Prophet for help. Joseph Smith prayed about the matter and received the revelation known as Doctrine and Covenants 18. In verse 1 of section 18 we learn that the Lord gave this revelation because of "the thing" which Oliver Cowdery desired to know. Oliver Cowdery wanted to know what to write.

The Lord told Oliver Cowdery he had manifested to him many times that the things he had written were true. (D&C 18:2.) Oliver Cowdery had written the Book of Mormon as the Prophet dictated it.

The Lord told Oliver Cowdery to rely on the things he had written that he already knew were true. (D&C 18:3.) That is, he was to get the information he needed for the articles and covenants of the Church from the Book of Mormon.

The Lord said he placed "all things . . . concerning the foundation of [his] church" in the Book of Mormon. (D&C 18:4.) The Lord had already inspired prophets to put in that book the basic principles Oliver Cowdery needed for the articles and covenants.

The Lord told Oliver to "build up my church, upon the foundation of my gospel." (D&C 18:5.) If he did, the gates of hell could not prevail against him. Note that Oliver Cowdery included the phrase "build up my church" in the introduction of the Ryder document. Oliver Cowdery then composed his three-page version of the articles and covenants of the Church from Book of Mormon scriptures. This is the same document that Symonds Ryder acquired.

Oliver Cowdery submitted his manuscript to Joseph Smith. Then Joseph Smith, or both he and Oliver Cowdery, revised that document.

They put it in the format now found in section 20. In its finished form, section 20 still retains some of the characteristics of the early draft by Oliver Cowdery.

The importance attached to Doctrine and Covenants 20 by early members of the Church is obvious from the many historical accounts of its use. Joseph Smith had the complete articles and covenants of the Church read aloud at the first conference of the Church in June 1830. The members of the church then received it as the word of the Lord by the "unanimous voice of the whole congregation."[7] Thus, section 20 became the first revelation of this dispensation canonized by the Church.[8] Since that time, the leaders of the Church have made sure that the basic practices of the Church correspond with this revelation. Joseph Smith and other leaders read the articles and covenants to the congregation at succeeding conferences. Presumably they did that so members and new converts might retain in their minds the truths revealed in it.[9]

Such men as Zebedee Coltrin, Orson Hyde, A. Sidney Gilbert, Orson Pratt, and others had manuscript copies of this revelation. They took their copies with them when they went on short missionary journeys or on preaching assignments to branches of the Church. They read the articles and covenants of the Church aloud in the meetings they conducted for the benefit of those people.[10]

A major division of section 20 is correlated to the priesthood of God. Many priesthood certificates of that time recorded that the bearer had been ordained "according to the Articles and Covenants of the Church."[11]

Several other revelations in the Doctrine and Covenants refer to the articles and covenants of the Church, including 28:12, 14; 33:14; 42:13; 51:4; 68:24; and 107:12, 63. The Lord, in each of these passages, requested the Saints to remember the articles and covenants and to obey the principles revealed there.

The articles and covenants of the Church may have served an additional purpose. Some researchers feel that it may be the certificate of incorporation that the State of New York required of churches. Any group that wanted recognition as a legally organized religious society had to submit such a certificate. Researchers have never found any document submitted by this Church in the government archives in New York. There is even a possibility that no one ever submitted it.[12]

The beginning verses of section 20 are certainly reminiscent of a legal document, and some think it may be the missing certificate.

The importance of section 20 has not diminished over the years. For example, President Harold B. Lee emphasized the principles revealed in section 20 during his administration.[13] Also, according to my own statistics, the General Authorities since 1974 cite only sections 84, 88, and 121 from the Doctrine and Covenants more often than they cite section 20.[14]

Doctrine and Covenants 20 contains some passages of scripture quoted directly from the Book of Mormon. Several other passages are paraphrased or summarized. The sacrament prayers are probably the most widely known of these scriptures. Moroni recorded them in Moroni 4:3 and 5:2, and Joseph Smith published them as verses 77 and 79 of section 20. Joseph Smith also included the instruction in Moroni 6:6 to partake of the sacrament frequently as verse 75 in section 20.

Verse 73 of section 20 contains the baptismal prayer from 3 Nephi 11:25. The phrase "having authority given me of Jesus Christ" appears in all sources of section 20 before 1835, including the manuscripts of section 20 and the published accounts in the Book of Commandments and *The Evening and the Morning Star*. Joseph Smith altered the phrase to read "having been commissioned of Jesus Christ" in the 1835 edition of the Doctrine and Covenants. That is the form of the prayer we use today. Joseph Smith also included the additional instructions concerning baptism from 3 Nephi 11:23–26 in verses 73 and 74 of section 20.

Moroni taught, in Moroni 3:4, how men are to be ordained to the priesthood. Joseph Smith included these same instructions in verse 60. He also placed in verse 37 the prerequisites for baptism that are given in Moroni 6:1–3.[15]

The elders are to conduct church meetings as the Holy Ghost directs them. This teaching comes from Moroni 6:9. Joseph Smith published this same doctrine in verse 45. Moroni recorded his teachings concerning transgressors in Moroni 6:7, and Joseph Smith included this material in verses 80 through 83.

President Ezra Taft Benson said: "In the twentieth section of the Doctrine and Covenants, the Lord devotes several verses to summarizing the vital truths which the Book of Mormon teaches. (See vs. 17–36.) It speaks of God, the creation of man, the Fall, the Atonement, the ascension of Christ into heaven, prophets, faith, repentance, baptism, the Holy Ghost, endurance, prayer, justification and sanctification through grace, and loving and serving God.

"We must know these essential truths. Aaron and Ammon and their brethren in the Book of Mormon taught these same kinds of truths to the Lamanite people (see Alma 18:22–39), who were 'in the darkest abyss' (Alma 26:3). After accepting these eternal truths, the Book of Mormon states, those converted Lamanites never did fall away. (See Alma 23:6.)"[16]

Joseph Smith included a large number of passages from the Book of Mormon in Doctrine and Covenants 20. The placement of these scriptures in the articles and covenants of the Church affirms that present Church leaders are to implement the same doctrines and teachings that the Savior gave anciently to the people of the Book of Mormon. Many of these passages of scripture come from the book of Moroni. We can be eternally grateful that Moroni was granted the time and had the inclination to include this book in the record, because including it was "contrary to that which [he] had supposed." (Moroni 1:4.)

Doctrine and Covenants 20 also instructs us about the Book of Mormon. Verses 6–9 include information about the origin of the Book of Mormon and the mission of Moroni to Joseph Smith. The Lord states in verse 9 that the Book of Mormon contains the fulness of the gospel of Christ. Moroni revealed this truth to Joseph Smith in his first visit to the Prophet in September 1823. (See Joseph Smith–History 1:34.) The Lord further stated it in Doctrine and Covenants 27:5 and 42:12. President Ezra Taft Benson explained precisely what this phrase means:

"The Lord Himself has stated that the Book of Mormon contains the 'fulness of the gospel of Jesus Christ' (D&C 20:9). That does not mean it contains every teaching, every doctrine ever revealed. Rather, it means that in the Book of Mormon we will find the fulness of those doctrines required for our salvation. And they are taught plainly and simply so that even children can learn the ways of salvation and exaltation. The Book of Mormon offers so much that broadens our understandings of the doctrines of salvation. Without it, much of what is taught in other scriptures would not be nearly so plain and precious."[17]

In Doctrine and Covenants 20:10, the Lord uses the testimony of the Three Witnesses and the Eight Witnesses to declare to mankind that the Book of Mormon is true.[18] Those testimonies are part of every copy of the Book of Mormon, and every reader of the book has access

to them. Angels who ministered to the witnesses "confirmed" the
testimonies they bear. Elder Sterling W. Sill made an interesting point
about the power of the testimony of these witnesses:

"I said to my friend, 'If you were on trial for your life and you had
this kind of testimony out against you, you wouldn't have a chance.
This kind of testimony where eleven men say they saw and they heard
and they know would be accepted in any court of law, either human
or divine.' And I patted him on the leg again and said, 'Now my friend,
I think you have great abilities, but if you understood this testimony
then I don't think you have enough courage to disbelieve in the Book
of Mormon. In this case, you have the kind of courage my little granddaughter has. I have a granddaughter two years old and she is very
courageous. If you were to put her here on the floor with three rattle-
snakes around her she would not have the slightest fear where I would
be almost scared to death. The difference being that I know more about
the situation than she does.' And I would say about anyone in this
assembly who understands this testimony that he would not dare disbelieve the Book of Mormon or disobey its counsel."[19]

Verse 11 of Doctrine and Covenants 20 adds two additional truths
concerning the Book of Mormon. First, the Book of Mormon proves
to the people of the world that the Bible is true. Brigham Young taught:
"No man can say that this book (laying his hand on the Bible) is true,
is the word of the Lord, is the way, is the guide-board in the path, and
a charter by which we may learn the will of God; and at the same time
say, that the Book of Mormon is untrue; if he has had the privilege of
reading it, or of hearing it read, and learning its doctrines. There is
not that person on the face of the earth who has had the privilege of
learning the Gospel of Jesus Christ from these two books, that can say
that one is true, and the other is false. No Latter-day Saint, no man or
woman, can say the Book of Mormon is true, and at the same time say
that the Bible is untrue. If one be true, both are; and if one be false,
both are false."[20]

The Book of Mormon verifies the truths of the Bible in several
ways. The Book of Mormon testifies that the Bible is a true record of
God's dealings with Israel. (See Mormon 7:9, for example.) It also states
that wicked men have removed many "plain and precious" truths from
the record. The Book of Mormon tells of the modern Bible and how
early settlers brought it to the Americas. Also, prophets in the Book
of Mormon quote many Old and New Testament passages in their

writings. Finally, many historic events in the one are corroborated in the other.

The second truth we learn in Doctrine and Covenants 20:11 is that the Book of Mormon establishes the actuality of prophets in our own day. President Ezra Taft Benson explained how the Book of Mormon does that:

"We are to use the Book of Mormon in handling objections to the Church. God the Father and his Son Jesus Christ revealed themselves to Joseph Smith in a marvelous vision. After that glorious event, Joseph Smith told a minister about it. Joseph was surprised to hear the minister say that there were no such things as visions or revelations in these days, that all such things had ceased. [See Joseph Smith–History 1:21.]

"This remark symbolizes practically all of the objections that have ever been made against the Church by nonmembers and dissident members alike. Namely, they do not believe that God reveals his will today to the Church through prophets of God. All objections, whether they be on abortion, plural marriage, seventh-day worship, etc., basically hinge on whether Joseph Smith and his successors were and are prophets of God receiving divine revelation. Here, then, is a procedure to handle most objections through the use of the Book of Mormon.

"First, understand the objection.

"Second, give the answer from revelation.

"Third, show how the correctness of the answer really depends on whether or not we have modern revelation through modern prophets.

"Fourth, explain that whether or not we have modern prophets and revelation really depends on whether the Book of Mormon is true.

"Therefore, the only problem the objector has to resolve for himself is whether the Book of Mormon is true. For if the Book of Mormon is true, then Jesus is the Christ, Joseph Smith was his prophet, The Church of Jesus Christ of Latter-day Saints is true, and it is being led today by a prophet receiving revelation."[21]

In Doctrine and Covenants 20:12 the Lord draws the conclusion that God is the same yesterday, today, and forever. This conclusion can be drawn because the Book of Mormon establishes the truth of the Bible and because there are living prophets on the earth. Living prophets and additional scripture are features of all past dispensations. This dispensation is no different from past ones, and so God is the same today.

The Lord reveals in Doctrine and Covenants 20:13 that he will judge those who "come to a knowledge" of the Book of Mormon. Those who accept the Book of Mormon and who obey the commandments in it will "receive a crown of eternal life." (D&C 20:14.) Those who reject the Book of Mormon will find that that decision "shall turn to their own condemnation." (D&C 20:15.)[22]

One important truth that the Lord revealed in section 20 is that he will hold all those who "come to a knowledge" of the Book of Mormon accountable for what they know. Moroni said he will meet every person who has had knowledge of the Book of Mormon at the judgment bar of God. In Ether 12:38–39, he says they will then know that his (Moroni's) garments are not spotted with their blood. He taught them all God commanded him to teach them, and they are now accountable for their own actions.

In Moroni 10:27–29, Moroni says the Lord will ask every one of them if they had the words "written by this man." God will then declare that he revealed his word to Moroni. He will also declare that Moroni wrote the truth. Moroni then urges those who have the Book of Mormon to come to Christ and forsake all evil so they won't be condemned.

Moroni made a third statement to the readers of the Book of Mormon in Moroni 10:34. This is the last verse of scripture in the Book of Mormon. Moroni promises he will meet them at the "pleasing bar of the great Jehovah, the Eternal Judge of both quick and dead." Judgment will be a pleasant experience for those who have made their lives conform to the standards taught in the Book of Mormon. They will stand with Moroni at the judgment bar of God and receive a crown of eternal life. (See D&C 20:14.)

Nephi also promised that he would meet the readers of the Book of Mormon at the time of judgment. In 2 Nephi 33:11–15 Nephi attests that the Lord will then declare that Nephi wrote the truth. Nephi urges the readers to abide by the principles he taught. If they will not, he bids them an everlasting farewell. Nephi knew that he would have eternal life. He knew that those who read his record would not have the same reward unless they would also obey the truth.

Jacob, who was Nephi's brother, also promised to meet the readers of the Book of Mormon at the time of judgment. In his account, Jacob 6:13, he speaks of the pleasing bar of God. The bar is pleasing to those who have not wasted their probation; however, this bar "striketh the wicked with awful dread and fear." They are fearful because they are facing the condemnation the Lord promised in Doctrine and Covenants 20:15.

All the Book of Mormon scriptures found in Doctrine and Covenants 20 teach that the Book of Mormon is a significant component of the work of the Lord in this dispensation.

Until the revelations were put in chronological order in the 1876 edition of the Doctrine and Covenants, section 20 was always the second revelation in the book, immediately following the Lord's preface to this book of scripture. Section 20 of the Doctrine and Covenants integrates the teachings of the Book of Mormon into the Church of this dispensation. It emphasizes the eternal covenants and commitments required by the Lord of the Nephites and also of us. It sets the same standard of conduct for us that the Savior set during his ministry to the Book of Mormon people. It is, in reality, a constitution to guide us in these latter days.

NOTES

1. The Lord called Symonds Ryder on a mission. Unfortunately Joseph Smith's scribe who wrote the letter notifying him of the call misspelled his name. Symonds Ryder complained about the Spirit that called him on a mission. If it could not spell his name correctly, then perhaps it erred in calling him on a mission. And so he refused to go. His name is still not spelled correctly in the Doctrine and Covenants and other Church publications. His tombstone and his signature give the spelling as *Symonds Ryder*, not Symonds Rider or Simonds Ryder.

2. Virginia Ryder Watters's father recovered, however, and was upset that they had given the document away. The Historical Department of the Church did supply him with a photocopy.

3. Dean Jessee, then of the Historical Department of the Church, verified that the handwriting was that of Oliver Cowdery.

4. For the complete text of this document, see Robert J. Woodford, "The Historical Development of the Doctrine and Covenants" (Ph.D. dissertation, Brigham Young University, 1974), 1:287–90.

5. Many other churches have formulated similar confessions of their faith. Some have designated these confessions as their creed, others as their platform, and still others as their articles of faith. In these confessions they intended to give a brief statement about their basic beliefs and doctrine. They also would include something about requirements for church membership and other information that would be useful to church members and investigators. These confessions have many parallels to Doctrine and Covenants 20. See an example in Milton V. Backman, Jr., *American Religions and the Rise of Mormonism* (Salt Lake City: Deseret Book

Co., 1965), pp. 446–56. See also Williston Walker, ed., *Creeds and Platforms of Congregationalism* (New York, 1969), pp. 367–402; and The Confession of Faith and Covenant, of the Baptists Church of Christ in Middleborough, Bridgewater and Rayniam (prepared by the Rev. Isaac Backus, and adopted by the First Baptist Church in Middleboro, at its organization, 16 Jan. 1756). This document is subtitled Articles of Faith.

6. Lyndon W. Cook, *The Revelations of the Prophet Joseph Smith* (Provo: Seventies Mission Bookstore, 1981), p. 31.

7. Far West Record, Archives of The Church of Jesus Christ of Latter-day Saints, Salt Lake City, Utah, p. 1.

8. The members of the Church first voted on the other revelations in the Doctrine and Covenants in 1835. They voted on the revelations again in 1880 after Brigham Young had Orson Pratt add twenty-six additional sections to the book. In 1890 Lorenzo Snow presented Official Declaration–1 in general conference, and the members sustained it. In 1976 N. Eldon Tanner presented sections 137 and 138 in conference, and the members sustained them. He also presented Official Declaration–2 in 1978, and they sustained it.

9. Far West Record, pp. 2, 27, 36–37.

10. See, for example, in the Archives of The Church of Jesus Christ of Latter-day Saints, Salt Lake City, Evan Melbourne Green Journal (1833–35), pp. 4, 15; see also Orson Pratt Journal, 27 Mar. 1834; Wilford Woodruff Journal, 26 Feb. 1836; Archives of The Church of Jesus Christ of Latter-day Saints, Salt Lake City, Utah.

11. Cook, *Revelations of the Prophet Joseph Smith*, p. 125.

12. Larry C. Porter, "A Study of the Origins of the Church of Jesus Christ of Latter-day Saints in the States of New York and Pennsylvania" (Ph.D. dissertation, Brigham Young University, 1971), pp. 374–86.

13. While I was doing research on the Doctrine and Covenants during the spring of 1973, Lauritz G. Petersen of the Historical Department of the Church requested a copy of anything I might find concerning Doctrine and Covenants 20. When I asked him why he wanted it, he said that President Lee had requested copies of any document historically connected with section 20. He wanted to administer the affairs of the Church using principles revealed in that section.

14. Database of scriptural quotations by General Authorities kept by the author.

15. Joseph Smith added to these prerequisites that persons must also "truly manifest by their works that they have received of the Spirit of Christ unto a remission of their sins." During the summer of 1830, Oliver Cowdery wrote to the Prophet and commanded Joseph to delete this addition. (See *History of the Church*, 1:104–5.) Eventually Joseph was able to convince Oliver Cowdery and the Whitmer family (who agreed with Oliver that it should be removed) that the phrase was doctrinal and should be retained. Even though Oliver Cowdery was presumptuous in commanding the Prophet to remove this phrase, we can appreciate his forceful approach when we remember that he wrote the first draft of section 20 and had a definite interest in the final version.

16. Ezra Taft Benson, "A New Witness for Christ," *Ensign*, Nov. 1984, p. 7.

17. Ezra Taft Benson, "The Book of Mormon—Keystone of Our Religion," *Ensign*, Nov. 1986, p. 6.

18. The Savior's own testimony concerning the Book of Mormon is in Doctrine and Covenants 17:6. Elder Bruce R. McConkie said of that testimony:

"One of the most solemn oaths ever given to man is found in these words of the Lord relative to Joseph Smith and the Book of Mormon. 'He [meaning Joseph Smith] has translated the book, even that part which I have commanded him,' saith the Lord, 'and as your Lord and your God liveth it is true.' (D&C 17:6.)

"This is God's testimony of the Book of Mormon. In it Deity himself has laid his godhood on the line. Either the book is true or God ceases to be God. There neither is nor can be any more formal or powerful, language known to men or gods." (*Ensign*, May 1982, p. 33.)

19. Sterling W. Sill, "Mormon and Moroni," address delivered at Salt Lake Institute of Religion Devotional Assembly, 26 Oct. 1973, pp. 8–9.

20. Brigham Young, in *Journal of Discourses*, 26 vols. (London: Latter-day Saints' Book Depot, 1855–86), 1:38.

21. Ezra Taft Benson, "The Book of Mormon Is the Word of God," *Ensign*, May 1975, pp. 64–65.

22. This same doctrine is also taught in Doctrine and Covenants 5:15–19, and to a lesser extent in Doctrine and Covenants 10:23 and Doctrine and Covenants 93:32.

Index

Aaron, 45

Aaronic Priesthood: preparatory nature of, 42, 45; covenant of, 49; work of, 233

Abraham: seed of, 46, 186–88; promises of restoration made to, 187

Abrahamic covenant, 46, 187; fulfilment of, through Joseph Smith, 188–89; passed on to descendants, 189–90; priesthood blessings as part of, 193

Abuse, forgiving brother for, 124

Adam: as grand patriarch, 79; baptism of, 145; holds keys of dispensation of fulness of times, 159–60; holds keys of First Presidency, 161–62; fall of, 227–28

Adams, James, 152

Africa, black: collecting oral histories in, 127–28; "restoration" of gospel in, 128; church units in, with LDS name, 129, 130; Eliases in, 129–31; converts in, quality of, 133; rapidity of Church growth in, 133; people of, God's love for, 138

Agency, 69, 75 n. 58, 125, 229

Ammon, 116–17, 143–44

Angels: ministering of, 50; as messengers bringing revelation, 90; definition of, 163–64; will not do work of mortals, 164–65; at Christ's tomb, 166

Anger, 123–24

Animals: supposed lack of spirit in, 59; spirits of, 68; in heaven, 75 n. 59

Aquinas, Thomas, 56

Arrington, Leonard, 98

"Articles and Covenants of the Church of Christ," 263–65

Arts, refinement of, in Zion, 181–82

Asay, Carlos E., 43, 47, 49

Atonement of Jesus Christ, 234, 240

Augustine, 56

Authority: channels of, 110; chain of, beginning with Adam, 160; of Melchizedek Priesthood, tracing of, 187–88

Babylon, 12, 178

Backman, Milton V., 97, 108

Ballard, Melvin J., 220

Baptism, 145; for the dead, 20–21, 84; as part of new and everlasting covenant, 228; covenants involved in, 230–31; of fire, 231; prayer for performing, 266

Benson, Ezra Taft, 117, 158, 254, 266–67, 269

Bible: differing interpretations of, 87; Joseph Smith Translation of, 171–72; truth of, Book of Mormon proves, 268

Billings, Titus, 103–5

Bishop, 99, 102–3

Blacks, priesthood extended to, 127. *See also* Africa, black

Blessings: law of, 152; to come after tribulation, 249

Bodies: renewing of, 44; spirit and physical, resemblance between, 68, 73 n. 36; happiness depends on, 70

Bois-Reymond, Emil du, 60

Book of Mormon: concept of Zion in, 170–71; treating lightly, 254; as foundation for Church "constitution," 264; vital truths of, summarized in D&C 20, 266–67; contains fulness of gospel, 267; witnesses to, 267–68; proves truth of Bible, 268; use of, in handling objections to Church, 269; knowledge of, accountability for, 270; God's testimony of, 273 n. 18

Booth, Ezra, 108, 114, 117–18

Boyle, Robert, 57–58

Brotherhood: coming unto Christ through, 141–42; spirit of, characterizes Zion, 176–77

Brown, Norman A., 108

Brucke, Ernst, 60

Brunson, Seymour, 20, 84

Burtt, E.A., 70

Calling and election made sure, 48, 52–53

Callings, magnifying, 42–43

Canonization of revelations, 265, 272 n. 8

Carnal, sensual, and devilish, 225

Celestial kingdom: Joseph Smith's vision of, 18, 83; principles of, Zion built on, 260

Chamberlain, Solomon, 131

Charity, 237

Children: parents' responsibilities toward, 6, 119; teaching light and truth to, 30; hearts of, turning to fathers, 78–79, 187

275